Ultimate Sticker Collection

SUPERMAN™

HOW TO USE THIS BOOK

Read the captions, then find the sticker that best fits in the space. (Hint: check the sticker labels for clues!)

•

Don't forget that your stickers can be stuck down and peeled off again.

•

There are lots of fantastic extra stickers too!

DK

LONDON, NEW YORK,
MELBOURNE, MUNICH, AND DELHI

Written and edited by Catherine Saunders, Alastair Dougall, and Garima Sharma
Inside pages designed by Anamica Roy and Suzena Sengupta
Cover designed by Suzena Sengupta

Superman created by Jerry Siegel and Joe Shuster

First published in the United States in 2013 by
DK Publishing
375 Hudson Street,
New York, New York 10014.

10 9 8 7 6 5 4 3 2 1

001–181689–April/13

DORL29437

Published in Great Britain by Dorling Kindersley Limited.

A catalog record for this book is available from the Library of Congress.

ISBN: 978-1-4654-0876-1

Color reproduction by Altaimage, UK.
Printed and bound by L-Rex Printing Co., Ltd, China.

The following DC artists have contributed to this book: Oclair Albert, Marlo Alquiza, Brad Anderson, Mahmud Asrar, Mark Bagley, Matt Banning, David Baron, Eddie Barrows, Moose Baumann, Ed Benes, Patrick Blanc, Blond, BIT, Brian Buccellato, Marc Campos, Bernard Chang, Cliff Chiang, Ian Churchill, Yildiray Cinar, David Curiel, Shane Davis, John Dell, Dale Eaglesham, Mark Farmer, Wayne Faucher, David Finch, Gary Frank, Renato Guedes, Gene Ha, HI-FI, Sandra Hope, Richard Horie, Tanya Horie, J. G. Jones, Kano, Andy Kubert, Andy Lanning, Jim Lee, Rob Lean, Aaron Lopresti, Art Lyon, Dave McCaig, Tom McCraw, Ed McGuinness, Mike McKone, J. P. Mayer, José Wilson Magalhaes, Francis Manapul, Doug Mahnke, Guy Major, Jesús Merino, Rags Morales, Tom Nguyen, Carlos Pacheco, Jimmy Palmiotti, Pete Pantazis, Joe Phillips, Kilian Plunkett, Joe Prado, Mark Propst, Jay David Ramos, Ivan Reis, Rod Reis, Alex Ross, Joe Rubinstein, Matt Ryan, Jesús Saiz, Nicola Scott, Steve Scott, Trevor Scott, Jon Sibal, R. B. Silva, Alex Sinclair, Cam Smith, Ryan Sook, Dave Stewart, Rob Stull, Art Thibert, CAFU, Glenn Whitmore, Wildstorm FX, Scott Williams, Jason Wright, Pete Woods.

Discover more at
www.dk.com

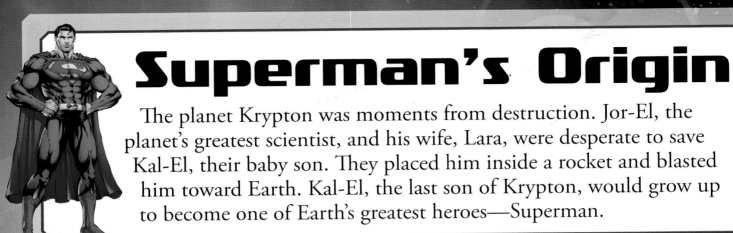

Superman's Origin

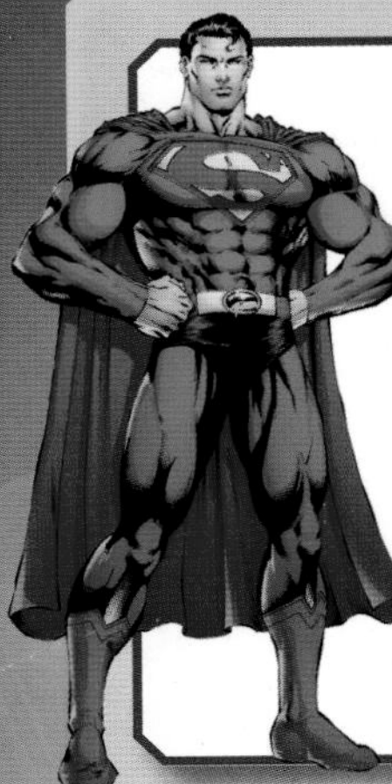

The planet Krypton was moments from destruction. Jor-El, the planet's greatest scientist, and his wife, Lara, were desperate to save Kal-El, their baby son. They placed him inside a rocket and blasted him toward Earth. Kal-El, the last son of Krypton, would grow up to become one of Earth's greatest heroes—Superman.

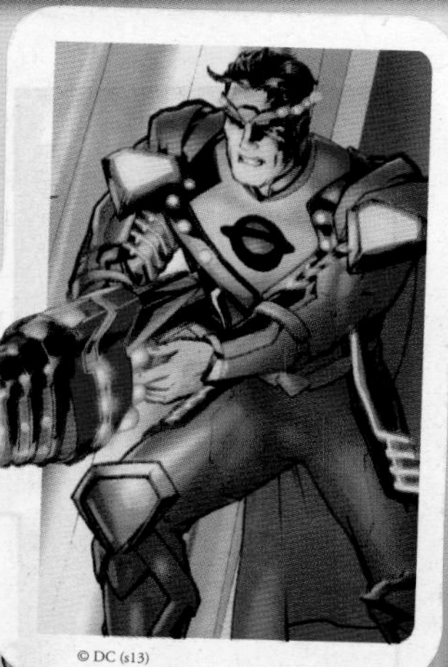

Loving Father

The journey to Earth was long and full of dangers. Jor-El hoped that baby Kal-El would be safe inside the Kryptonian capsule.

Worried Mother

Lara wanted her son to be safe, but she wasn't sure that Earth was the right place for him. It would be a very primitive place compared to Krypton.

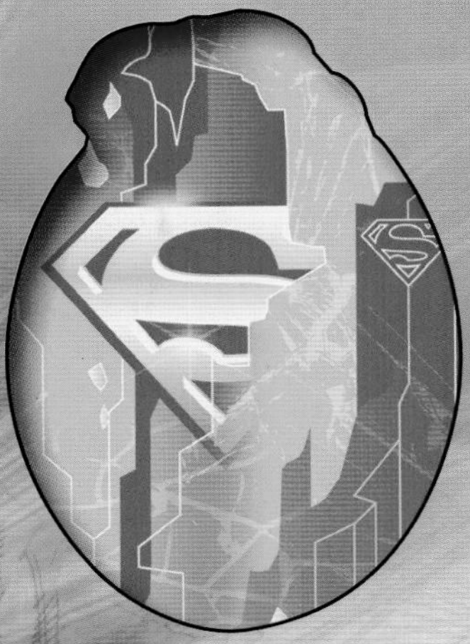

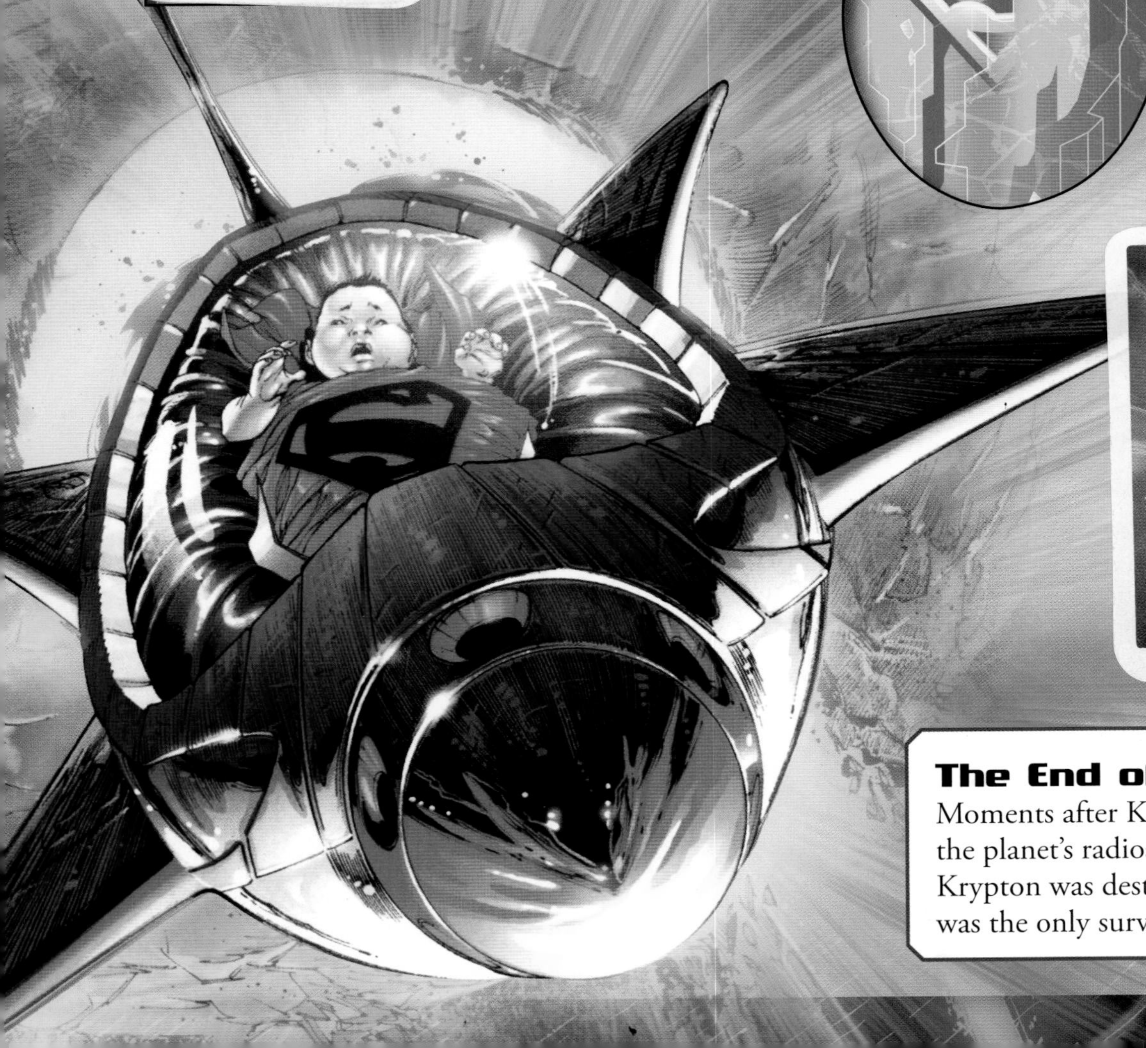

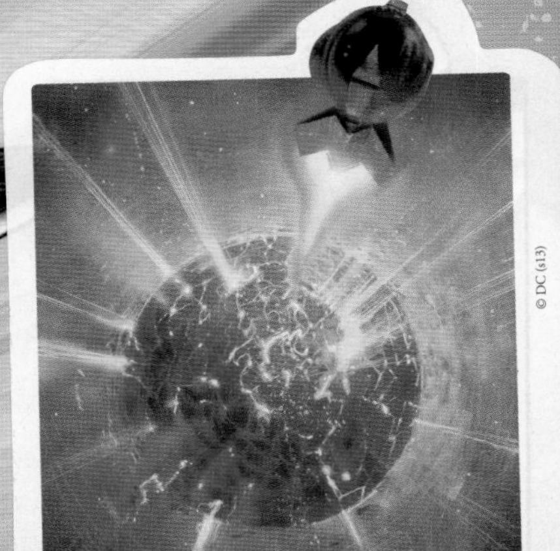

The End of Krypton

Moments after Kal-El left Krypton, the planet's radioactive core exploded. Krypton was destroyed and Kal-El was the only survivor. Or was he?

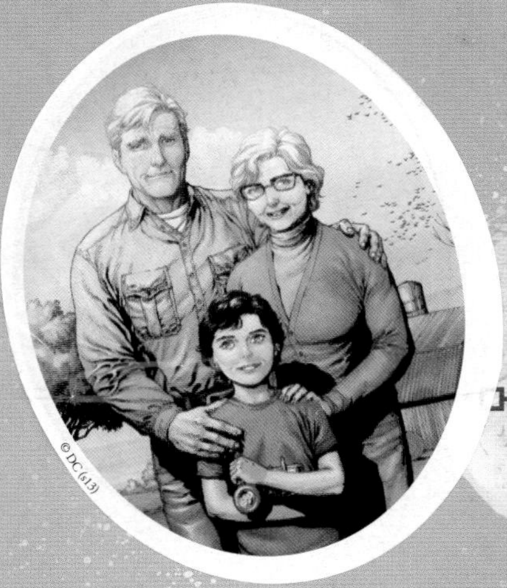
© DC (s13)

Becoming Clark

The rocket landed in Smallville, Kansas, and Kal-El was found by a kindly couple named Jonathan and Martha Kent. They adopted the baby and named him Clark.

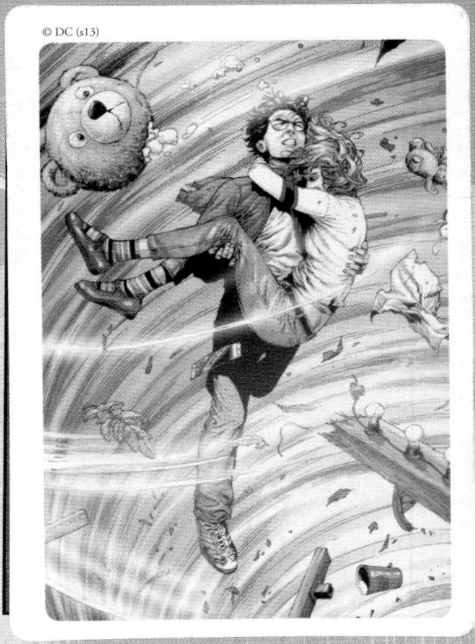
© DC (s13)

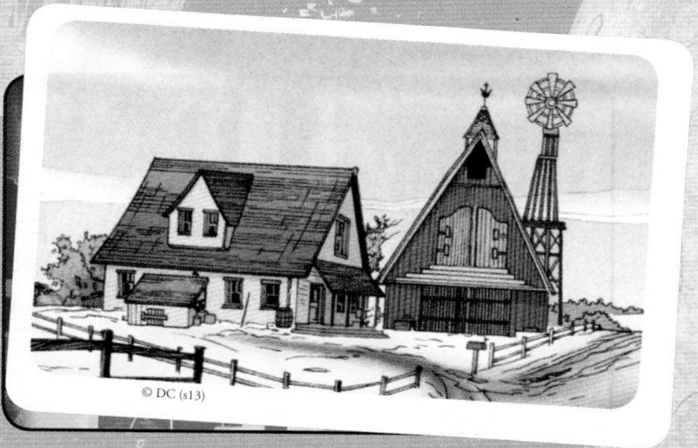
© DC (s13)

Simple Farmers

Clark had a happy childhood on the Kents' farm. His adoptive parents loved him very much and taught him to respect others and stand up for what was right.

Young Hero

Clark soon made a habit of rescuing people from danger. One of his first heroic acts was saving his sweetheart, Lana Lang, from a tornado.

Secret Talents

As Clark grew, his superpowers began to emerge. However, he had to keep them a secret so that no one would know that he was different.

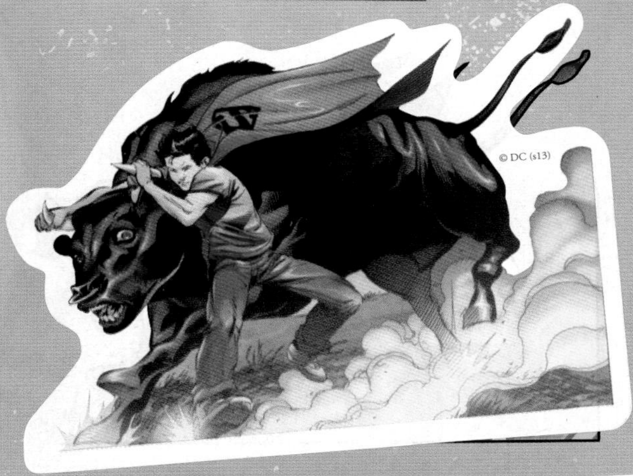
© DC (s13)

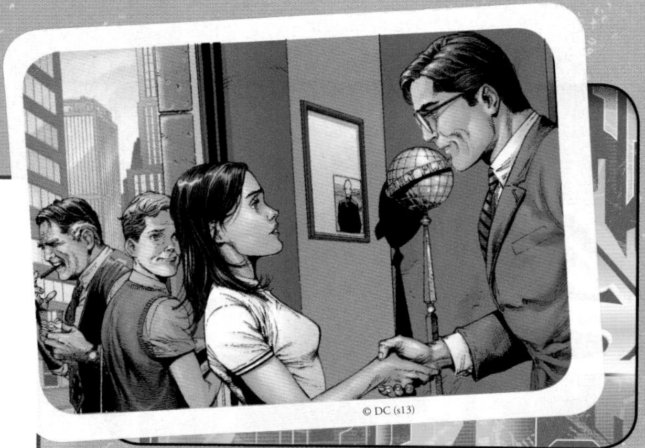
© DC (s13)

Grown Up

Clark decided to fight for justice as a super hero in Metropolis. He also took a job as a newspaper reporter, and met Lois Lane.

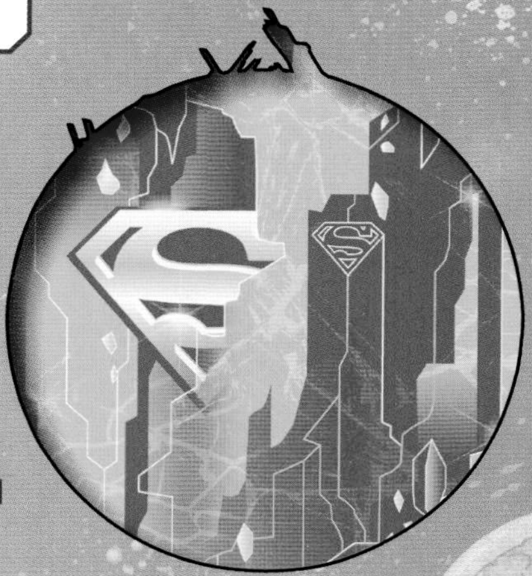

Hideaway

When Superman needs to take time out from saving the world, he heads to his secret Kryptonian sanctuary on Earth—the Fortress of Solitude.

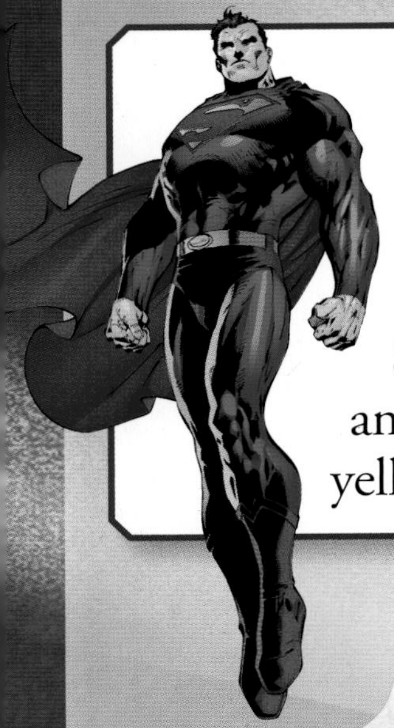

A Hero's Costume

Clark wanted to live quietly among ordinary folk, but he also wanted to use his superpowers to fight injustice. As Superman, he needed a costume that all people, both good and evil, could instantly recognize. He chose the red, yellow, and blue colors of his Kryptonian heritage.

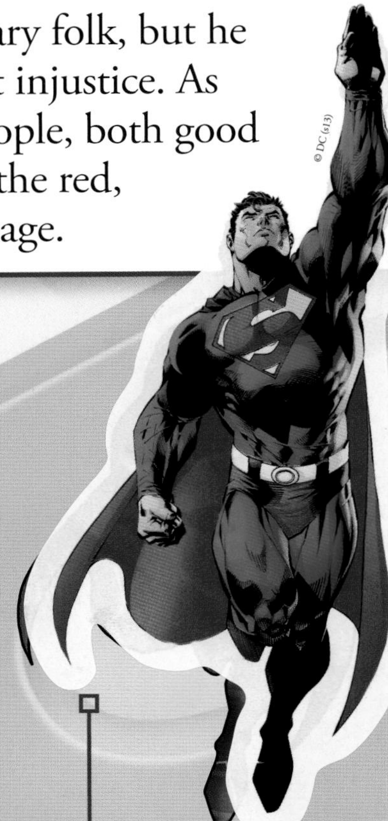
© DC (s13)

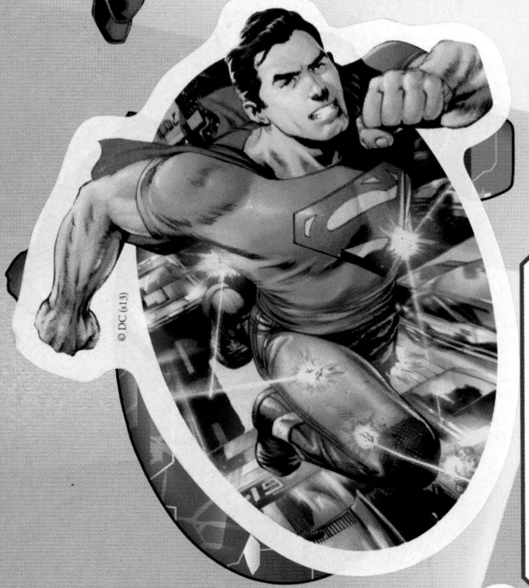
© DC (s13)

Indestructible Cape
When Superman first arrived in Metropolis, he wore ordinary jeans, t-shirt, and boots. Only his cape was made of indestructible Kryptonian fabric.

New Identity
His blue suit, with a red cape, has a red and yellow "S"—the symbol of Kal-El's House of El.

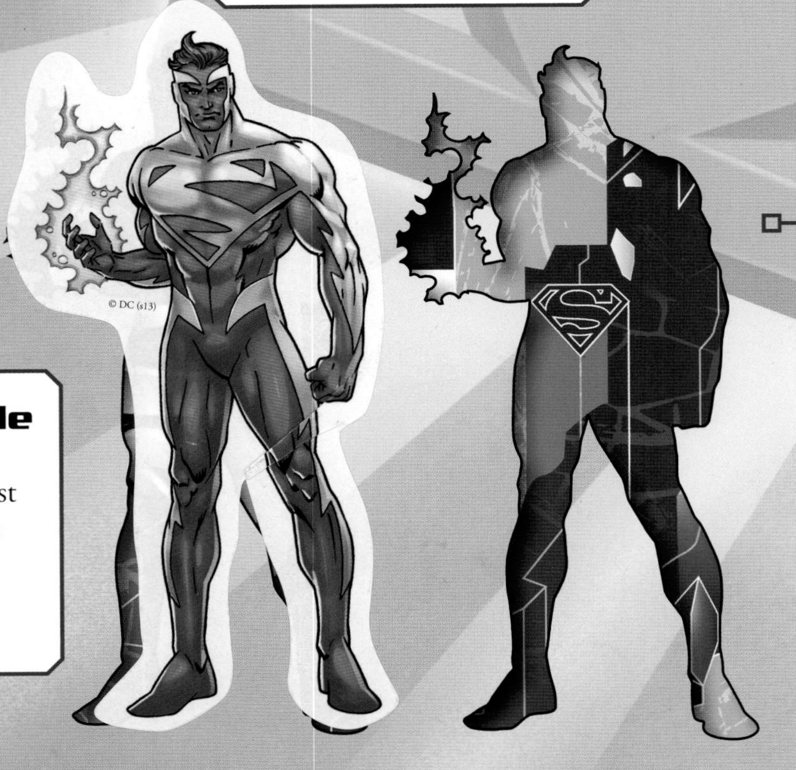
© DC (s13)

Double Trouble
When the sun was damaged, Superman lost his powers. His friends tried to help, but they accidentally split him into two Supermen.

Hot & Cold
Blue Superman was cool and sensible, but Red Superman was hot-headed and unpredictable. Fortunately, Superman soon returned to his complete self.

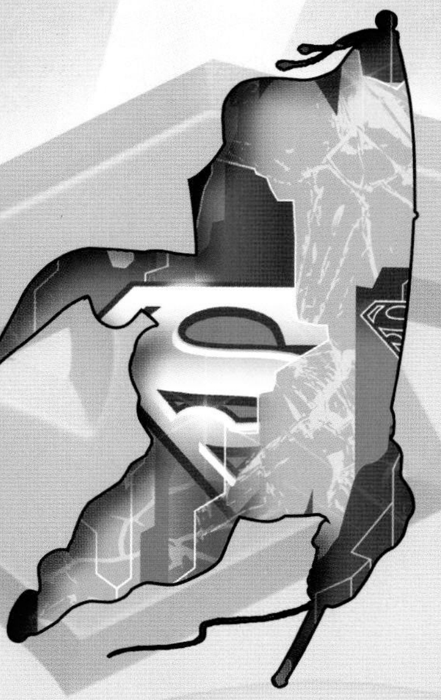

Mourning Suit

To honor those who died in the Imperiex War, Superman wore a special red and black "S."

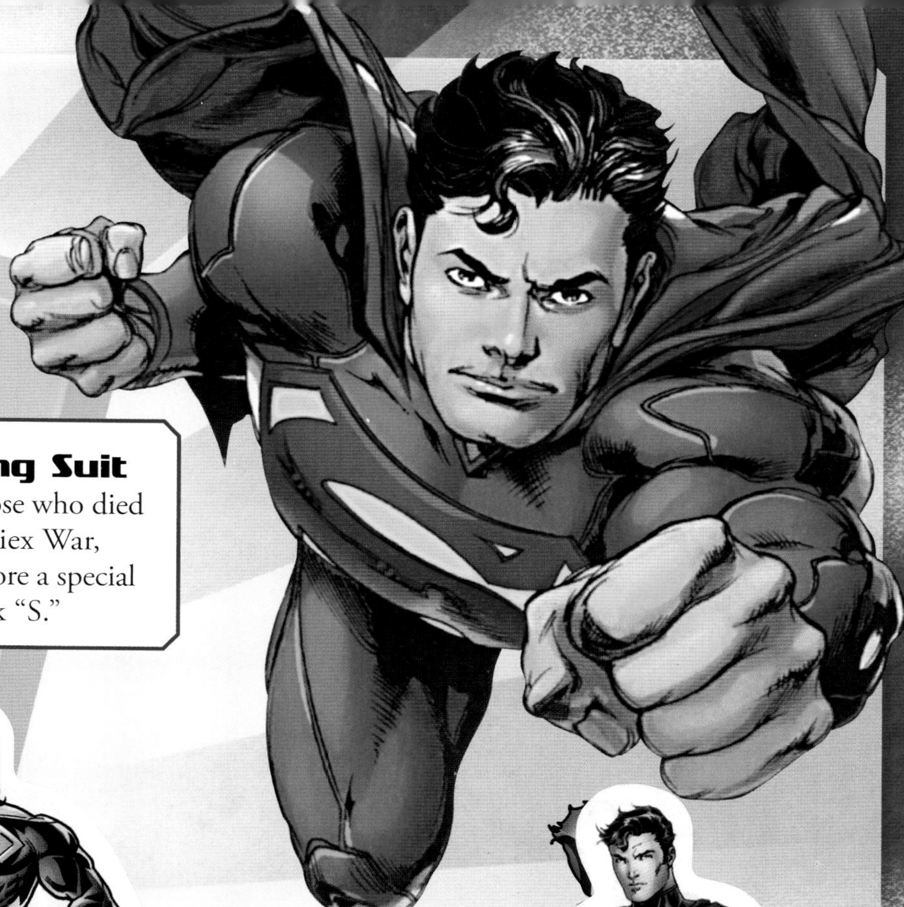

Regeneration

While recovering from his deadly clash with Doomsday Superman wore a special black regeneration suit.

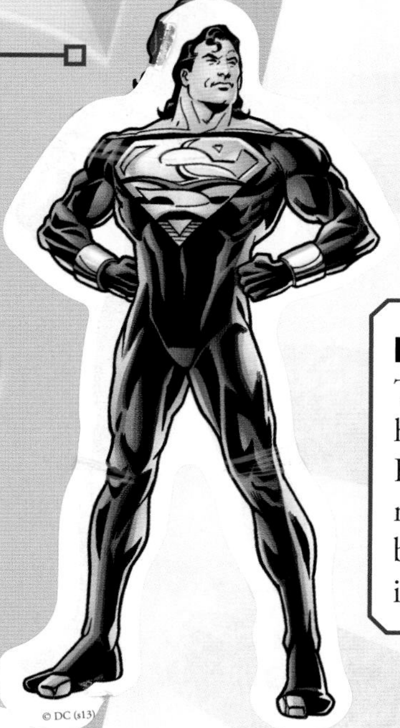
© DC (s13)

Latest Look

The new suit is his toughest yet. Kryptonian fabric molds to his body, becoming invulnerable armor.

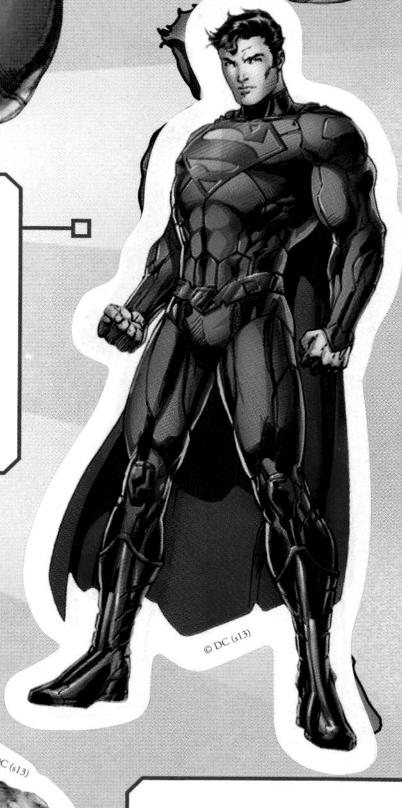
© DC (s13)

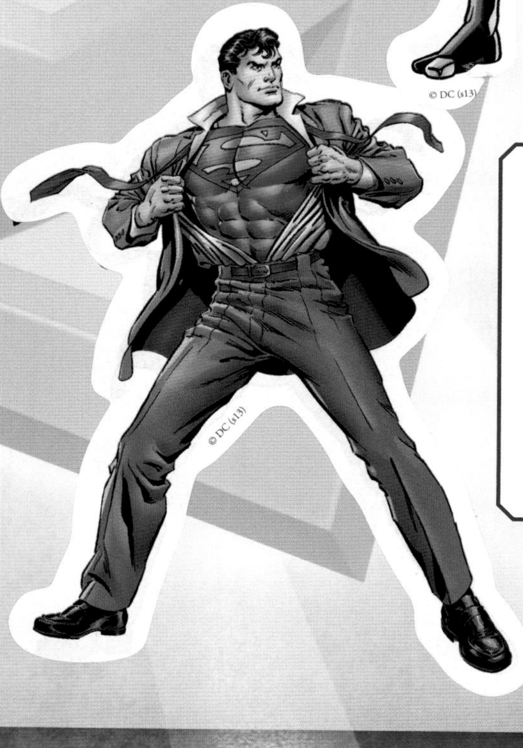
© DC (s13)

Quick Change

Clark is always ready to become Superman at super-speed—he wears his suit under his regular clothes.

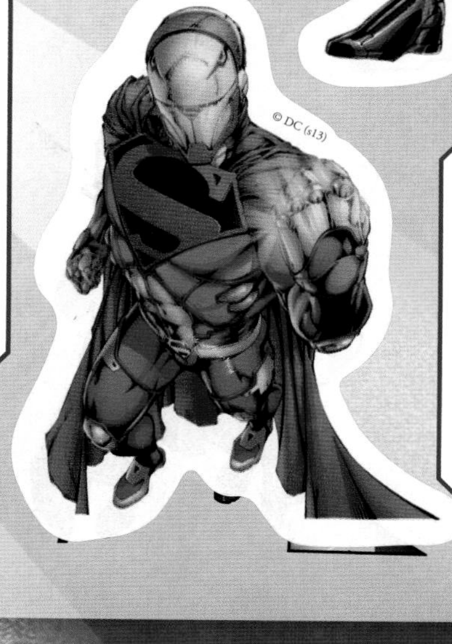
© DC (s13)

Special Suit

This suit looks like Superman's regular costume, but it is made from lead. That means it can protect him from Kryptonite.

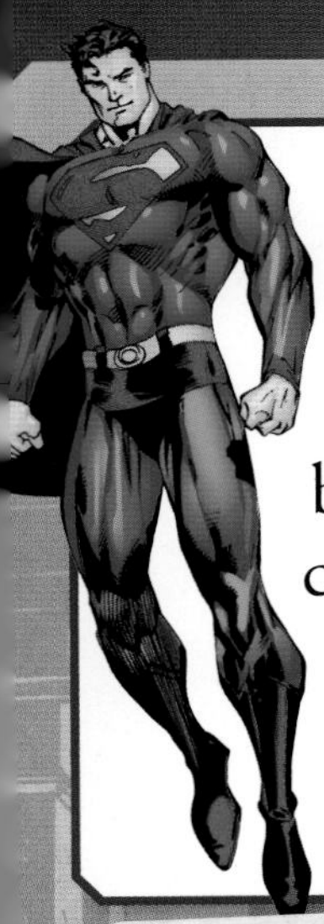

Superpowers

Superman is the ultimate super hero. He is fueled by the power of the sun and there is very little he cannot do. Few enemies are strong enough to defeat him. His strength and invulnerability have earned him the nickname "Man of Steel," but Superman has many other amazing powers, too.

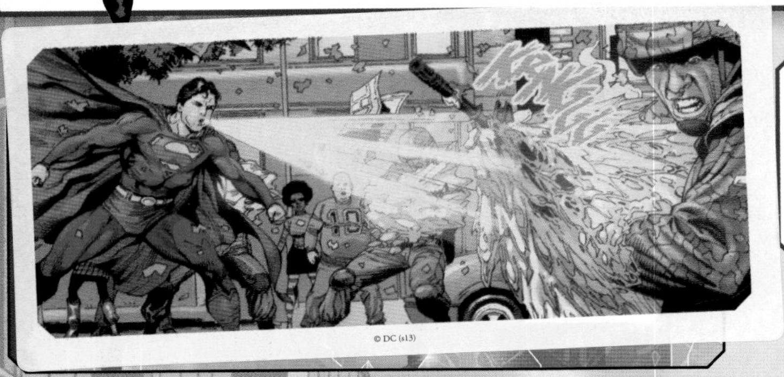

© DC (s13)

Super-speed

Superman can reach speeds of 3,219km (2,000 miles) per second!

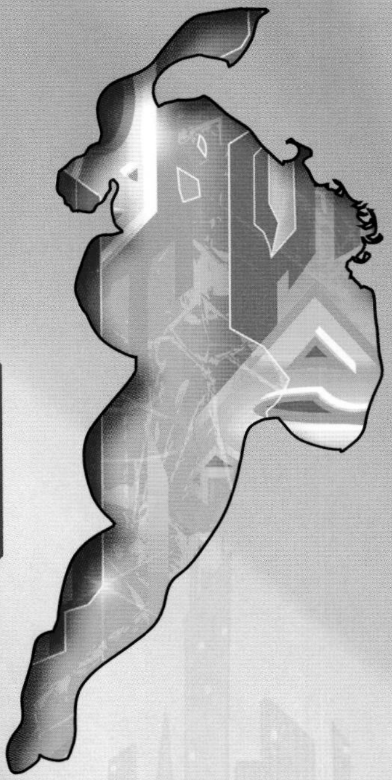

Super-breath

Even Superman's breath is awesome! He can hold it for long periods of time and even use it to put out fires or freeze enemies.

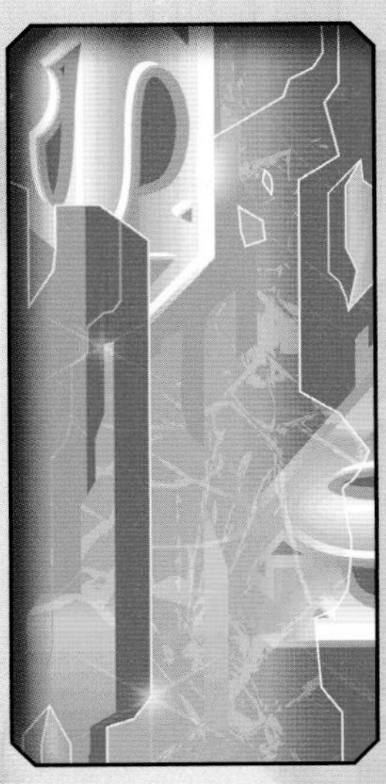

Bulletproof

Superman's solar-powered cells are like an invisible force field. His skin is tougher than any armor—bullets simply bounce off it!

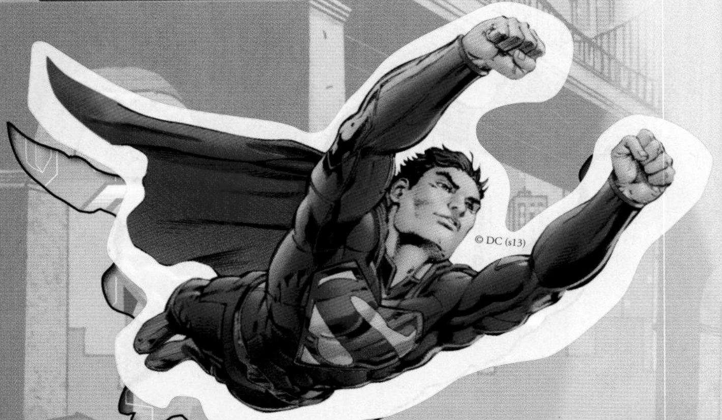

© DC (s13)

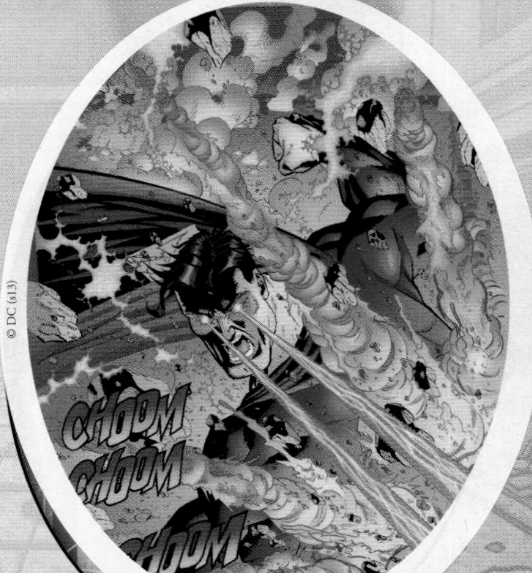

© DC (s13)
CHOOM
CHOOM

Flight

Faster than any bird or plane, Superman can fly from Earth to the moon in less than two minutes!

Heat Vision

Superman has super heat vision and can use it to melt solid rock or just warm up a cold cup of coffee!

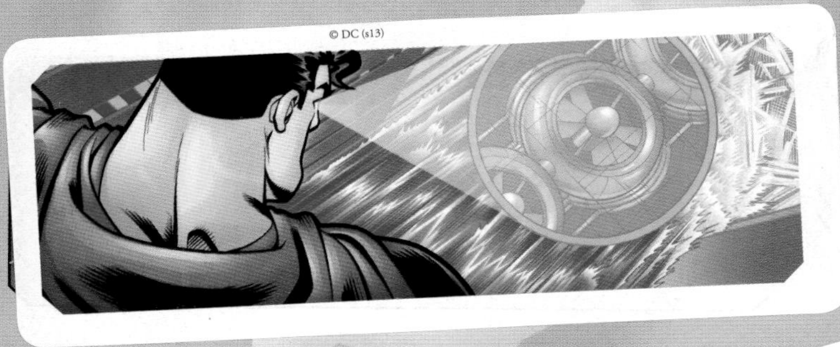

Solar-powered

When Jor-El chose Earth for his son, he knew that the yellow sun's rays would have a powerful effect on Kal-El's Kryptonian cells.

X-ray Vision

Superman can even see through solid objects, unless they are made of lead.

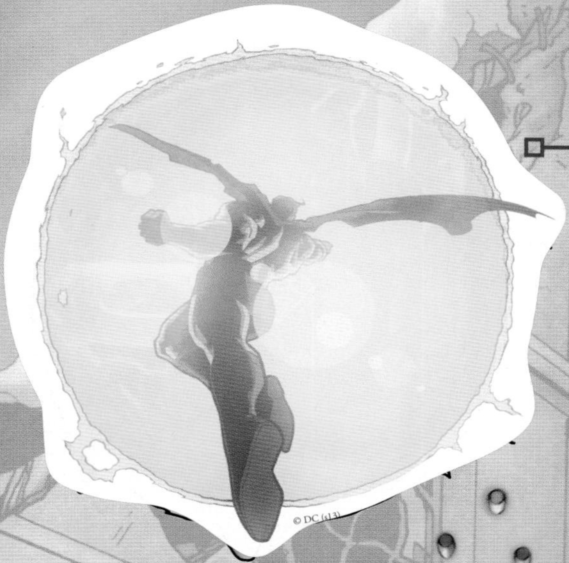

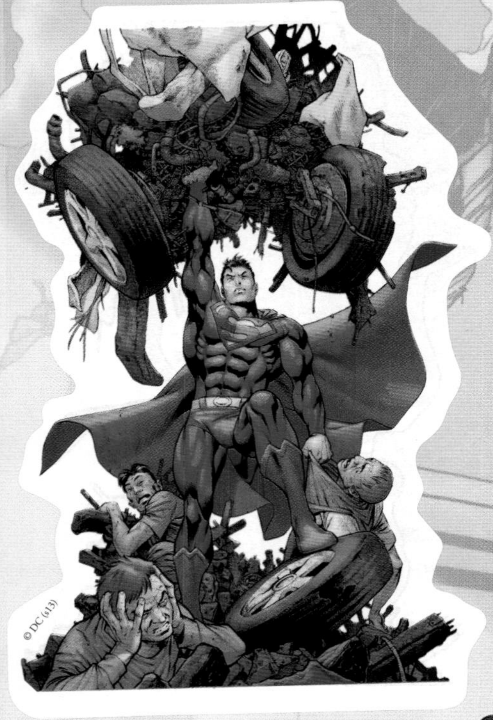

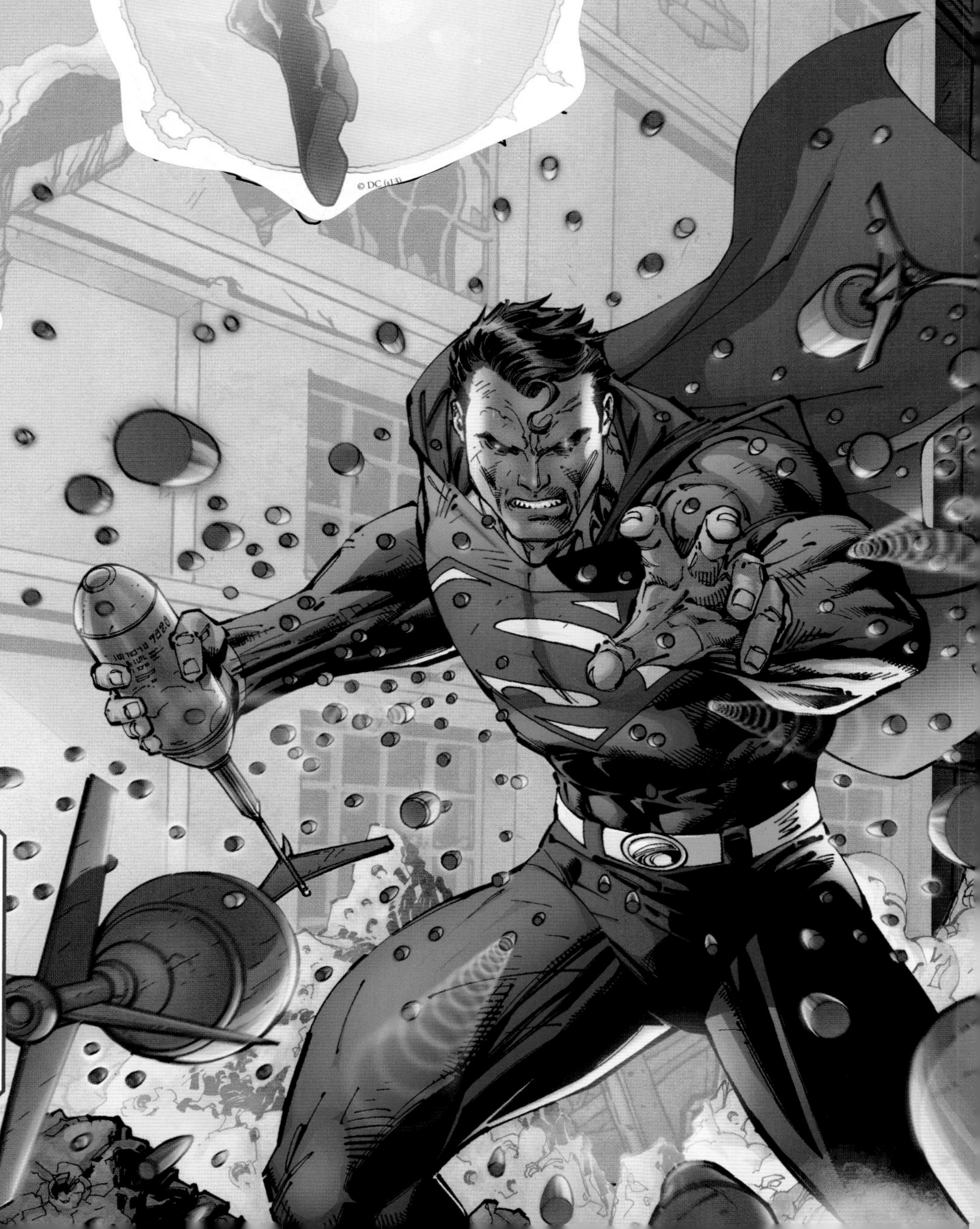

Super-strength

The only thing greater than Superman's strength is his ability to control his power. He only unleashes his super-strength when he has to.

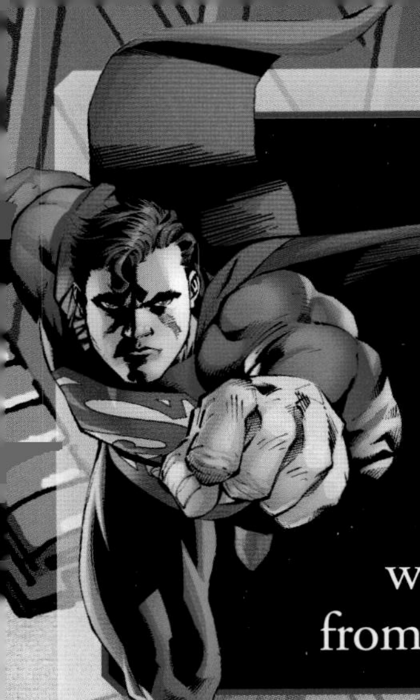

Weaknesses

The Man of Steel may be super-strong, super-fast, extremely tough, and be able to fly, but he is not totally invulnerable. Deprived of Earth's sunlight Superman can gradually lose his powers. However, far, far worse is the effect on him of a certain radioactive rock from his home planet—a rock named Kryptonite.

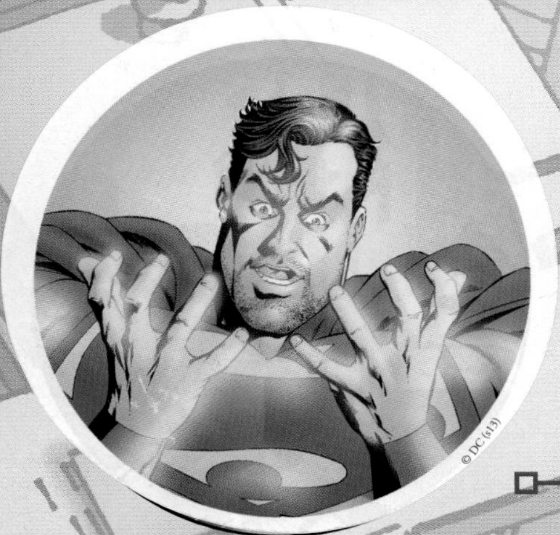

Green Pain

Kryptonite can cause Superman great pain, depending on its color. Prolonged exposure to green kryptonite would kill him!

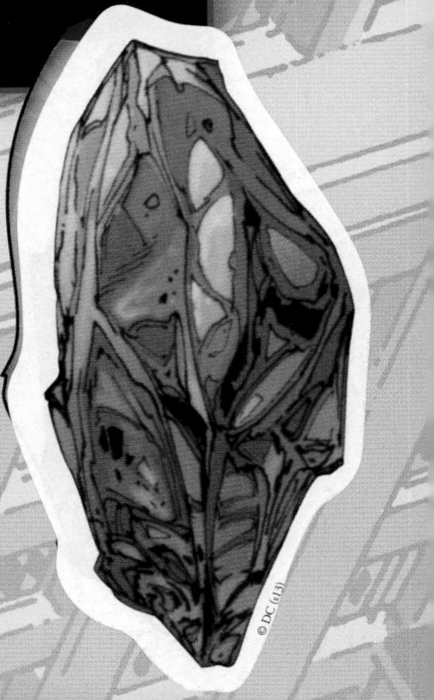

Kryptonite

When Superman's home planet exploded, fragments of Kryptonite were scattered across the universe.

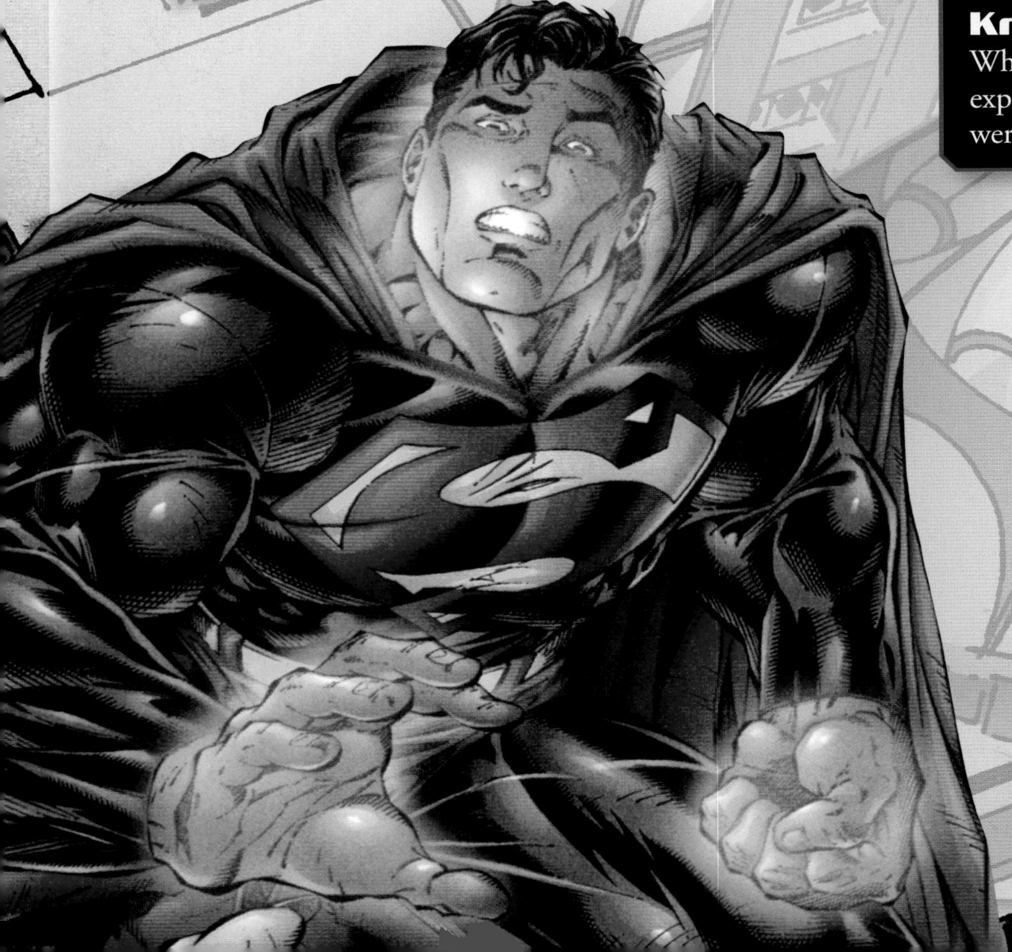

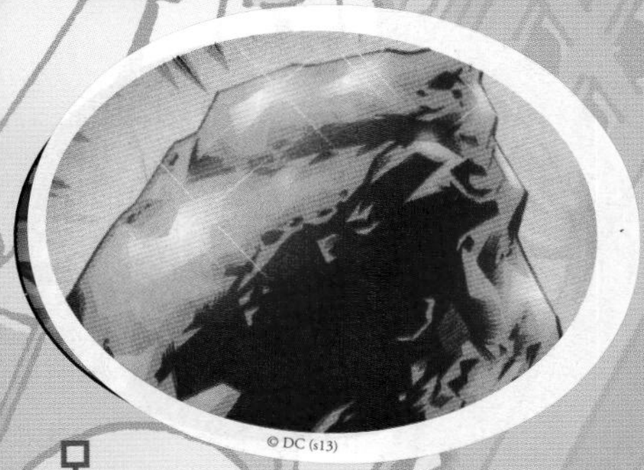

Red Kryptonite

This man-made version makes Superman's skin transparent. The sun shines directly into his cells, disrupting his powers.

Unwelcome Alien

Superman cares for the people of Earth, and is sad when they don't appreciate his efforts to help them.

Epic Battle

Metropolis was shaken to its foundations when Superman fought Doomsday. The villain won, but Superman would return even stronger.

Lonely Hero

Being a secret super hero can be lonely, but at least Superman has a faithful friend in his dog, Krypto.

Magic

Superman has no power over the supernatural. He was once transformed into the Ape of Steel by the powerful gorilla Ulgo.

The Red Sun

Earth's yellow sun gives Superman amazing abilities, but Krypton's red sun takes his powers away.

© DC (s13)

Air to Breathe

Even Superman cannot survive without air. He has, however, learned to hold his breath for long periods underwater and in space.

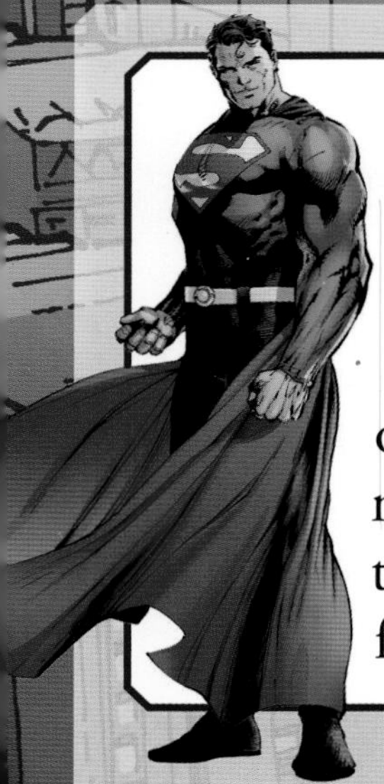

Heroic Friends

Superman believed he was the sole survivor of the planet Krypton, but he was wrong. Over the years, he has met other Kryptonians, both good and evil. Fortunately, many of Superman's Kryptonian allies not only have the same superpowers, but also share in his fight for truth and justice.

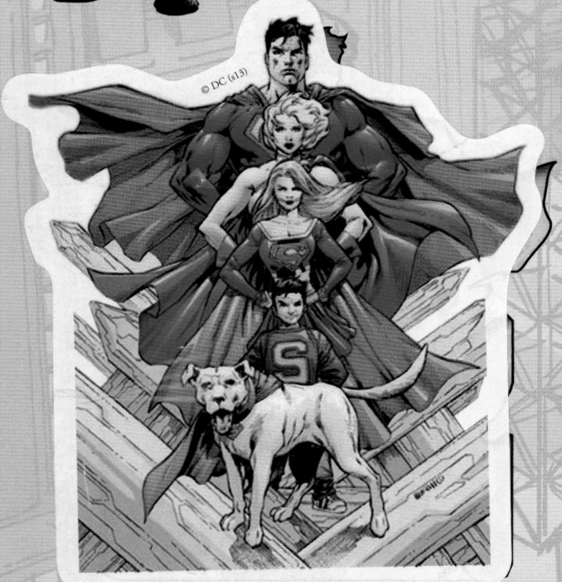
© DC (s13)

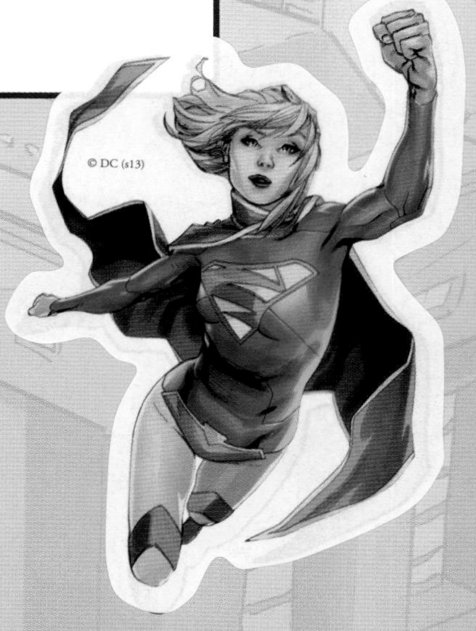
© DC (s13)

Supergirl
Kara Zor-El is Superman's cousin. She left Krypton shortly after Kal-El, but her journey to Earth took a lot longer!

Superman's Family
Although he loved the Kents, Superman enjoys having a family who understands what it's like to be a super hero.

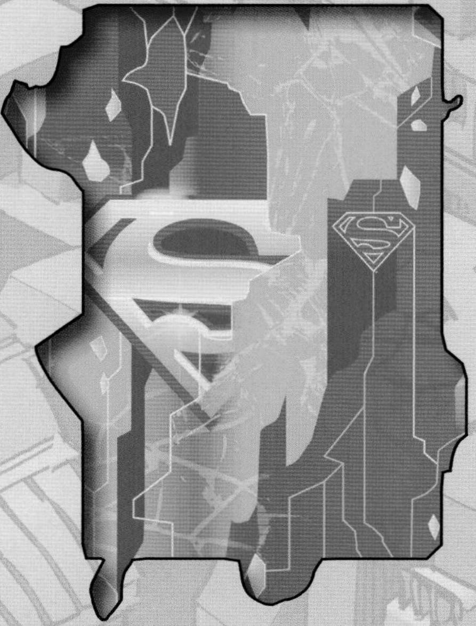

Steel
Superman inspired inventor John Henry Irons to become a super hero. He created a high-tech suit of armor and became Steel, Superman's ally and friend.

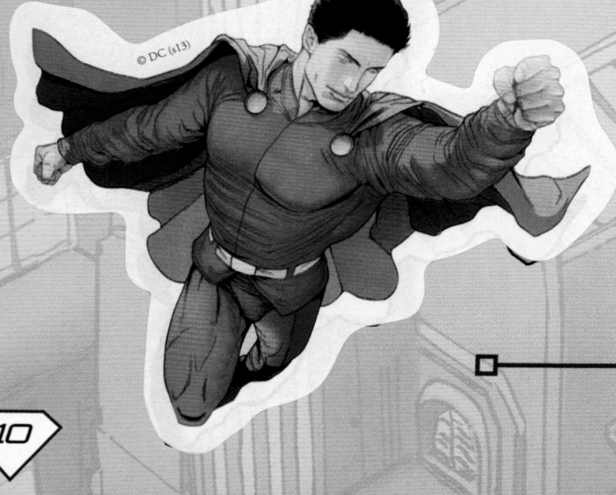
© DC (s13)

Mon-El
Superman thought that he and his good friend Mon-El were related because they had similar superpowers. But Mon-El is from the planet Daxam, not Krypton.

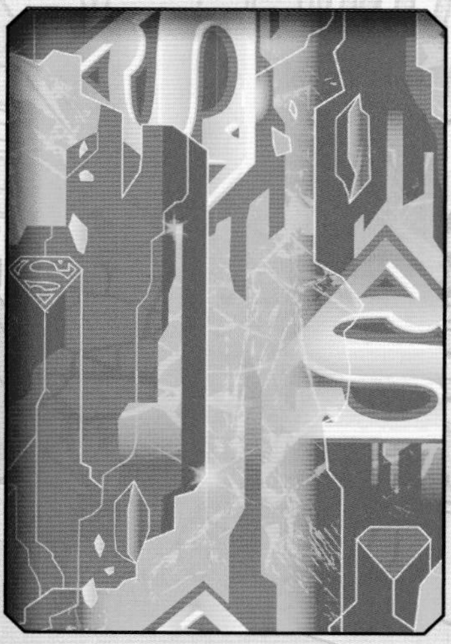

Krypto
Superman's super-dog, a Krypton survivor, has the canine version of his master's powers, including flight.

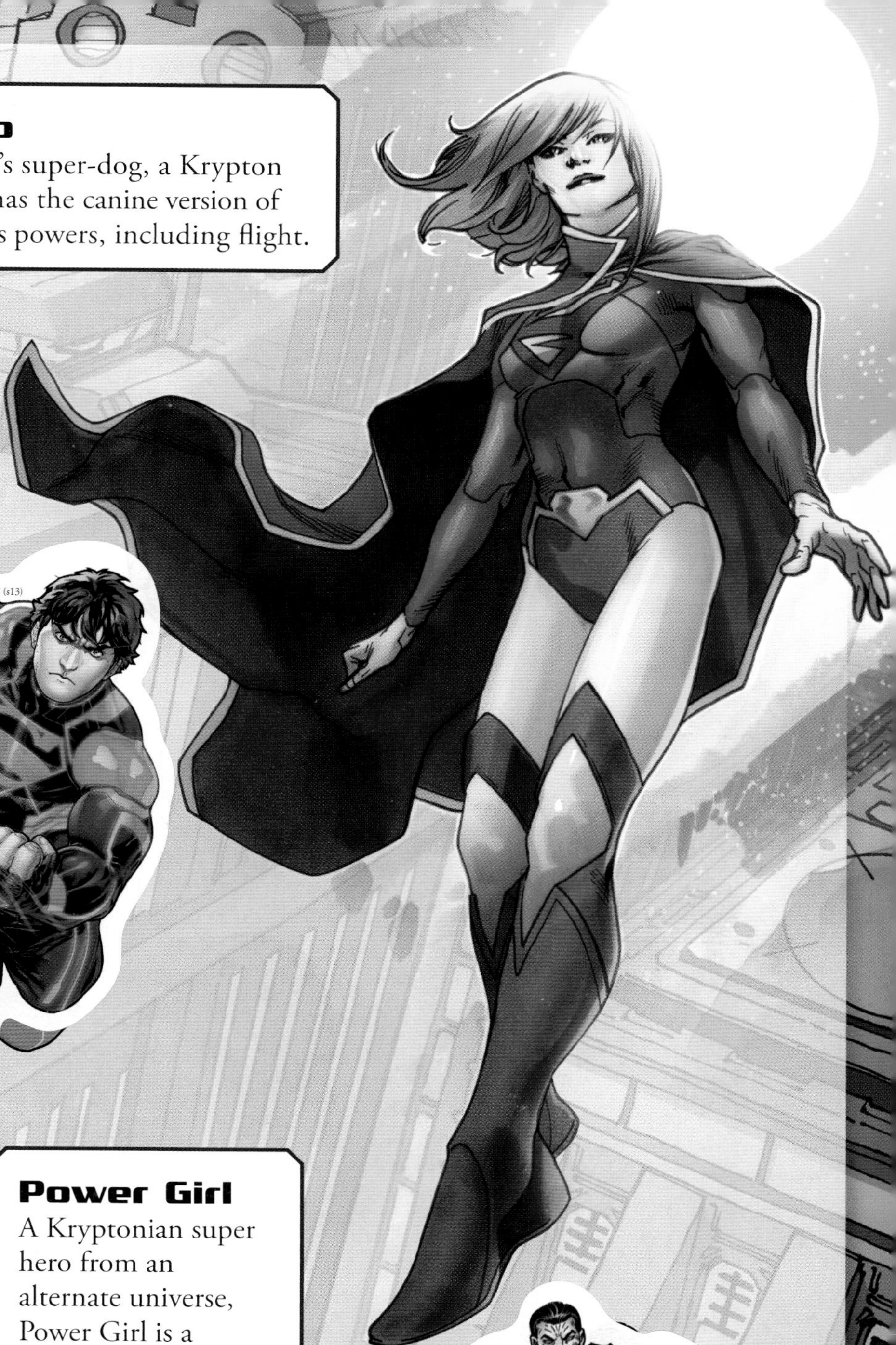

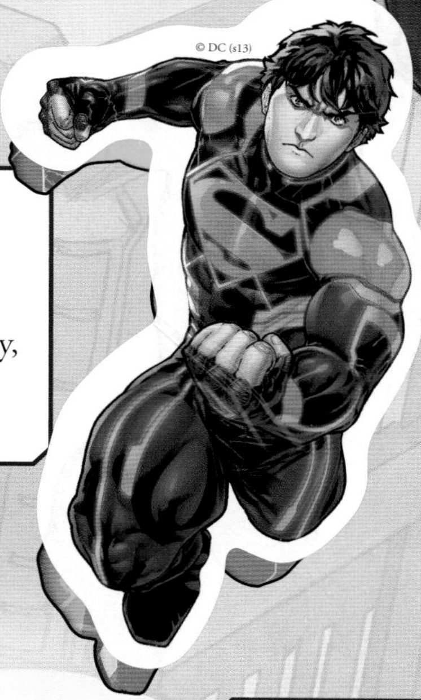
© DC (s13)

Superboy
This mixed-up teenager was created using Superman and Lex Luthor's DNA. Fortunately, Superboy's Kryptonian DNA is proving to be stronger!

Power Girl
A Kryptonian super hero from an alternate universe, Power Girl is a member of the super hero team the Justice Society of America.

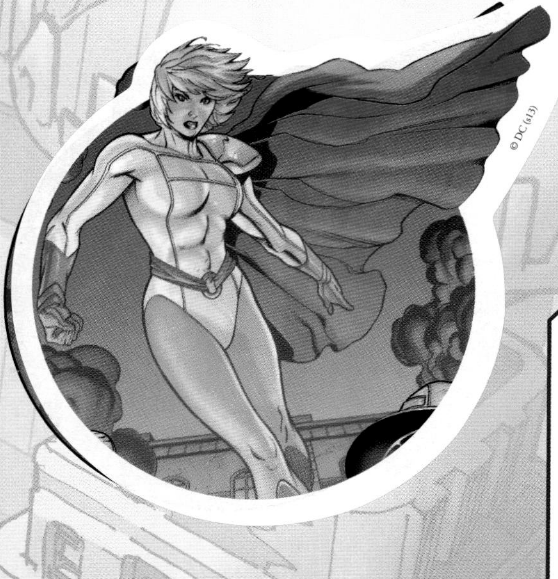
© DC (s13)

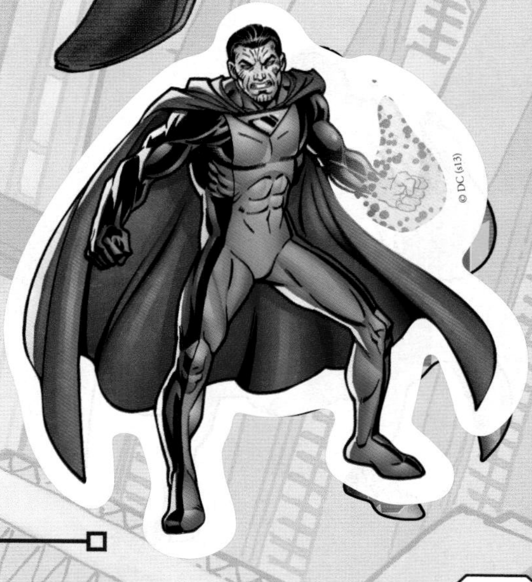
© DC (s13)

The Eradicator
This ancient Kryptonian saved Superman when Doomsday killed him. The Eradicator has since fought alongside the Man of Steel.

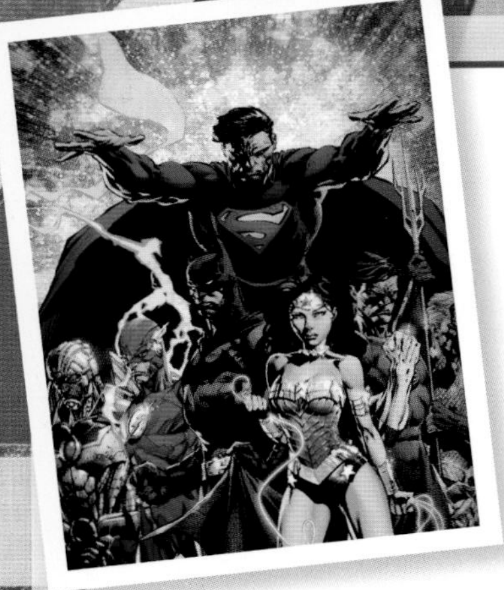

The Justice League

The Justice League is the ultimate super hero team. Superman, Batman, and Wonder Woman are founding members and the team is made up of the bravest, strongest, fastest, and cleverest heroes. The League aims to protect Earth from threats that no single hero can defeat.

Current Roster

Members come and go, but the current line-up is Superman, Batman, Wonder Woman, Green Lantern, Aquaman, the Flash, and Cyborg.

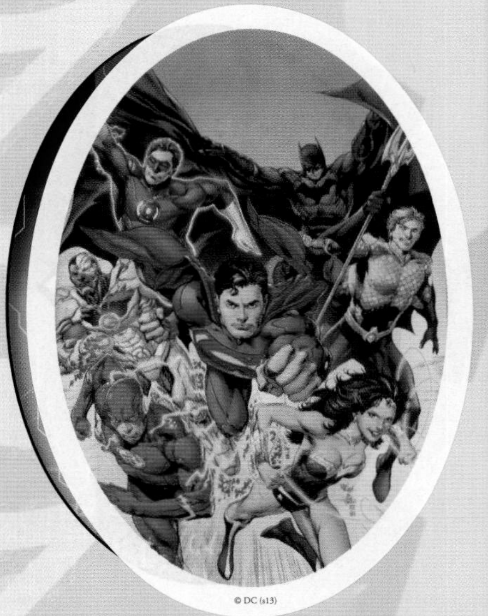

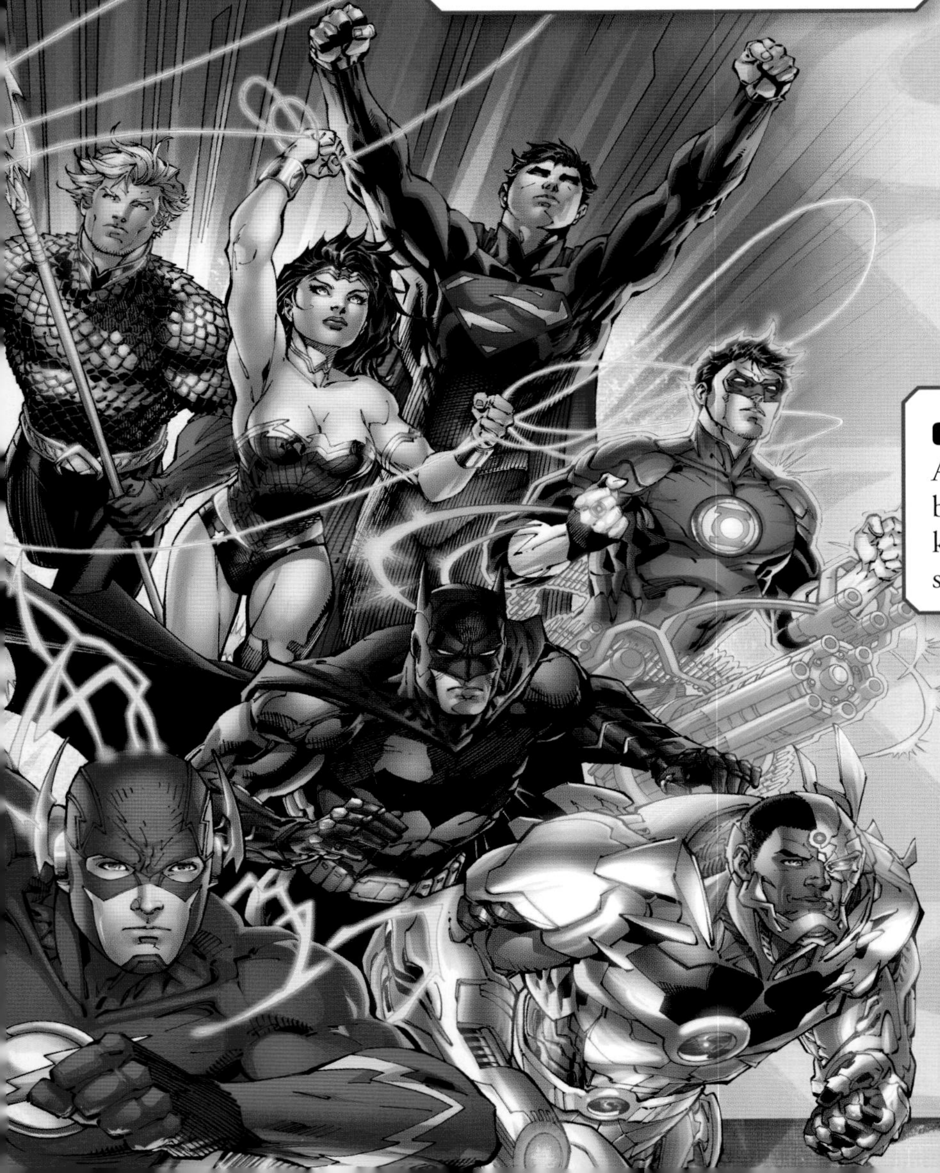

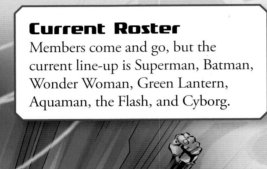

Cyborg

After a laboratory accident, Victor Stone's body was rebuilt using cybernetic parts. Now known as Cyborg, he has super-strength, speed, stamina, and some awesome weapons.

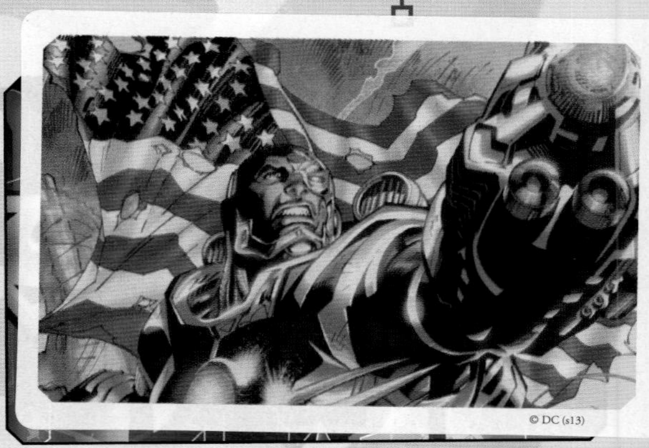

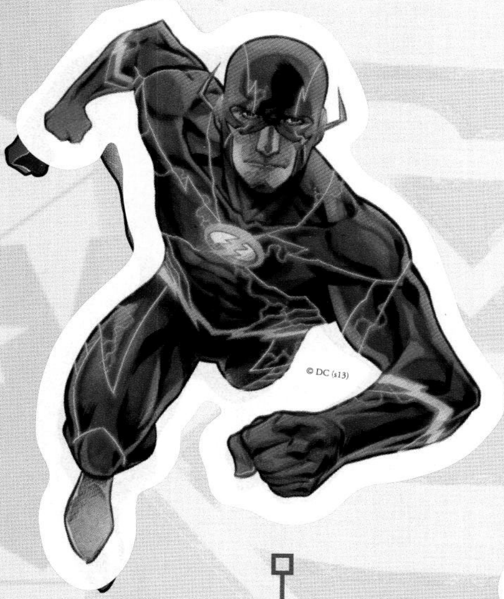

Batman

Bruce Wayne is a skilled fighter and a detective without equal. Armed with gadgets, he fights crime as Batman.

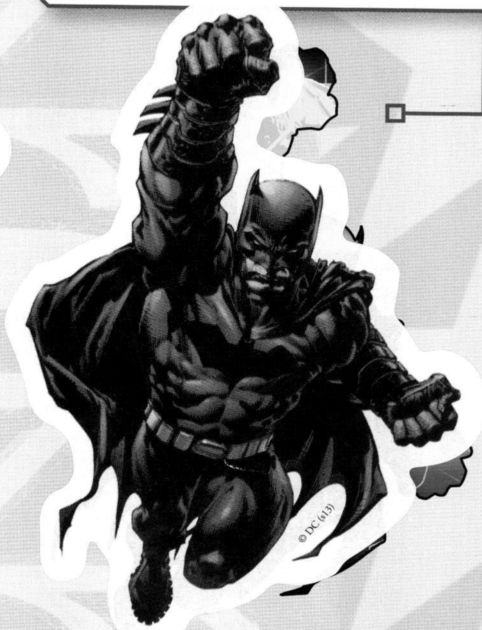

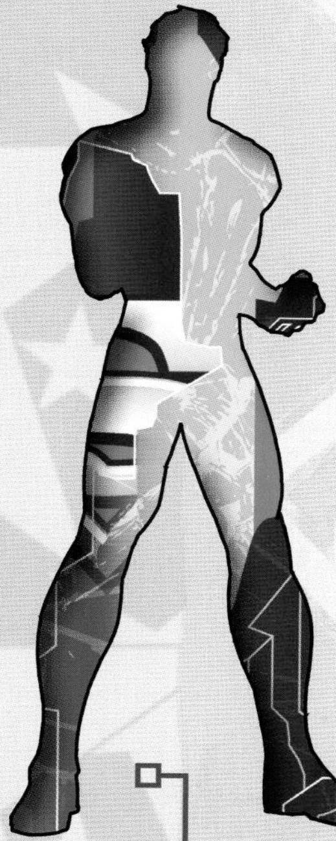

The Flash

A chemical spill and lightning transformed forensic scientist Barry Allen into the Fastest Man Alive. As the Flash, he is powered by an extra-dimensional energy named Speed Force.

Green Lantern

Law enforcer of the universe, Green Lantern uses his power ring to wield powerful light energy and travel through space.

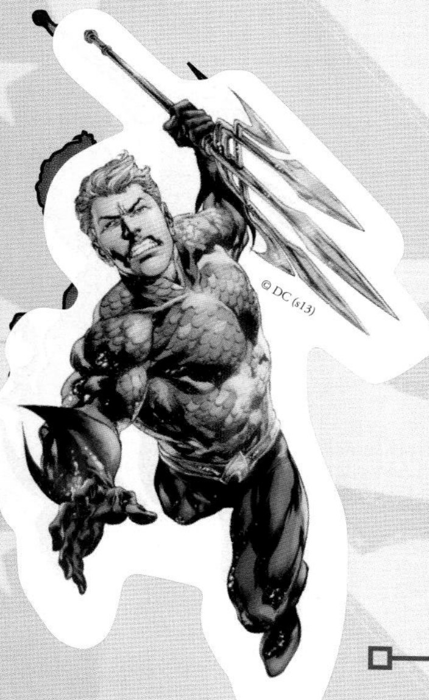

Wonder Woman

Super-strong and super-fast, this Amazonian warrior princess wields the Golden Lasso of Truth. Her wrist gauntlets have the ability to deflect bullets.

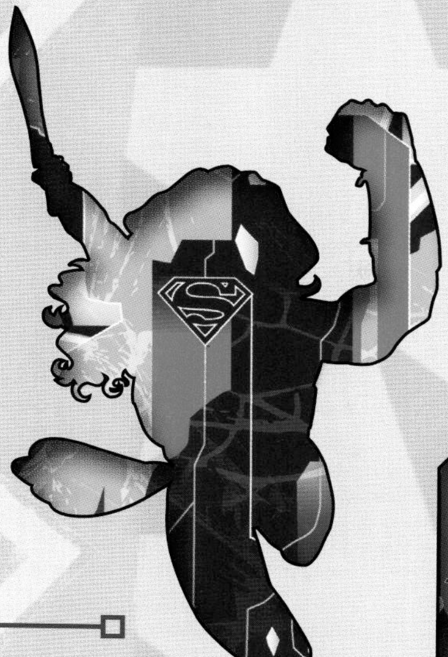

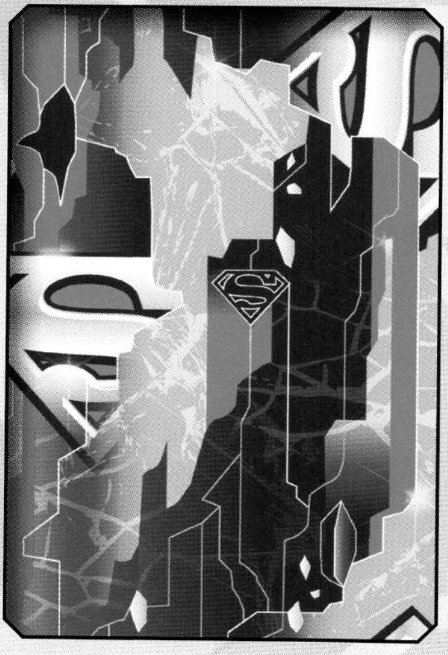

Aquaman

Powerful and fast, Arthur Curry can breathe underwater and telepathically talk with marine life. He rules the underwater kingdom of Atlantis.

Common Cause

The heroes of the Justice League may argue occasionally, but they stand united whenever Earth's in peril.

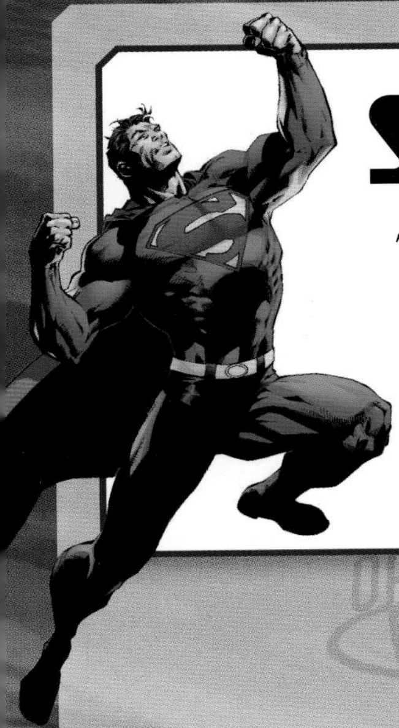

Standing Together

There are too many villains in the universe for even Superman to defeat alone. Fortunately, many brave super heroes are always ready to team up with the Man of Steel to defeat evildoers. Superman has also inspired many other individuals to become heroes and protect the people of Earth.

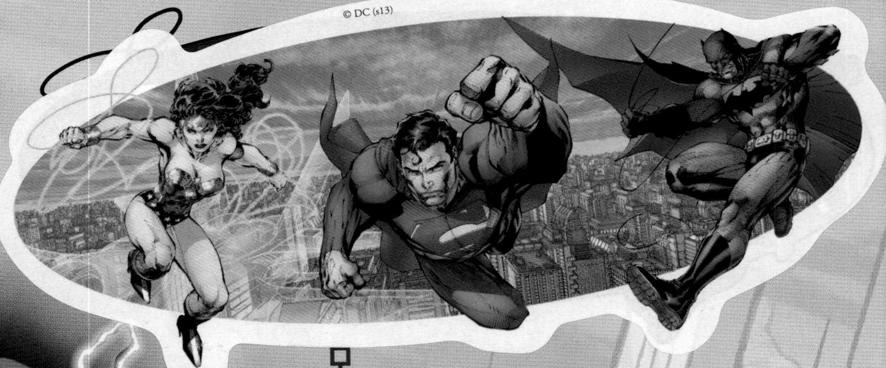

The Trinity

Before the Justice League, Wonder Woman, Superman, and Batman formed The Trinity to prevent Rā's al Ghūl, Bizarro, and Artemis from bringing chaos to Earth.

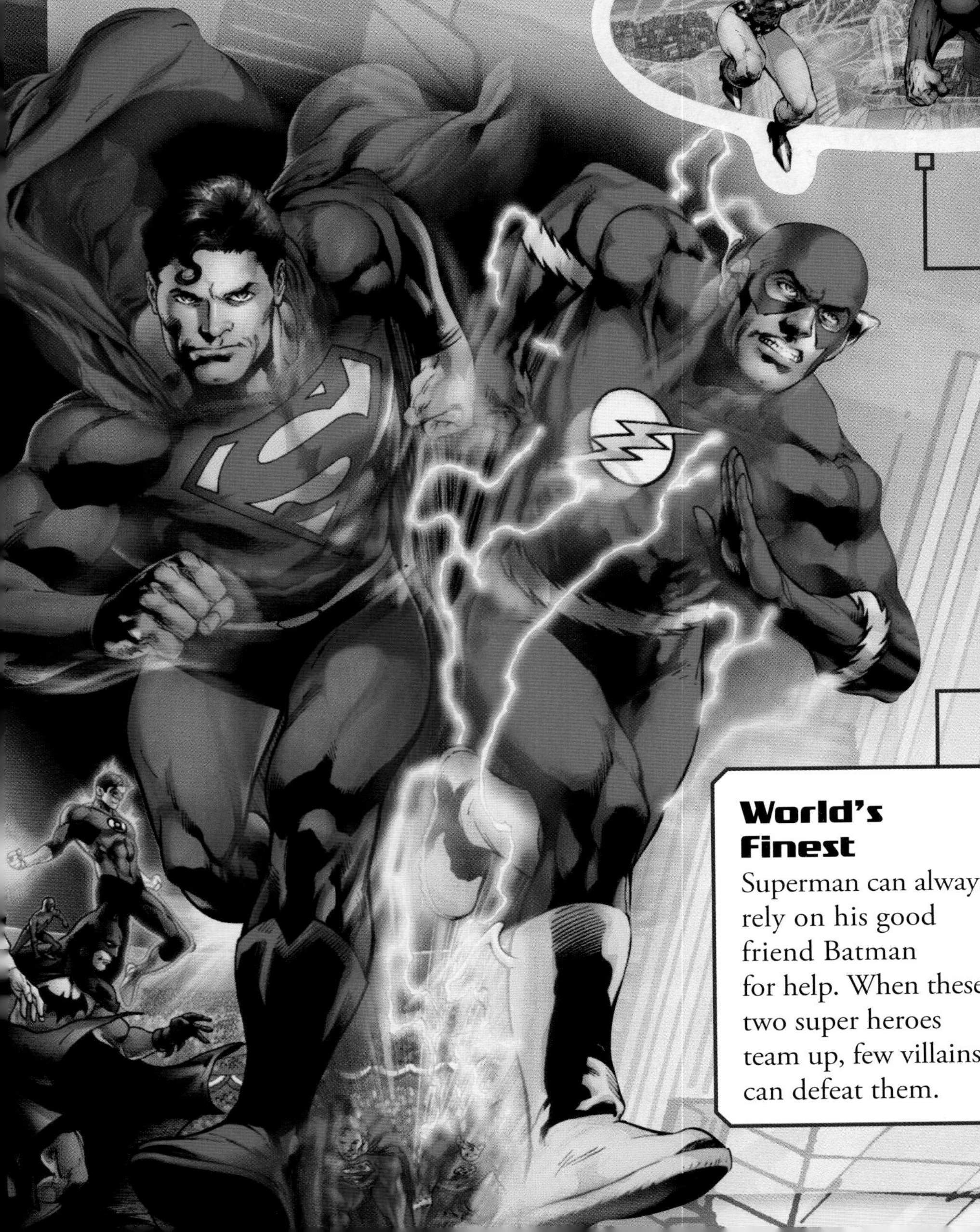

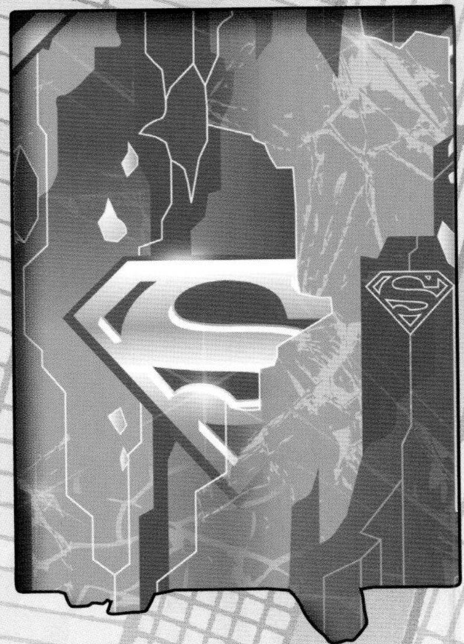

World's Finest

Superman can always rely on his good friend Batman for help. When these two super heroes team up, few villains can defeat them.

Fast Friends

If he needs help in a hurry, Superman can always turn to the Flash.

Guardian

Like Superman, Guardian cares about Metropolis. By day he is a police officer, by night he hunts down criminals the law cannot catch.

The Justice Society

Before the Justice League, Superman was an honorary member of the Justice Society of America, or JSA.

Martian Manhunter

This super hero from Mars has similar powers to Superman, including flight, super-breath, and X-ray vision.

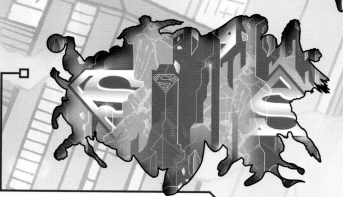

The Legion of Super-Heroes

Inspired by Superman, this group of teenagers from the 31st century have sworn to protect every planet from danger.

Gangbuster

Schoolteacher Jose Delgado, inspired by Superman, fights street gangs in Metropolis as the armored hero Gangbuster.

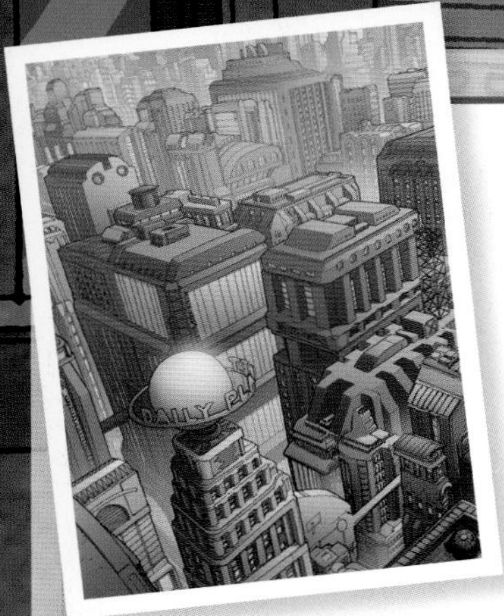
DAILY PLANET

Metropolis

Smallville was the only home Clark Kent had ever known, but he knew that Superman could help more people in a big city. And with a population of almost 11 million, Metropolis is certainly big! Clark works as a reporter at the *Daily Planet* and secretly fights for justice as Superman.

Breaking News

The *Daily Planet* team risk their lives to uncover the biggest news stories. Fortunately, Superman usually happens to be around when they need him…

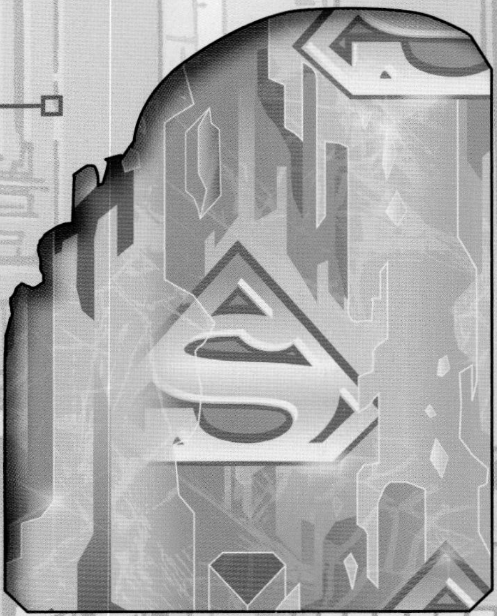

Lois Lane

Clark's fellow reporter, Lois Lane, invented the name "Superman" when he saved her life. Since then, Superman has saved her life many times.

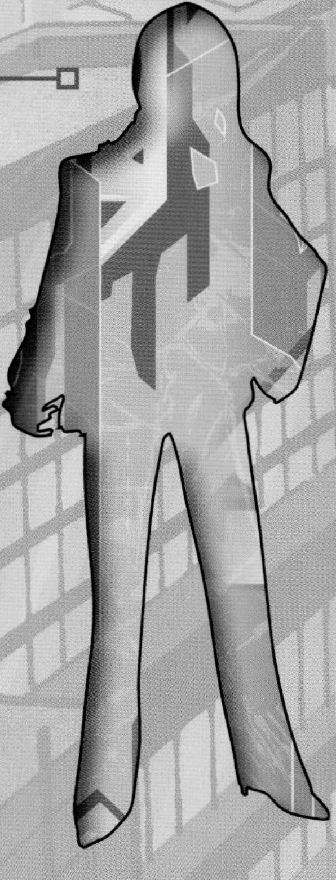

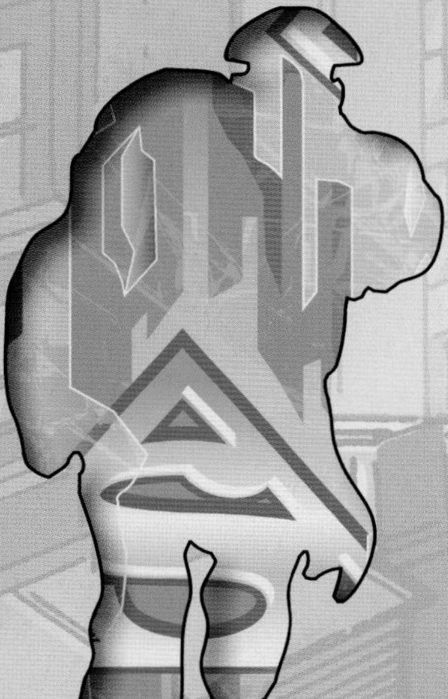

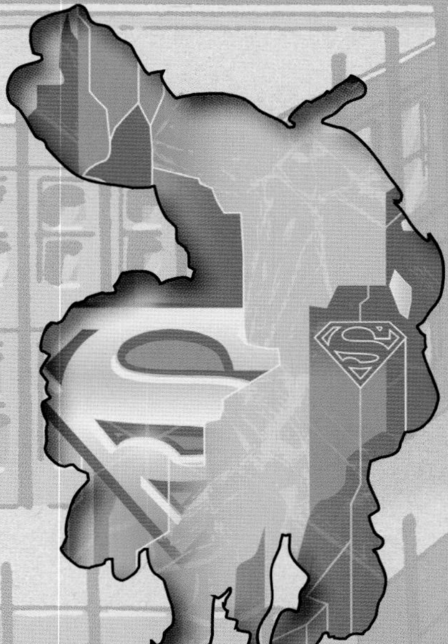

Bibbo

Mean-looking but big-hearted, Bibbo Bibbowski will do anything to protect his beloved Metropolis or to help his favorite super hero, Superman.

Special Crimes Unit

Metropolis's SCU (Special Crimes Unit) is trained to fight super-villains. Their high-tech armor is inspired by Superman's Kryptonian warsuit.

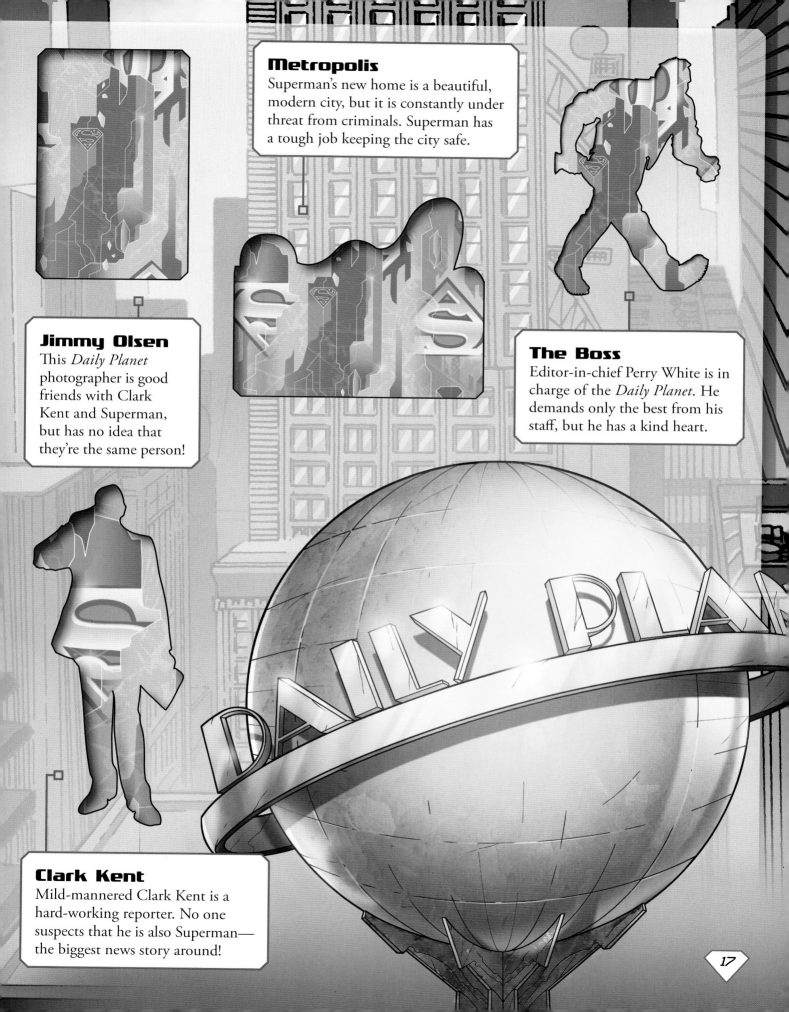

Metropolis

Superman's new home is a beautiful, modern city, but it is constantly under threat from criminals. Superman has a tough job keeping the city safe.

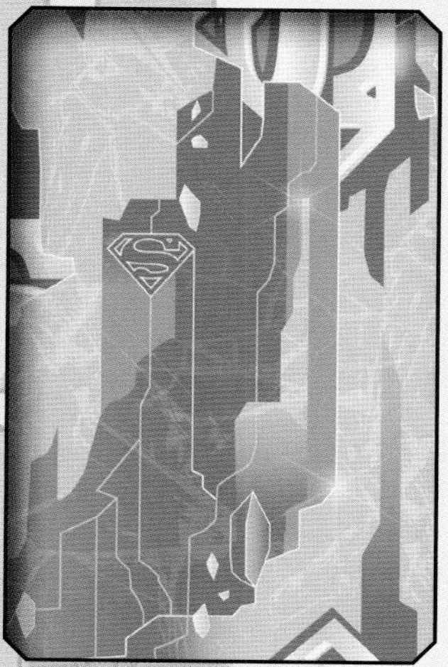

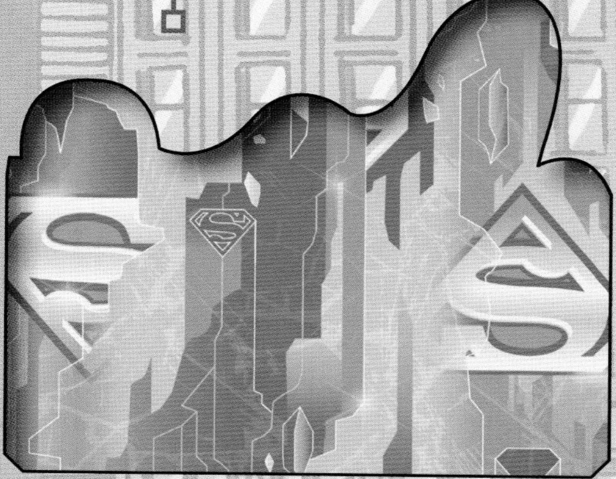

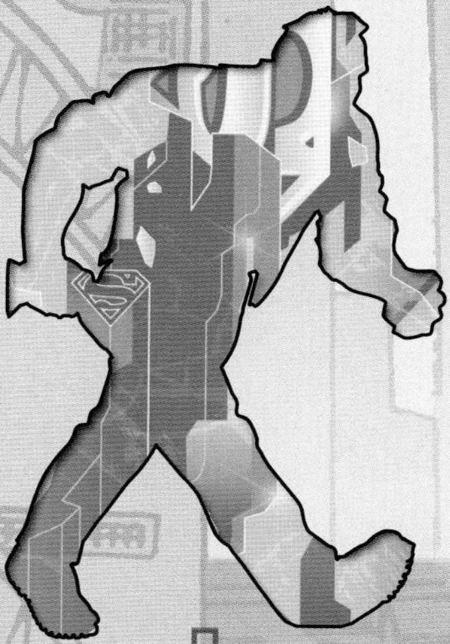

Jimmy Olsen

This *Daily Planet* photographer is good friends with Clark Kent and Superman, but has no idea that they're the same person!

The Boss

Editor-in-chief Perry White is in charge of the *Daily Planet*. He demands only the best from his staff, but he has a kind heart.

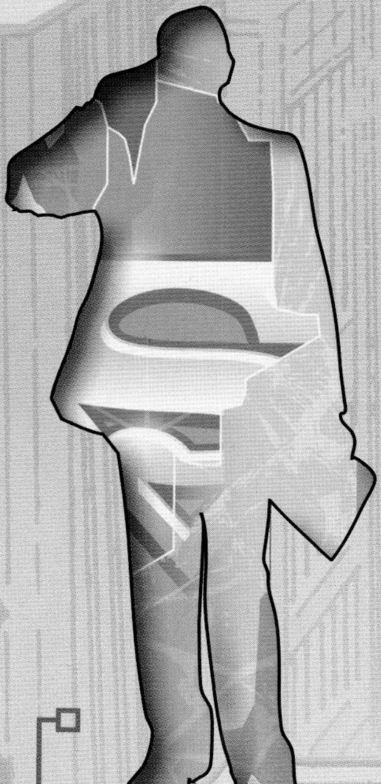

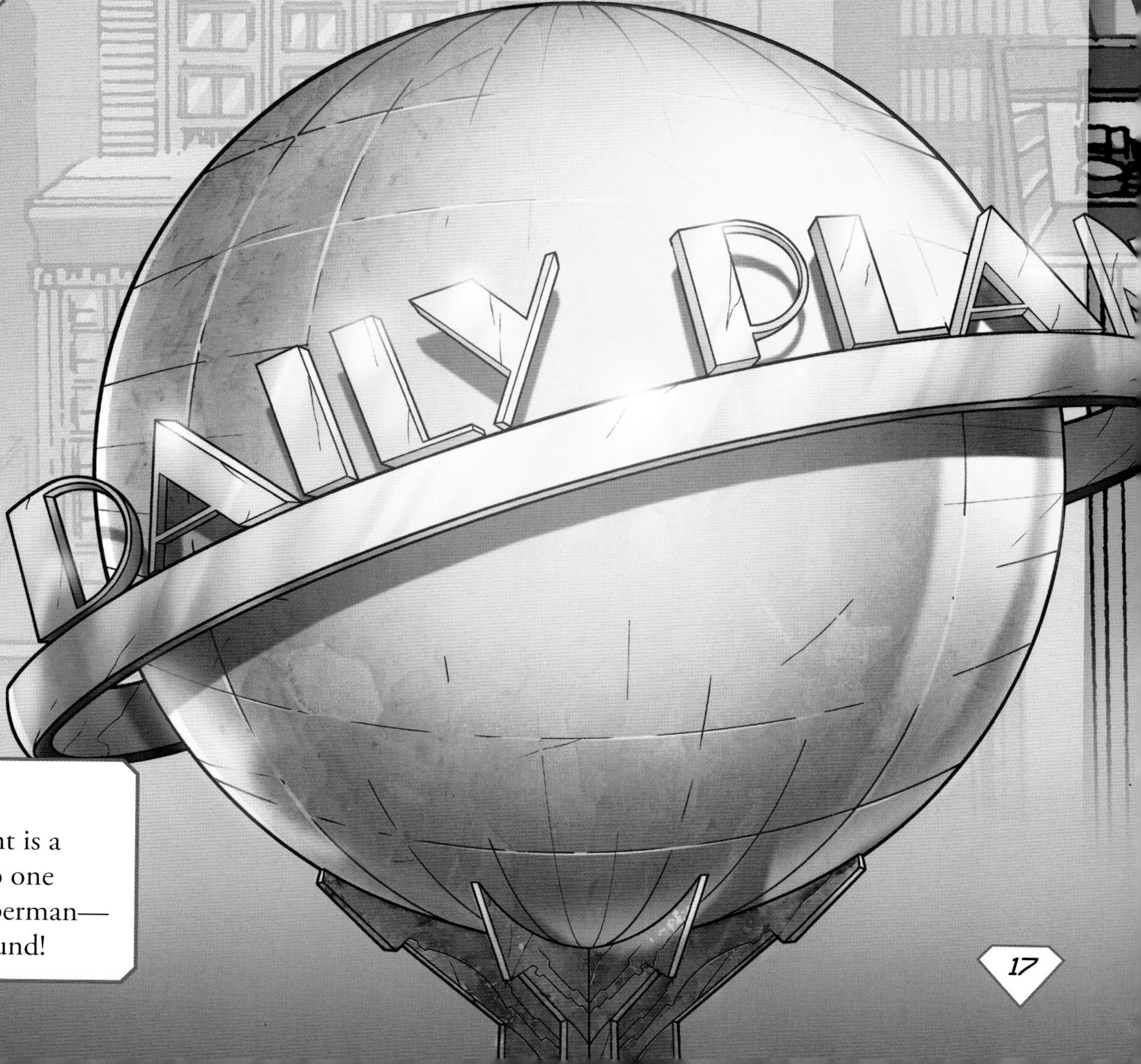
DAILY PLA

Clark Kent

Mild-mannered Clark Kent is a hard-working reporter. No one suspects that he is also Superman—the biggest news story around!

Lex Luthor

Lex Luthor is the richest man in Metropolis and his business empire, LexCorp, employs a large portion of the city's inhabitants. He is also the most ruthless schemer in Metropolis and will stop at nothing to get what he wants. And what he wants most of all is to destroy Superman.

President Luthor
Lex can be charming when he needs to be. He pretended to approve of Superman to win votes and become President of the United States.

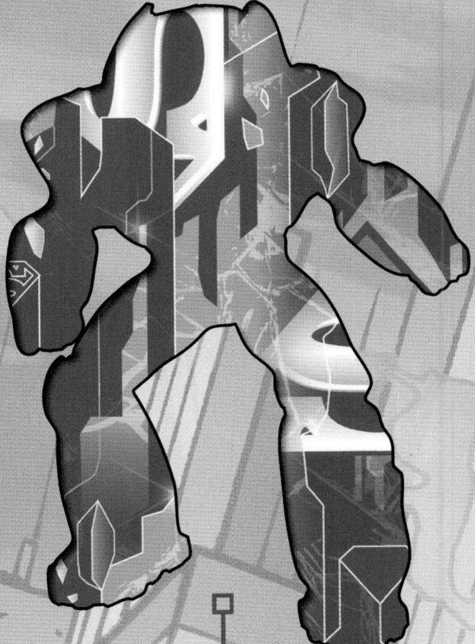

Damaged Child
Lex grew up in Smallville and knew Clark quite well. But after a lab accident in which he lost his hair, Lex became bitter and vengeful.

Battle Suit
Lex is no match for Superman in battle, so he created a special suit. It was made from impenetrable armor and equipped with deadly Kryptonite-powered weapons.

Injustice League
Lex formed a team of the world's greatest super-villains, including the Joker and Cheetah. Their mission was to conquer Earth and defeat the Justice League.

Infinity, Inc.
Lex acquired the technology to turn regular humans into super heroes. He created his own super hero team called Infinity, Inc. to carry out his orders.

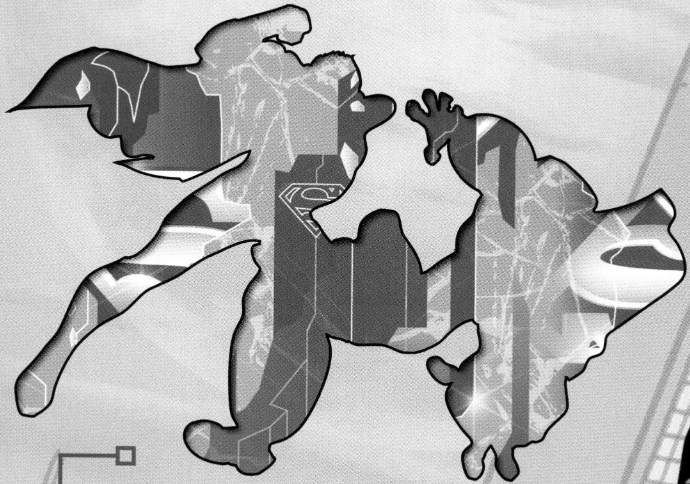

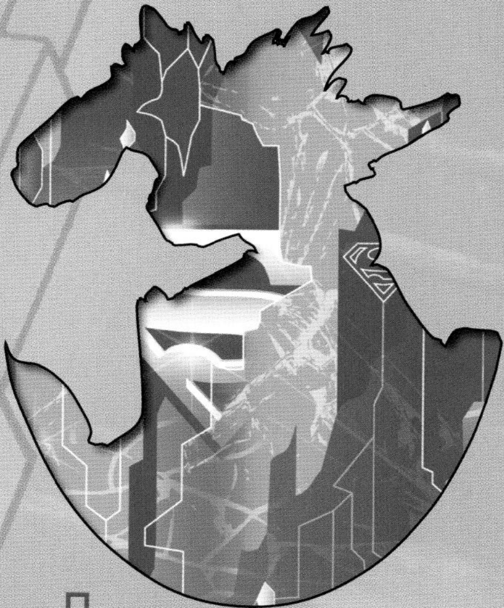

Knocked Out
Even wearing his special battle suit, Lex Luthor was defeated by the Man of Steel.

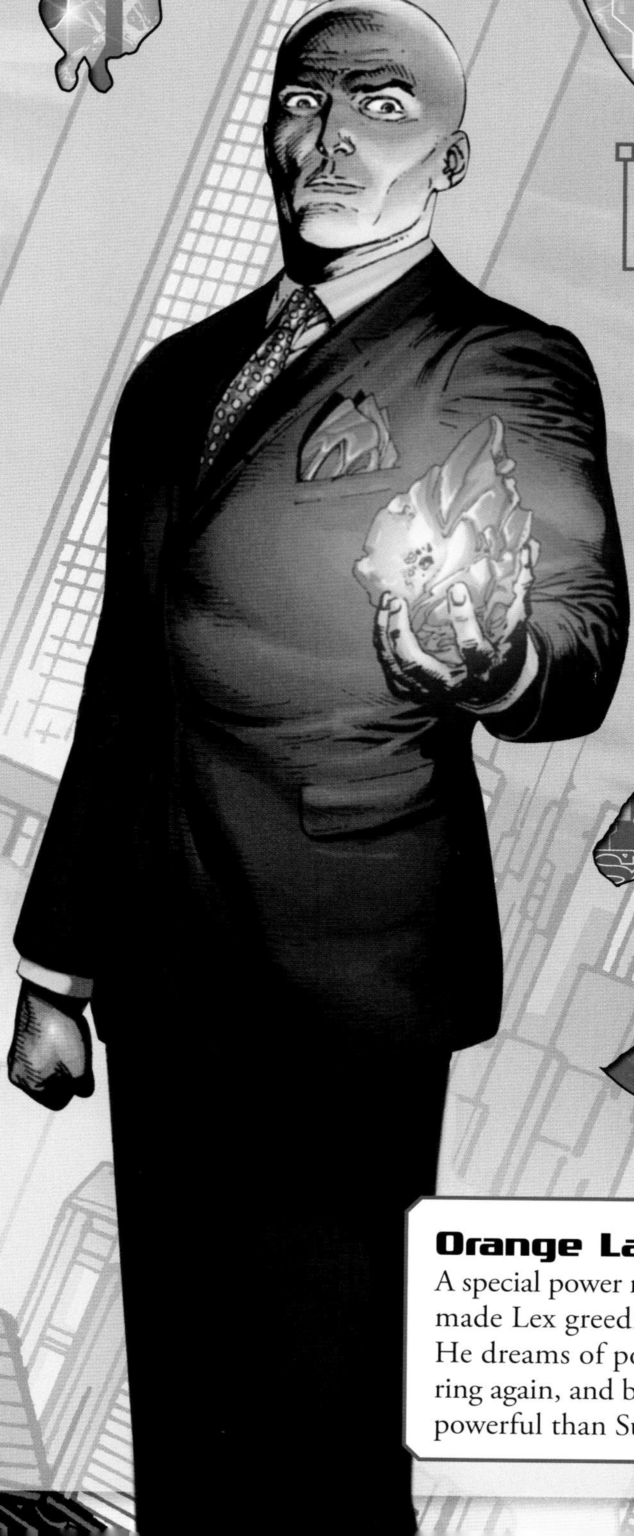

Nice Try
Lex Luthor hoped to defeat Superman when he turned an ancient Kryptonian warship into a giant Kryptonite robot.

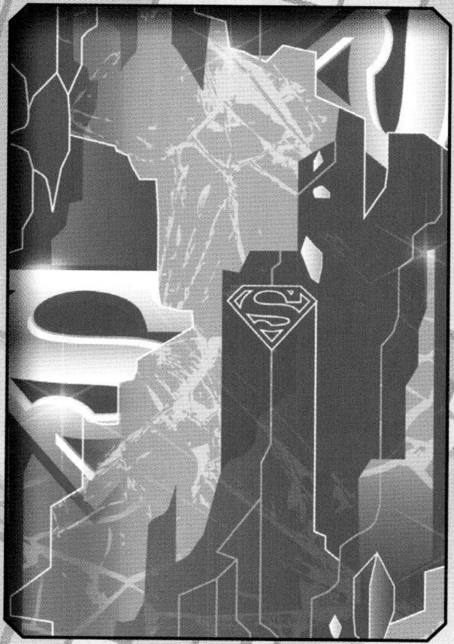

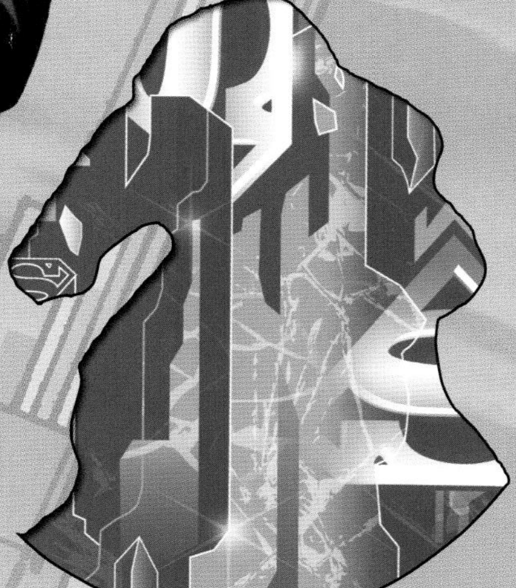

Revenge Squad
Lex Luthor's desire to destroy Superman and become the most powerful man in Metropolis led him to form the Superman Revenge Squad with villains Parasite, Metallo, and Bizarro.

Orange Lantern
A special power ring temporarily made Lex greedier than ever. He dreams of possessing the ring again, and becoming more powerful than Superman!

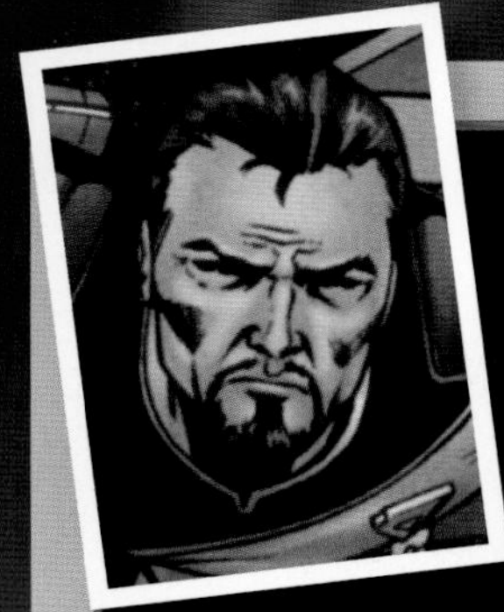

General Zod

Kryptonian villain General Zod tried to take over Krypton, and failed. His punishment was 40 years in the Phantom Zone, a prison outside space and time. As a result, Zod survived Krypton's destruction. When he was set free, Zod tried to conquer Earth.

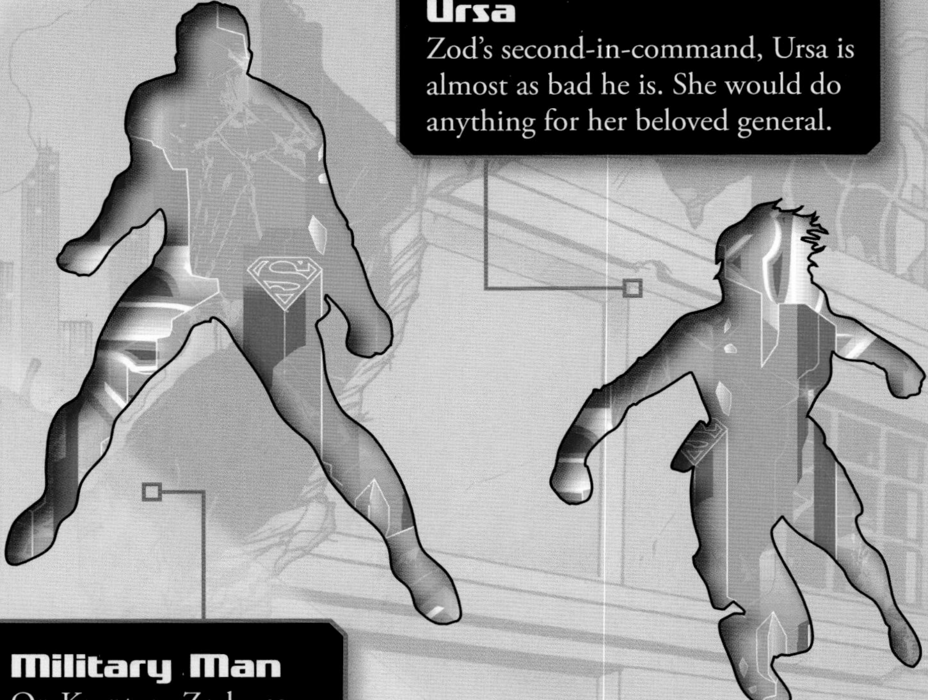

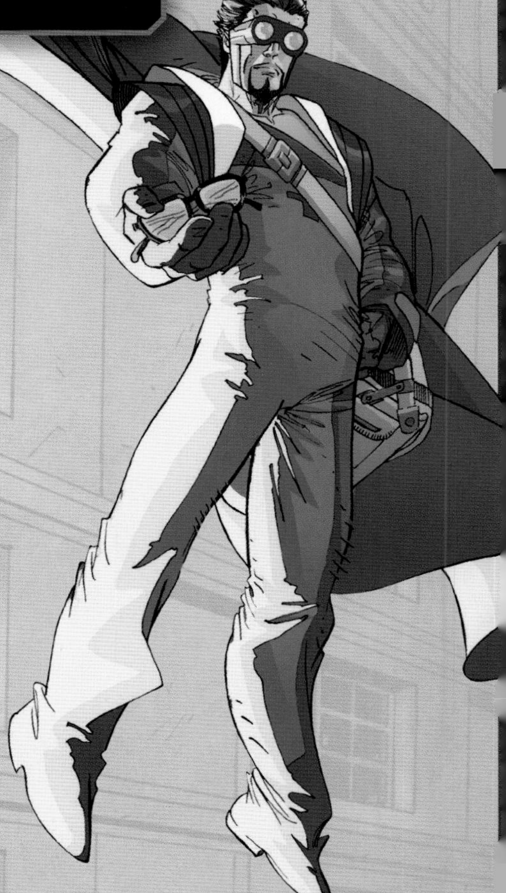

Ursa
Zod's second-in-command, Ursa is almost as bad he is. She would do anything for her beloved general.

Military Man
On Krypton, Zod was a ruthless general. He is a skilled fighter and an expert in military tactics.

Phantom Zone
Prisoners in the Phantom Zone do not speak, eat, sleep, or grow older. They merely exist there until they have served their sentences.

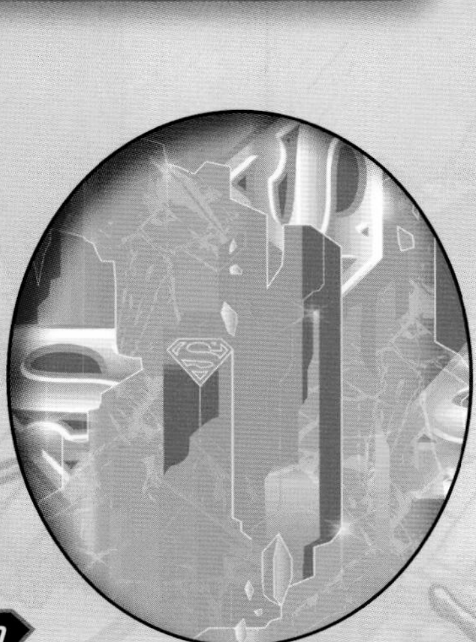

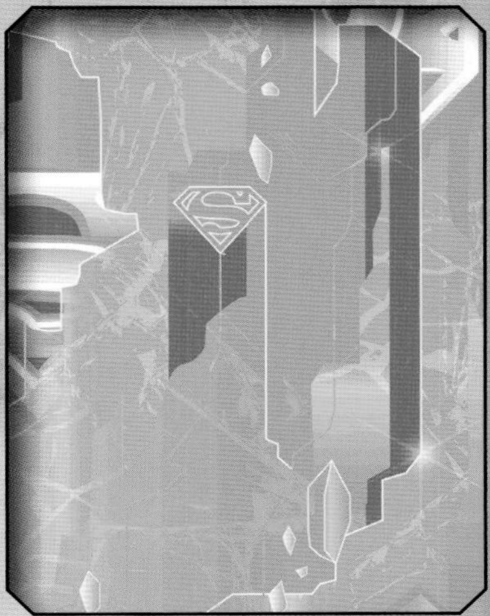

Dangerous Foe
Zod was determined to take over Earth, but Superman defeated him and sent him back to where he belonged—in the Phantom Zone.

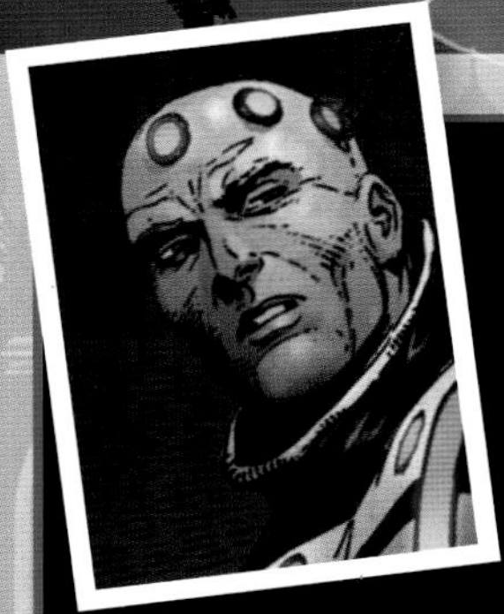

Brainiac

This evil alien is one of the most intelligent and dangerous beings in the universe. He travels through space looking for cities to shrink and store in bottles. Superman will never let Brainiac add Metropolis to his creepy collection.

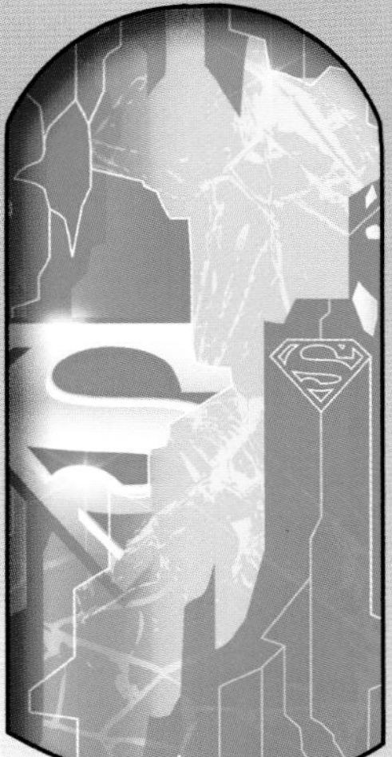

Skull Ship
Brainiac roams the universe in a skull-shaped spaceship. He stores all his treasures on board and can connect his mind to the ship's core.

Collector of Worlds
Knowledge is power to Brainiac. He uses his ship to capture a planet's city, its people, and its culture in a bottle. Once done, he destroys the planet.

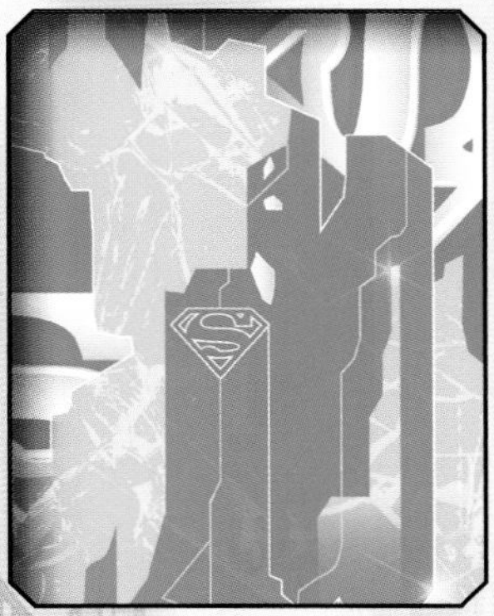

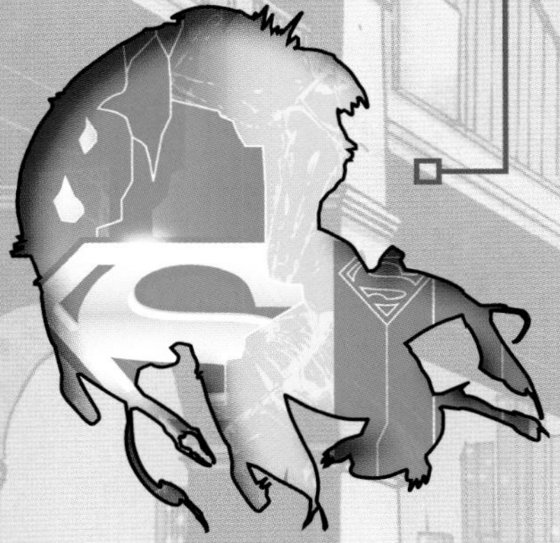

Brain Power
Brainiac is no fighter, but his mind is so powerful that he can control the actions of others. He took over Metallo to fight Superman.

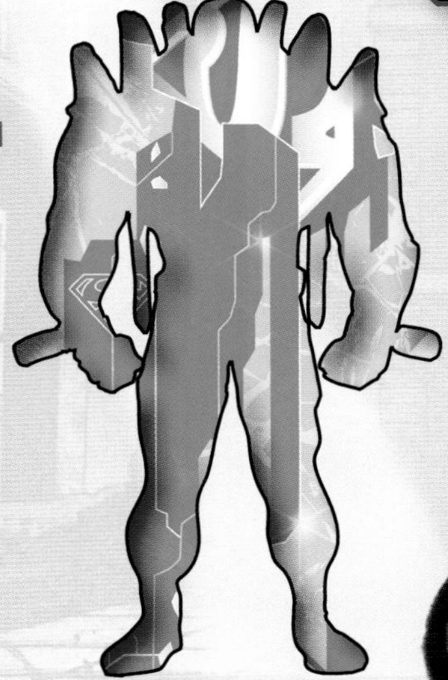

Brainiac 13
This villain often upgrades his body. Brainiac 13 was so advanced that he traveled from the future to 21st-century Metropolis to take over Earth.

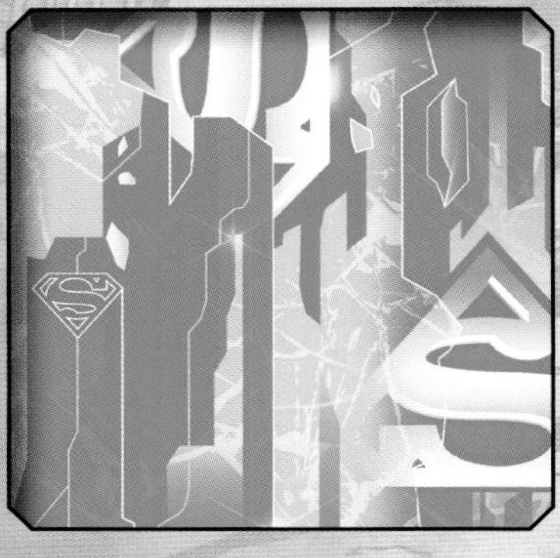

Ultimate Prize
Brainiac lured Superman aboard his ship hoping to fulfill his desire to add the Man of Steel to his collection of treasures.

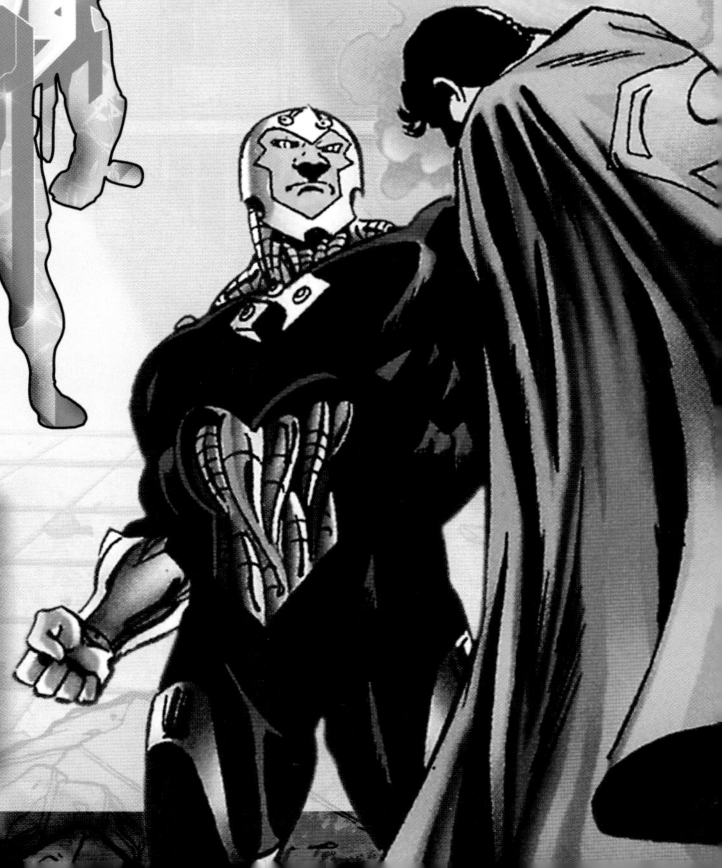

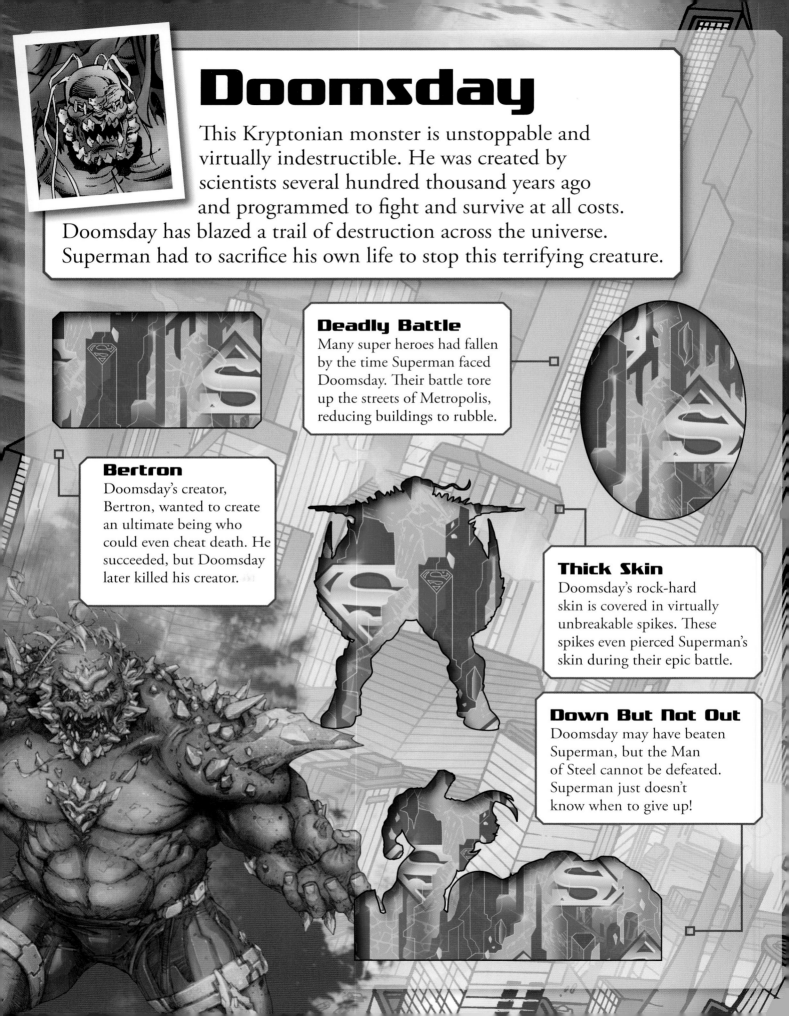

Doomsday

This Kryptonian monster is unstoppable and virtually indestructible. He was created by scientists several hundred thousand years ago and programmed to fight and survive at all costs. Doomsday has blazed a trail of destruction across the universe. Superman had to sacrifice his own life to stop this terrifying creature.

Deadly Battle

Many super heroes had fallen by the time Superman faced Doomsday. Their battle tore up the streets of Metropolis, reducing buildings to rubble.

Bertron

Doomsday's creator, Bertron, wanted to create an ultimate being who could even cheat death. He succeeded, but Doomsday later killed his creator.

Thick Skin

Doomsday's rock-hard skin is covered in virtually unbreakable spikes. These spikes even pierced Superman's skin during their epic battle.

Down But Not Out

Doomsday may have beaten Superman, but the Man of Steel cannot be defeated. Superman just doesn't know when to give up!

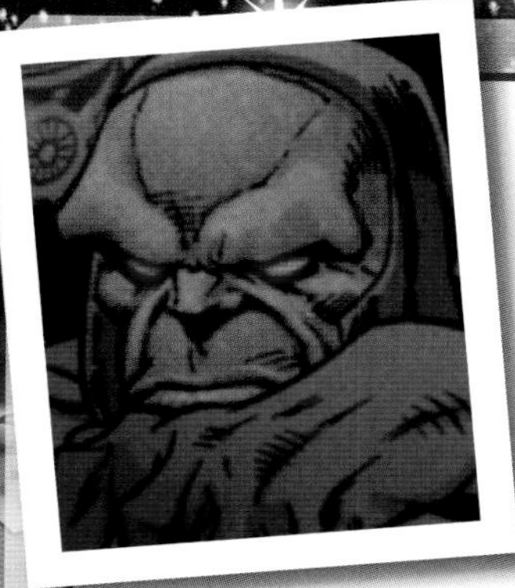

Darkseid

One of the universe's most powerful villains, Darkseid rules the planet Apokolips by fear. This tyrant seeks the legendary Anti-Life Equation, which would give him the power to enslave the whole universe. Superman will not let that happen!

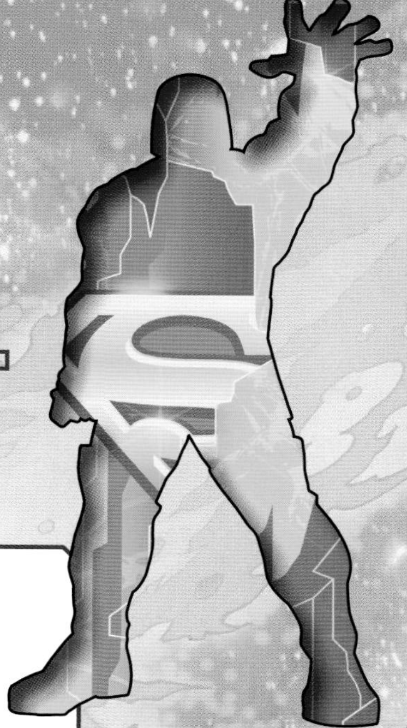

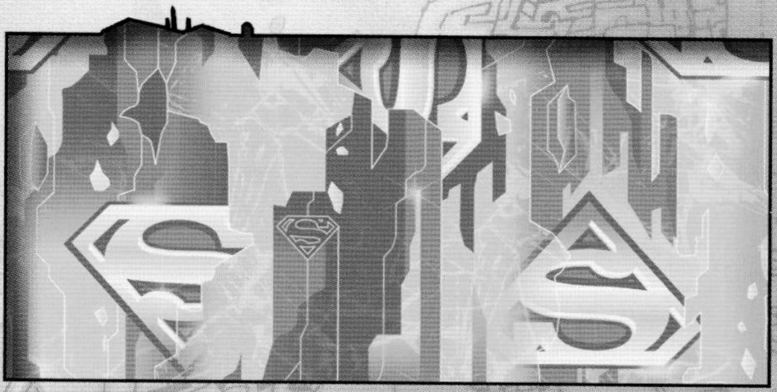

Deadly Powers

Darkseid's body is practically impenetrable, and he is extremely intelligent. He can also read minds and move objects with his mind.

Apokolips

Darkseid's army of Parademons patrols the planet, hunting down anyone who defies his rule. The people of Apokolips are slaves known as the Hunger Dogs.

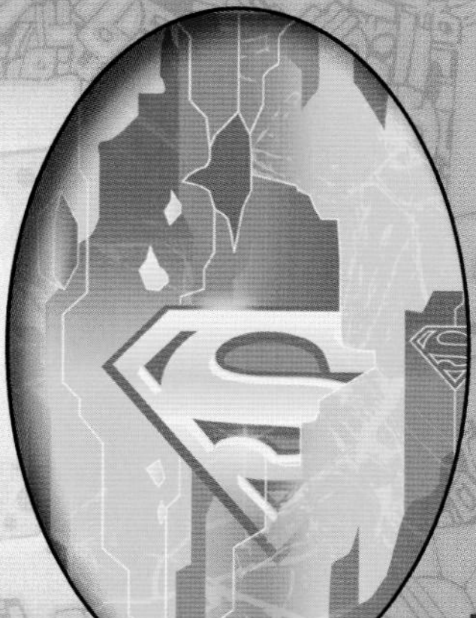

Omega Beams

Darkseid can project energy blasts, called Omega Beams, from his eyes. These can kill or transport a victim wherever Darkseid chooses.

Granny Goodness

Granny Goodness, Darkseid's evil minion, trains Darkseid's soldiers, turning them into brutal warriors who would die for their master.

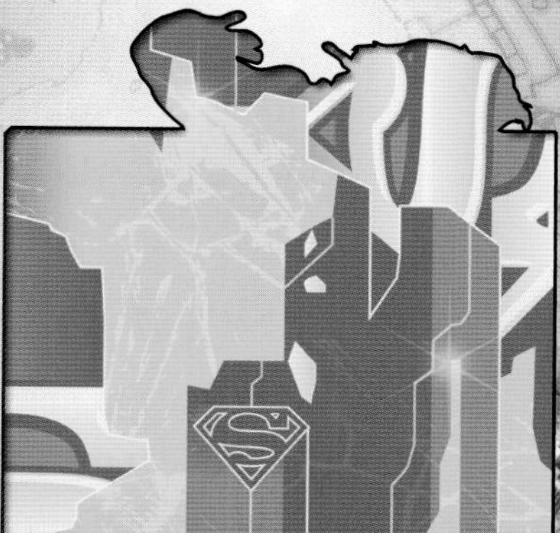

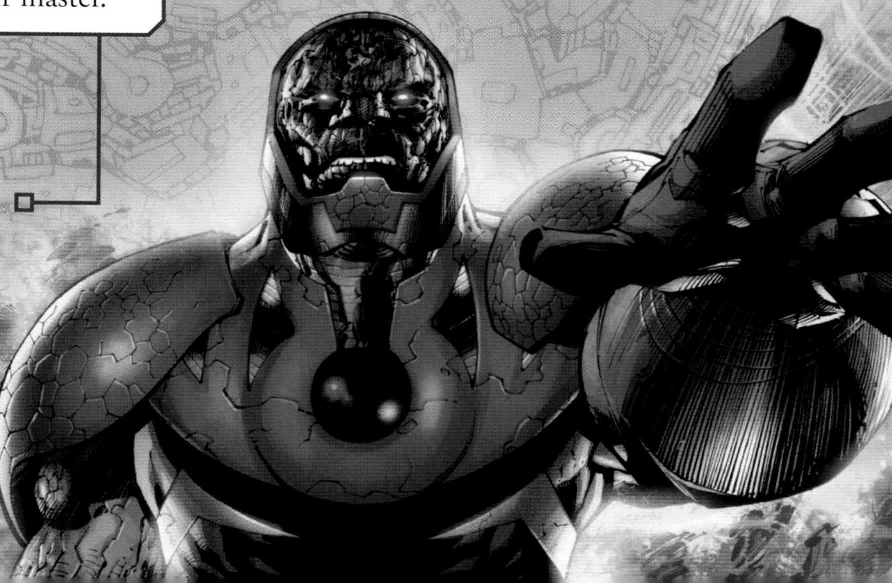

Alien Foes

Earth has had many visitors, not all of them welcome. Some of the Man of Steel's greatest challenges have come from evil aliens. While some plan to invade and conquer the planet, others just want to cause trouble. Whatever their evil plans, it's Superman's job to try and stop them.

H'el
This powerful Kryptonian explorer believes that Earthlings are unworthy of Superman and sees himself as the ultimate protector of Kryptonian culture.

Replikon
First Replikon tried to destroy life on Earth, and failed. He then tried to defeat Superman, but he failed at that, too.

Lobo
Unlike Superman, this superpowered bounty hunter doesn't care about right or wrong. He hires himself out for money and never gives up until the job is done.

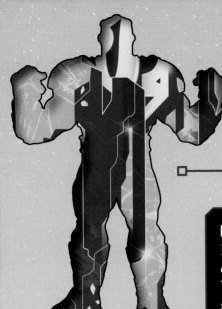

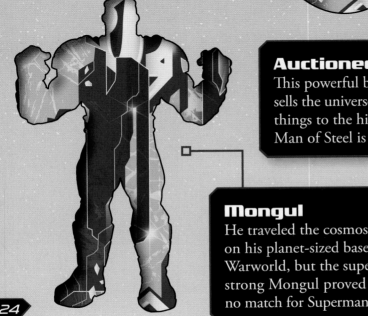

Auctioneer
This powerful being collects and sells the universe's most interesting things to the highest bidder. The Man of Steel is high on his list.

Mongul
He traveled the cosmos on his planet-sized base, Warworld, but the super-strong Mongul proved no match for Superman.

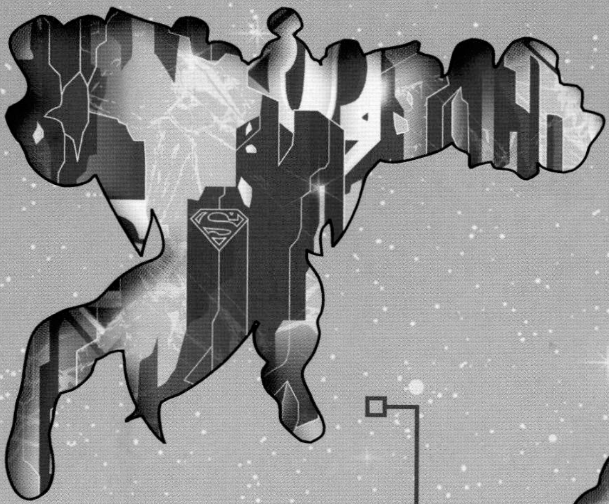

Anti-Monitor

This giant being is from a parallel universe. He is so tough that he can withstand a punch even from the Man of Steel!

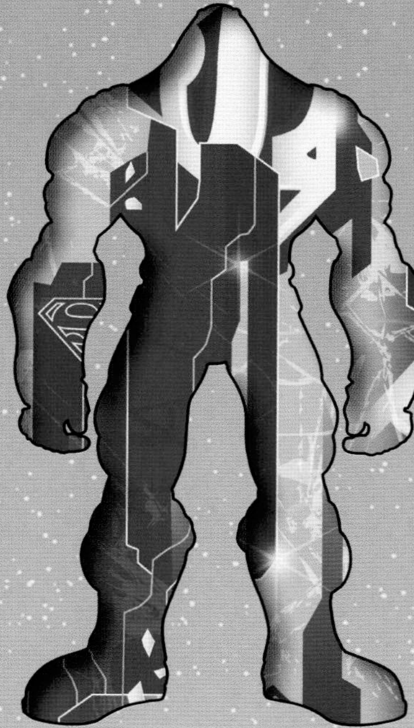

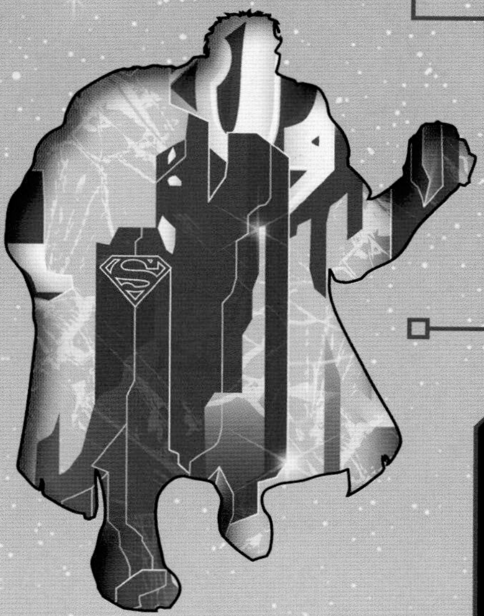

Imperiex

Also known as the Destroyer of Galaxies, Imperiex unleashed a massive attack on Earth. Superman joined forces with other super heroes—and even villains—to stop him.

Bizarro

Bizarro is an imperfect clone of the Man of Steel. This mixed-up bad guy is the opposite of Superman—Kryptonite only makes him stronger!

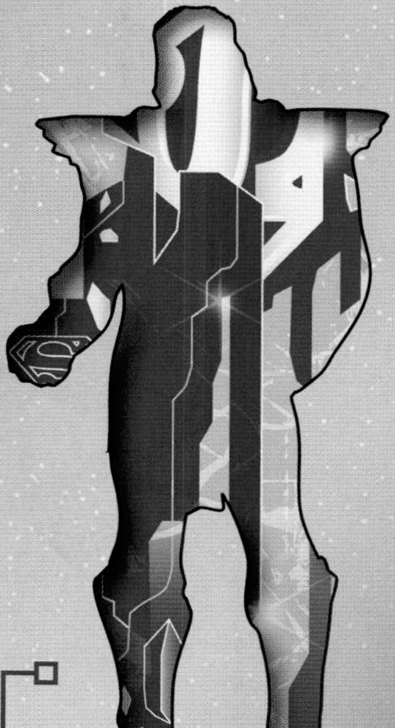

Grayven

The son of Darkseid, Grayven used his super-strength and endurance to destroy planets. No one was a match for him, until he met Superman.

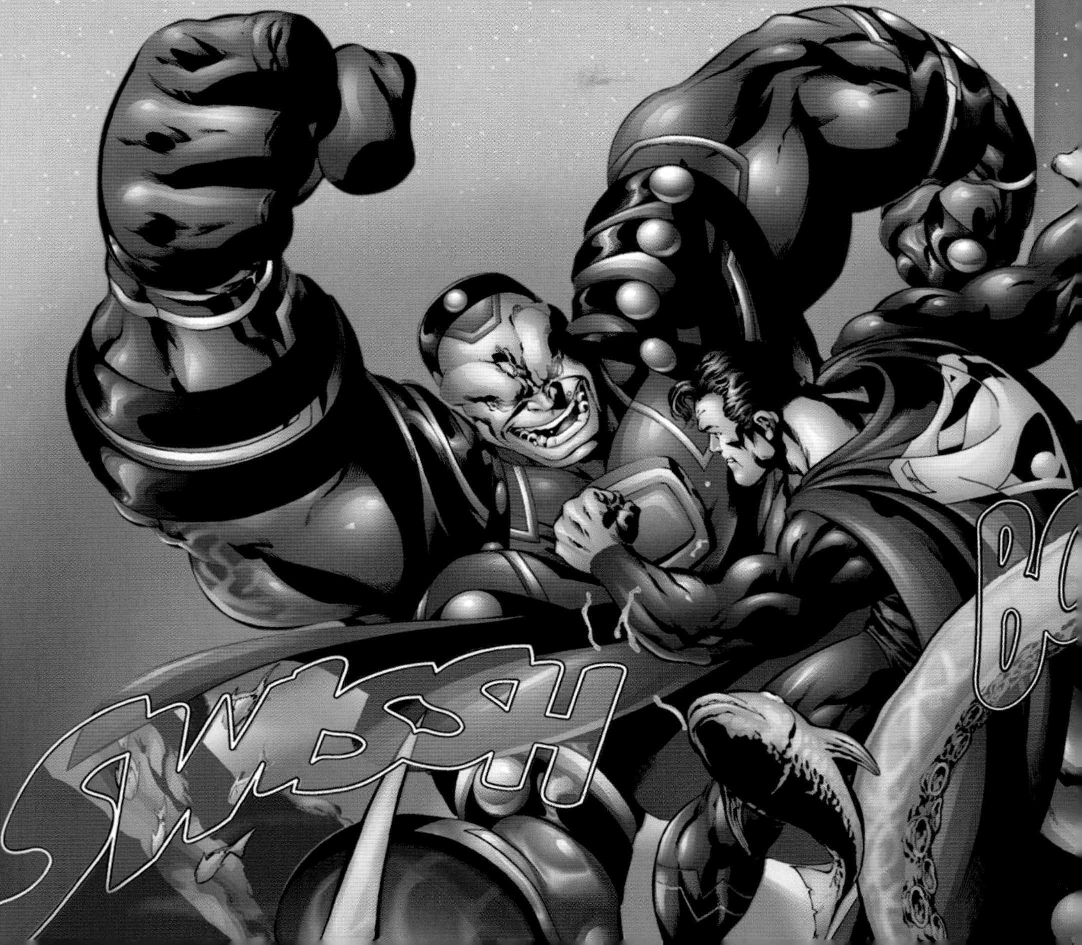

Parasite

Rudy Jones wanted more out of life, but he got more than he bargained for when he ate a donut covered in toxic waste. Jones was transformed into a greedy, power-absorbing villain named Parasite. This hideous monster is hungry for power—making Superman his primary target.

Monster Looks

Parasite is not a pretty sight. He has a blubbery body and a mouth full of sharp teeth that fasten on to his prey.

Greedy

Parasite only has to touch someone to absorb their powers. He can even assume their shape and personality.

Power Thief

Parasite is hungry for Superman's powers. He's come close, but so far hasn't been able to combat the Man of Steel's abilities.

Warming Up

When Supergirl faced Parasite, the evil monster absorbed all her abilities.

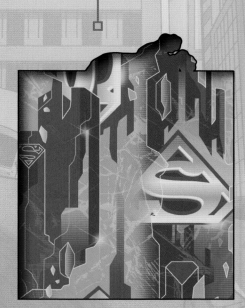

Metallo

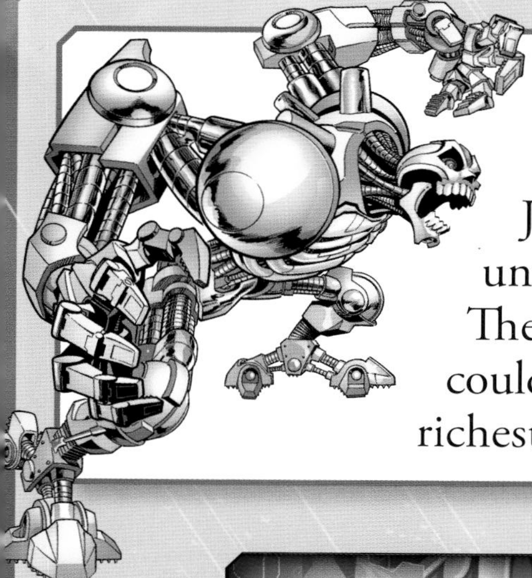

John Corben was an ordinary soldier in the US Army, until he underwent a top-secret military procedure. The experiment's real aim was to create a soldier who could defeat Superman, and it was funded by Superman's richest and most devious foe, Lex Luthor.

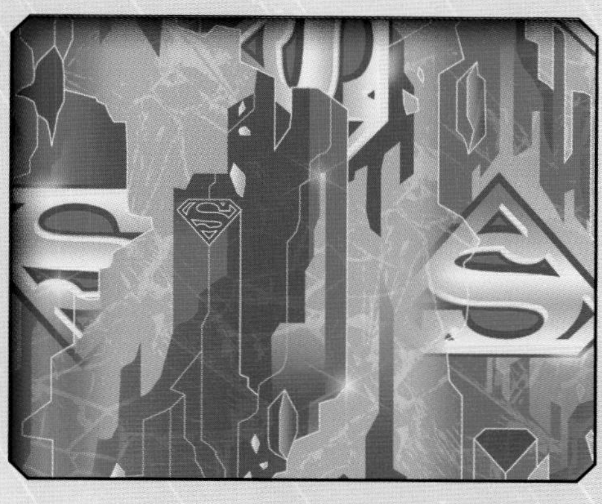

New Man

Corben became part human, part robot. The experiment also made his heart burst, so Luthor gave him a new one—made of Kryptonite.

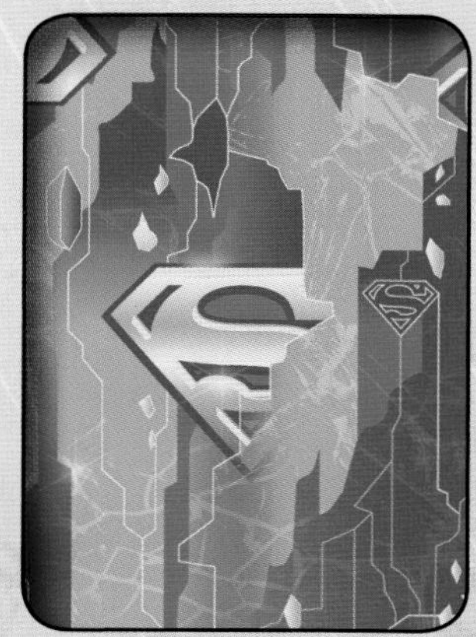

Heart to Kill

Superman is more than a match for Metallo—until the villain reveals his Kryptonite heart and weakens the Man of Steel.

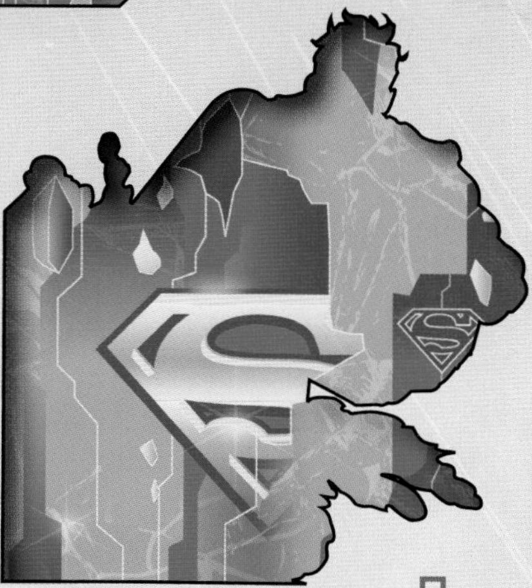

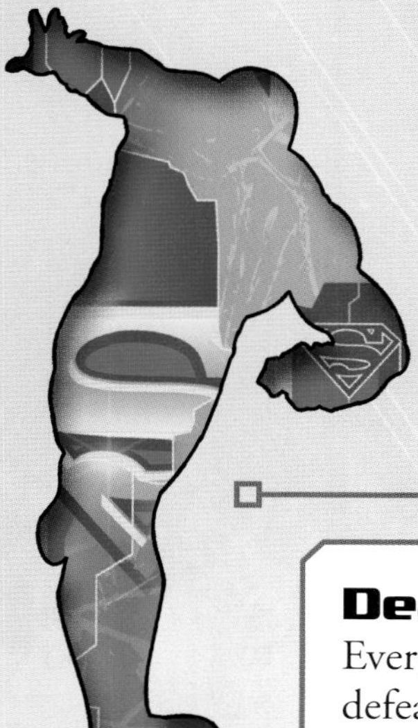

Getting Ahead

Superman once prevented Metallo from causing mayhem by destroying his body and removing his head!

Deadly Mission

Every time Metallo is defeated, he simply repairs his metallic body to continue his rampages.

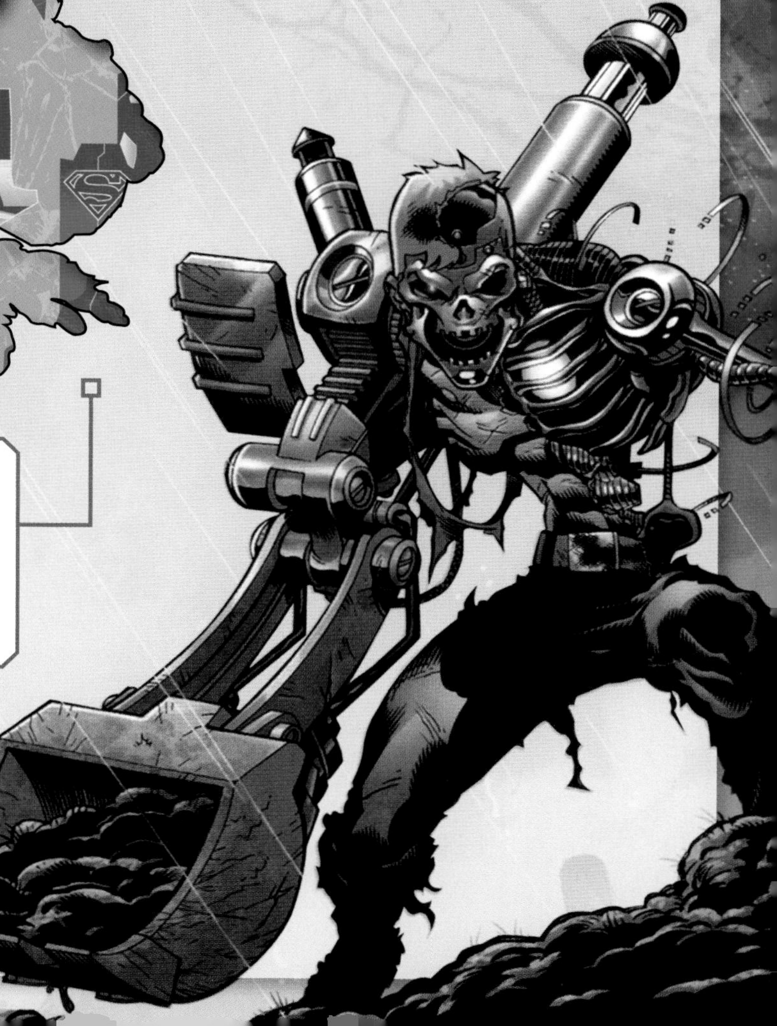

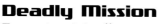

Other Foes

It's not just visitors from other worlds who cause problems for Superman, Earth has some pretty bad people, too. Many of them seem to really dislike the Man of Steel—he's always getting in their way, thwarting their evil plans, and protecting the people of Earth.

Livewire
Leslie Lewis became super-villain Livewire after losing her job. Born with the gift of manipulating electricity, her lightning blasts can stun Superman.

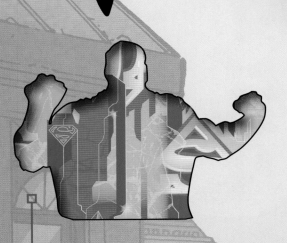

Cyborg Superman
A failed space mission turned Hank Henshaw into a cyborg. He once pretended to be a super hero to make Superman look bad.

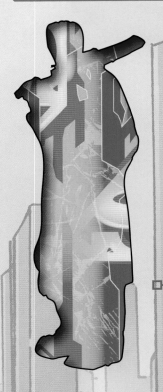

Manchester Black
He hated Superman for his belief in honor and justice, and tried to use his psychic powers against the Man of Steel.

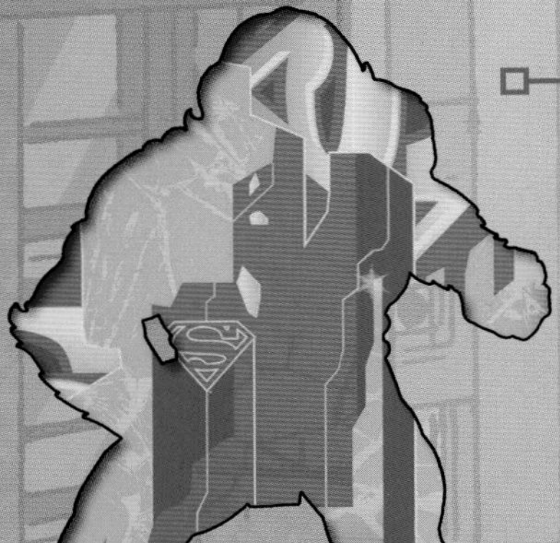

Ultra-Humanite
To save his powerful brain from his failing body, Ultra-Humanite began transferring his brain into powerful bodies—such as that of a large white gorilla.

Bruno Mannheim
The head of Metropolis's Intergang, this powerful criminal recently joined forces with the evil alien Darkseid.

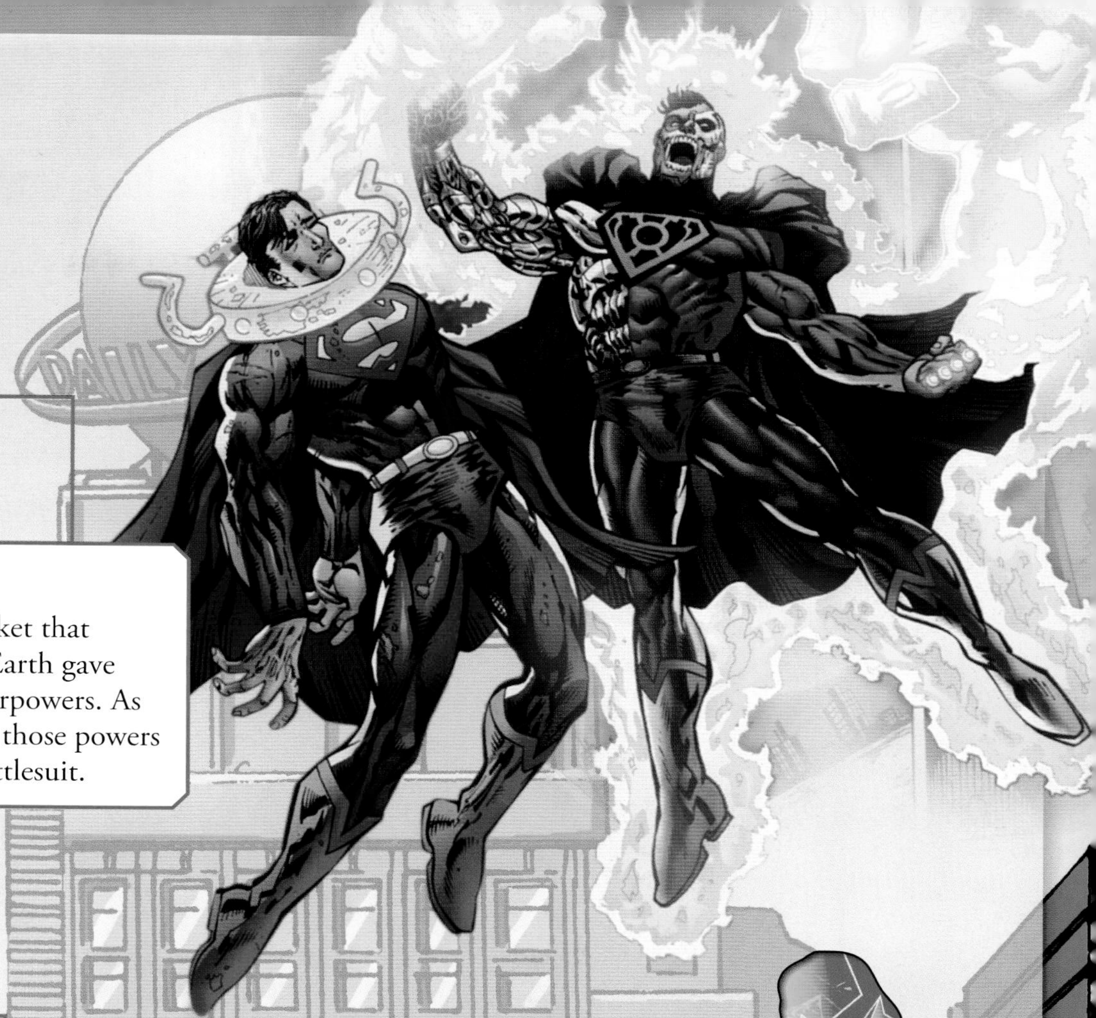

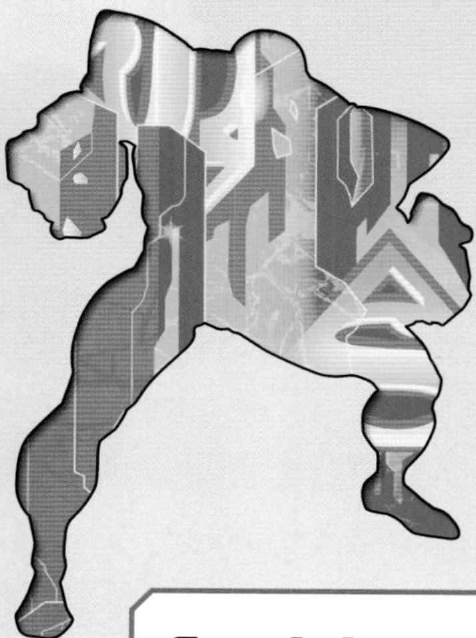

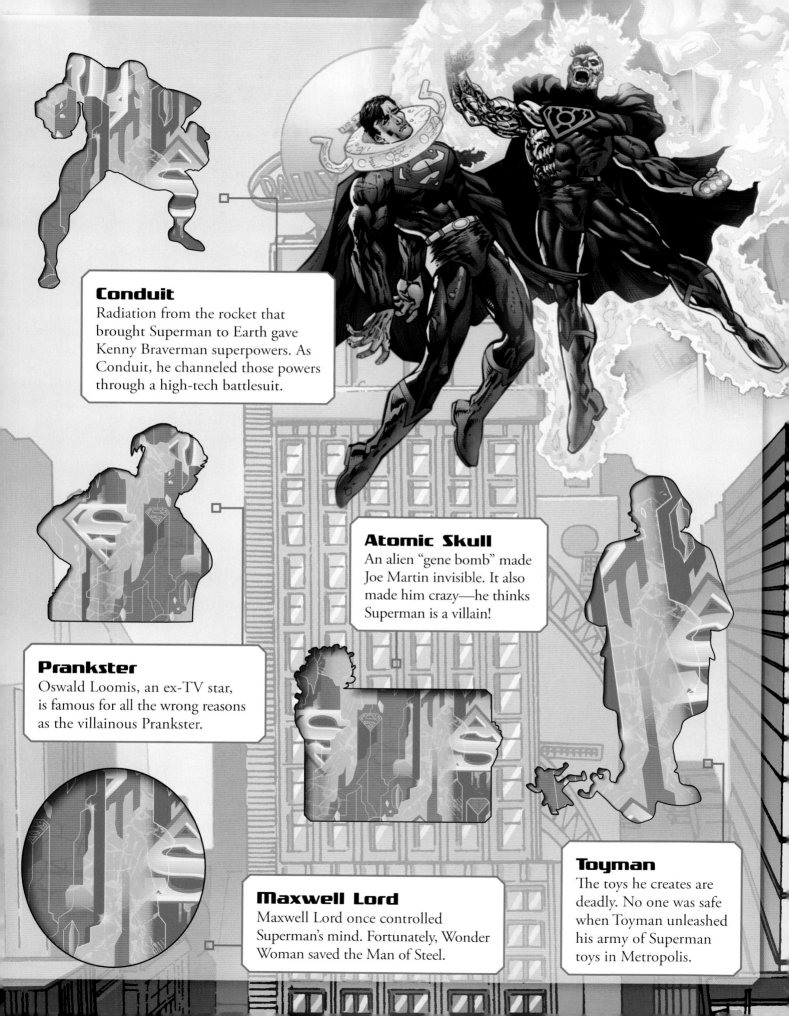

Conduit
Radiation from the rocket that brought Superman to Earth gave Kenny Braverman superpowers. As Conduit, he channeled those powers through a high-tech battlesuit.

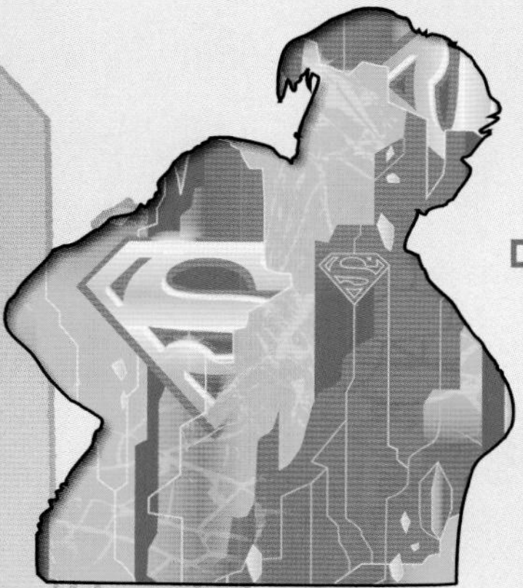

Atomic Skull
An alien "gene bomb" made Joe Martin invisible. It also made him crazy—he thinks Superman is a villain!

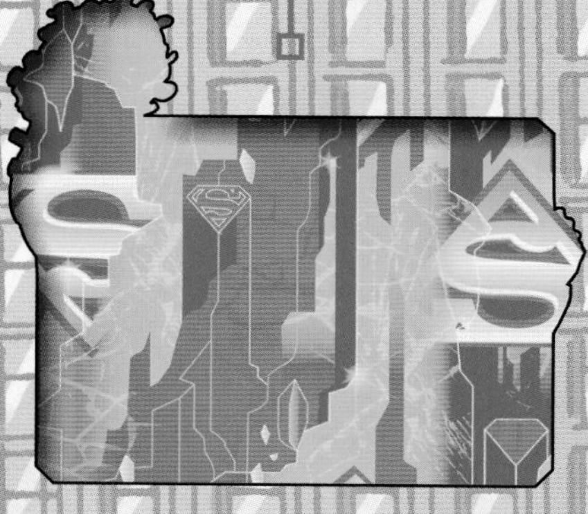

Prankster
Oswald Loomis, an ex-TV star, is famous for all the wrong reasons as the villainous Prankster.

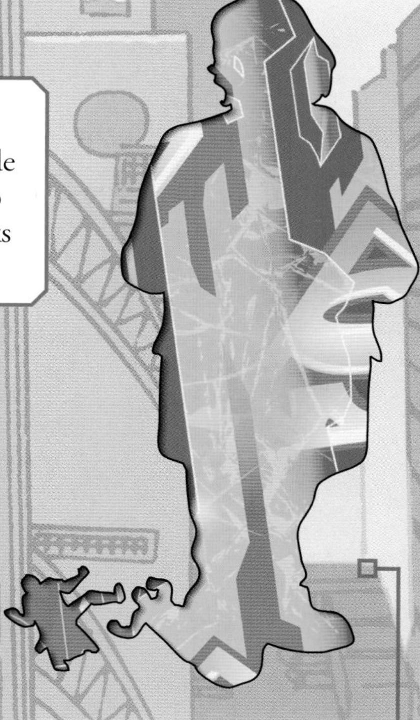

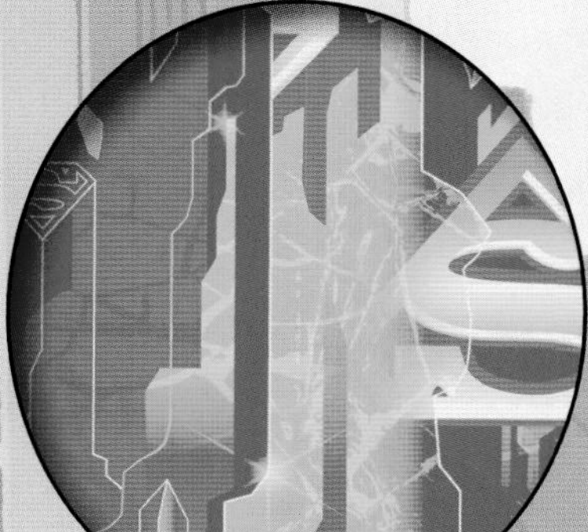

Toyman
The toys he creates are deadly. No one was safe when Toyman unleashed his army of Superman toys in Metropolis.

Maxwell Lord
Maxwell Lord once controlled Superman's mind. Fortunately, Wonder Woman saved the Man of Steel.

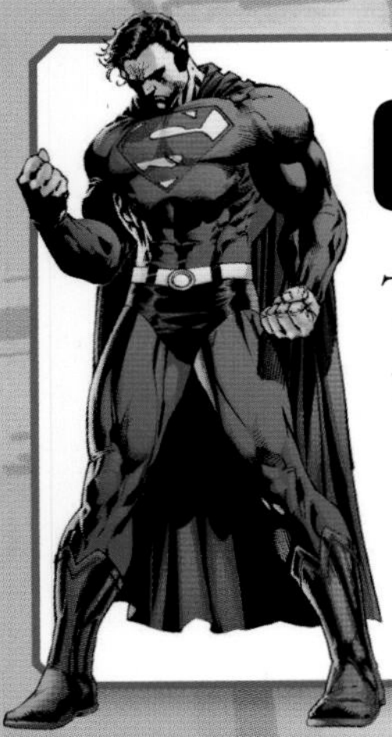

Great Battles

To most people of Earth, Superman is a hero for protecting their planet. However, to super-villains, Superman spells trouble. He's all that stands between them and world domination. When fiendish cunning fails, some villains resort to brute force, hoping to defeat the Man of Steel in battle.

Son of Mongul

The son of Superman's old foe, Mongul II actually helped him defeat Imperiex. But later he fought Superman, Batman, and Wonder Woman.

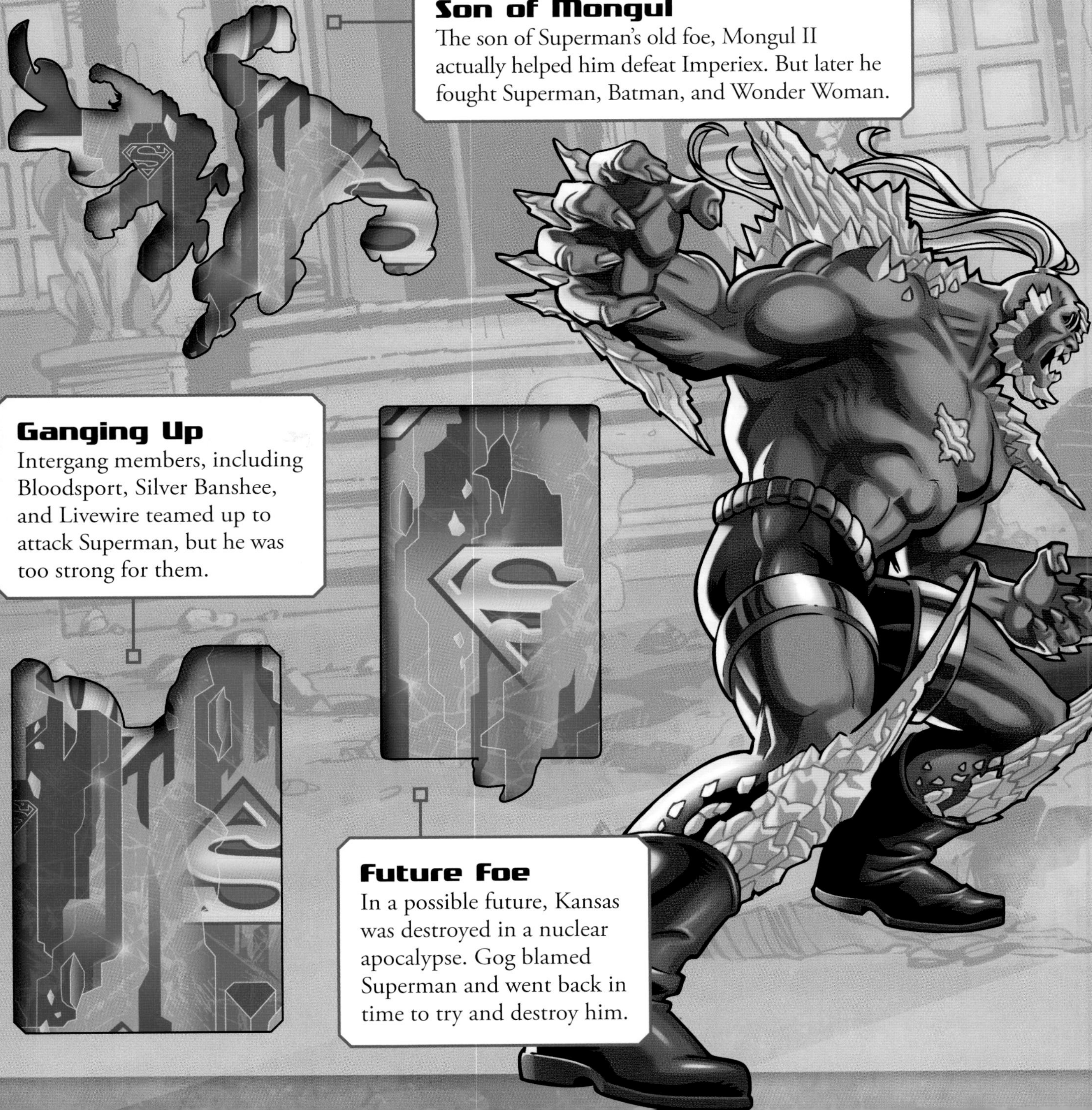

Ganging Up

Intergang members, including Bloodsport, Silver Banshee, and Livewire teamed up to attack Superman, but he was too strong for them.

Future Foe

In a possible future, Kansas was destroyed in a nuclear apocalypse. Gog blamed Superman and went back in time to try and destroy him.

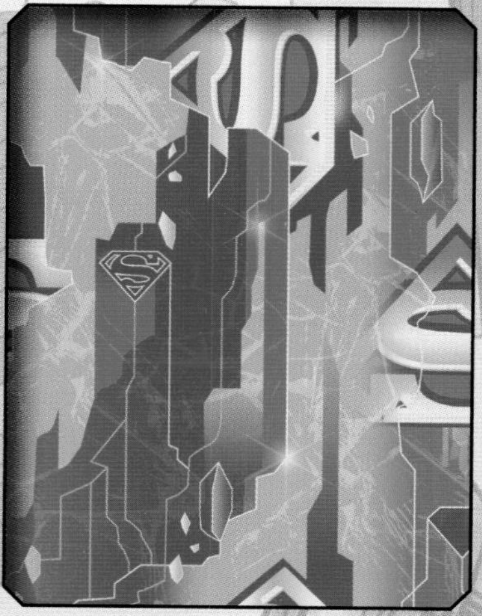

Hero Hater
Solomon Grundy, the undead monster, hates super heroes. Superman has fought him many times, but he keeps coming back!

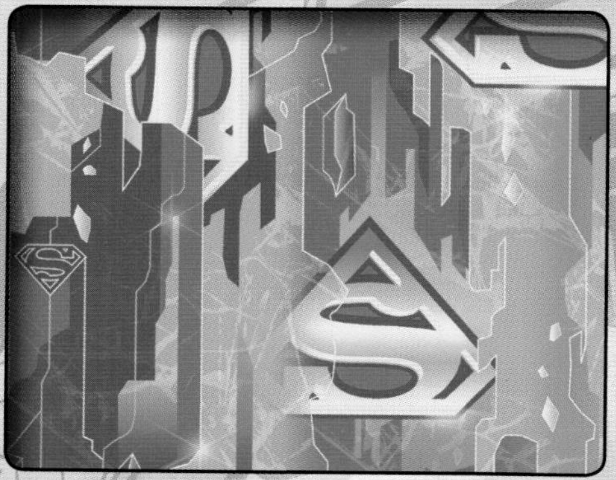

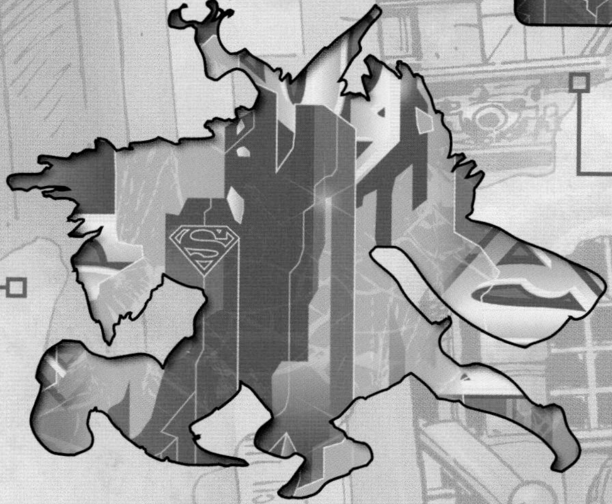

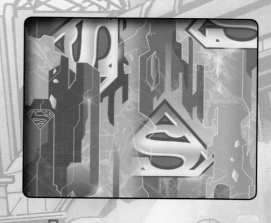

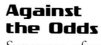

Odd Teamup
When Imperiex threatened to destroy the galaxy, major villains, including Darkseid and Brainiac, helped Superman to conquer him.

Not Dead Yet
So far, Doomsday is the only villain to have defeated Superman. The Man of Steel seemed dead, but he returned stronger than ever.

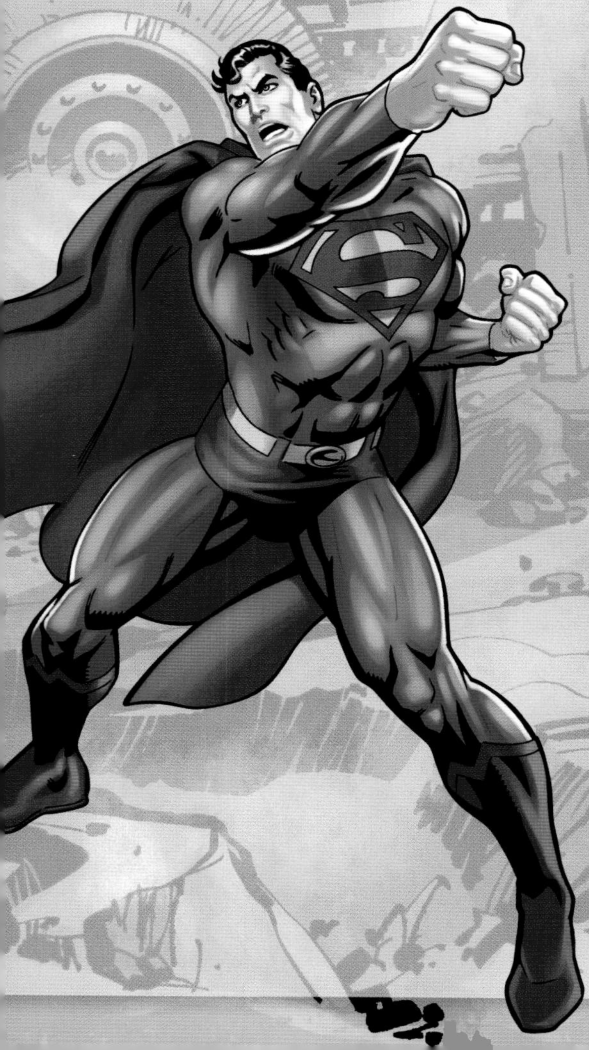

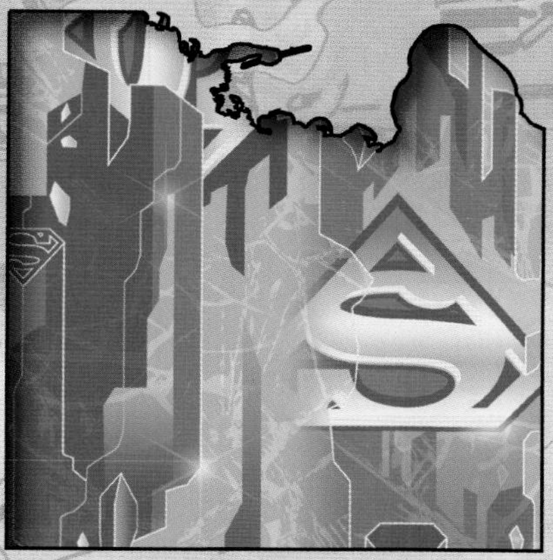

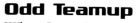

Against the Odds
Superman often takes on more than one foe at a time. He usually wins, especially if fellow crime fighter, Batman, lends a hand.

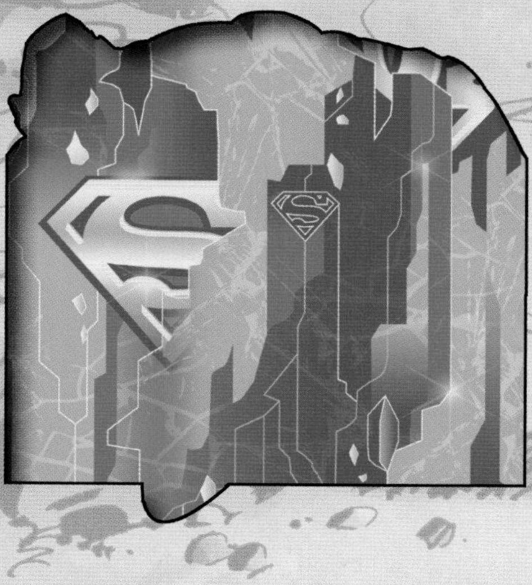

Victory!
Although injured by Darkseid's Omega Beams, Superman was able to defeat the tyrannical alien and banish him to another dimension.

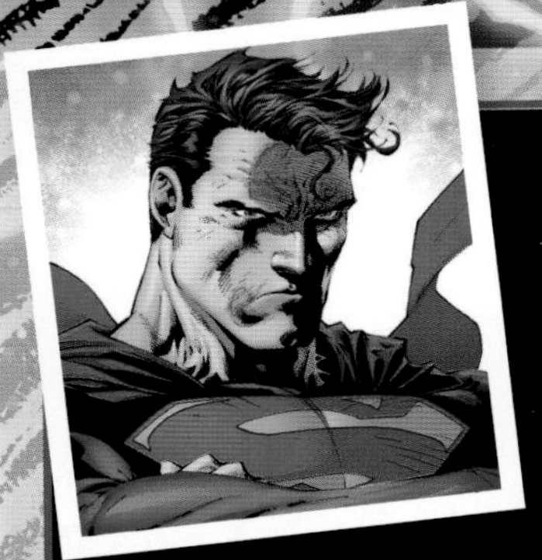

Magic Villains

Despite his awesome abilities, Superman has a surprising weakness—magic. The Man of Steel can be affected by magical forces, and he has no power over the supernatural. Superman can't explain why—there are no logical explanations when magic is involved!

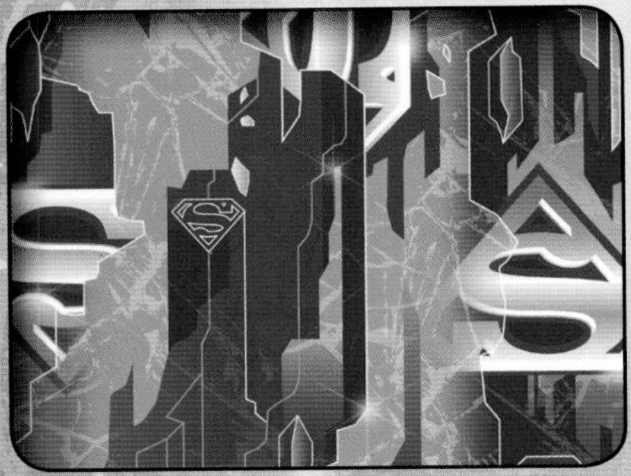

Mr. Mxyzptlk
This mischievous imp from the Fifth Dimension torments Superman with his magic. The Man of Steel does not find his practical jokes funny!

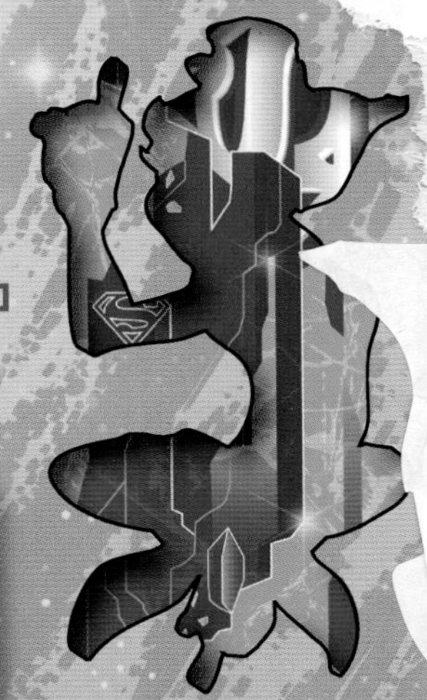

Encantadora
This troublesome enchantress gave Superman a Kryptonite kiss, nearly killing him. She then sold fake Kryptonite to Superman's enemies.

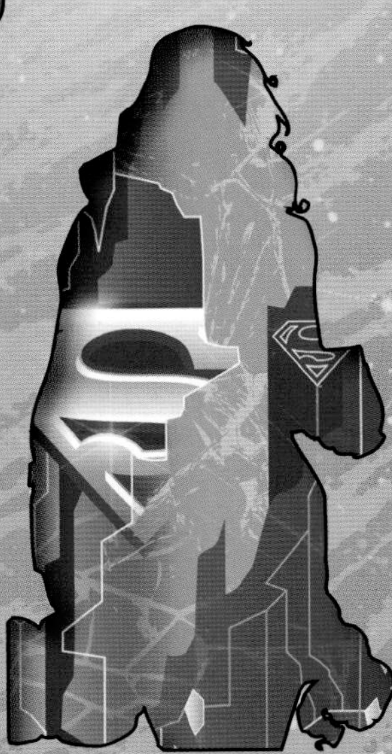

Eclipso
Using his magical black diamond, Eclipso once controlled Superman and made him attack the hero Shazam.

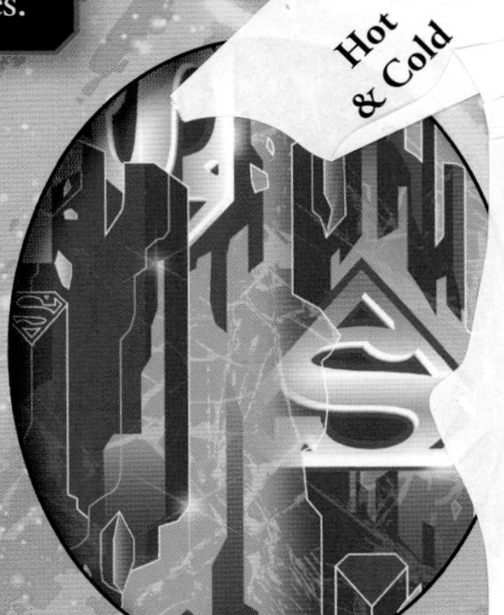

Hot & Cold

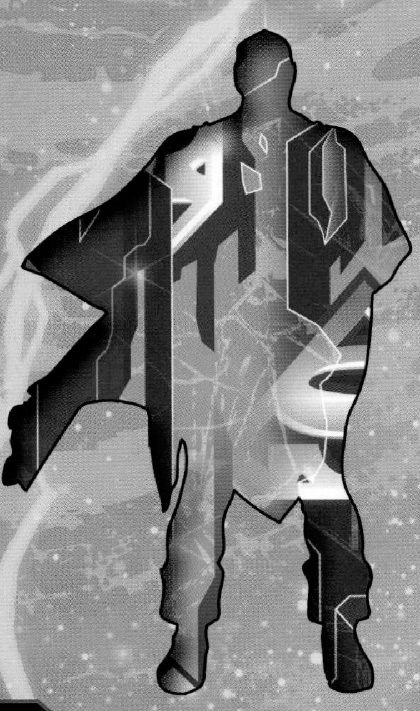

Black Adam
Black Adam is an ancient Egyptian prince with magical powers, who has clashed with Superman in the past.

Silver Banshee
Her high-pitched screams are deadly for humans. But Silver Banshee is equally dangerous to Kryptonians, too. She once turned Supergirl into a Banshee!

Stickers

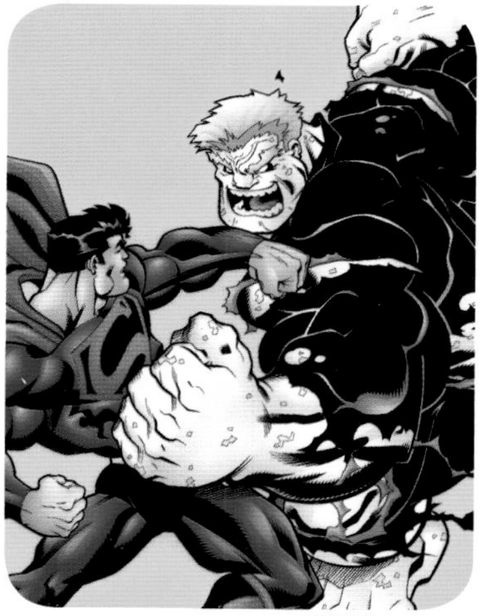

Hero Hater

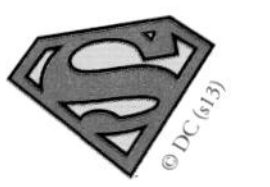

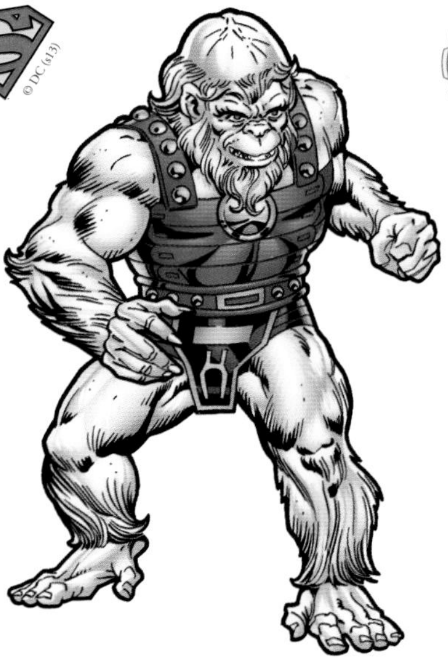

Ultra-Humanite

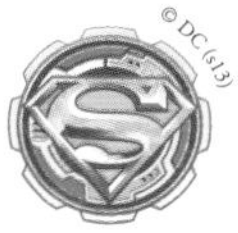

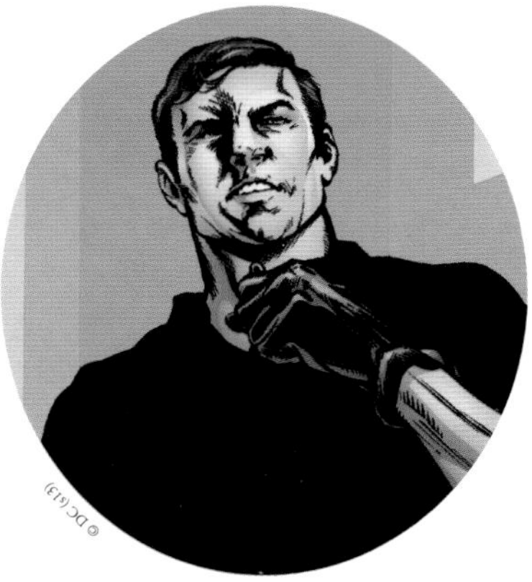

Maxwell Lord

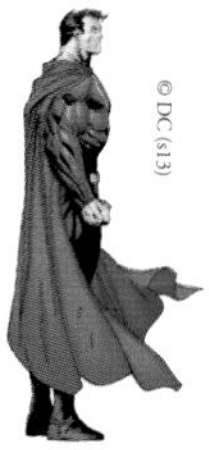

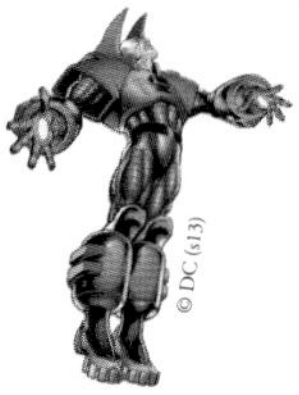

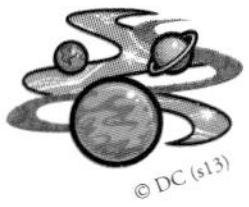

Deadly Mission

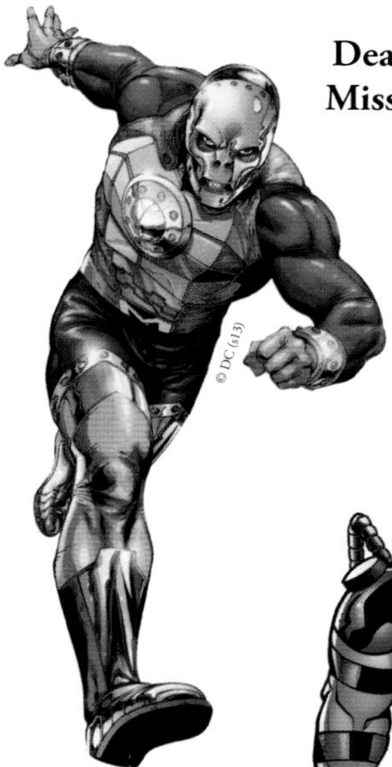

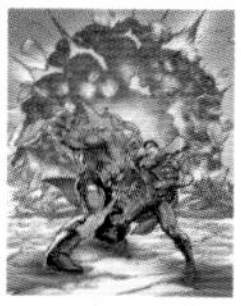

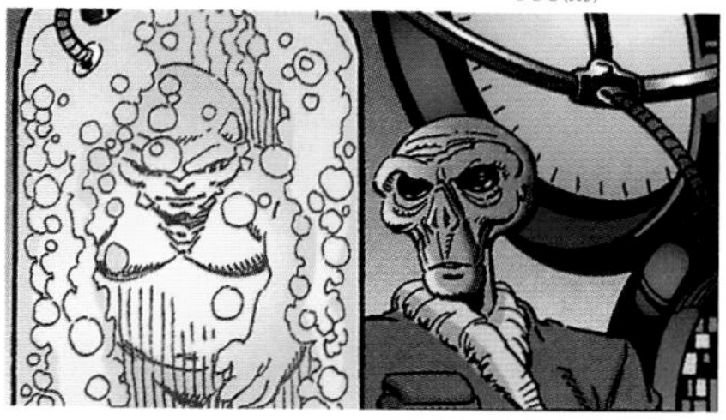

Bertron

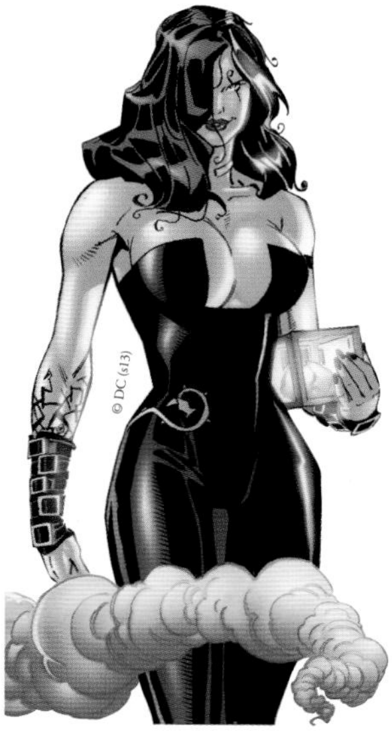

Encantadora

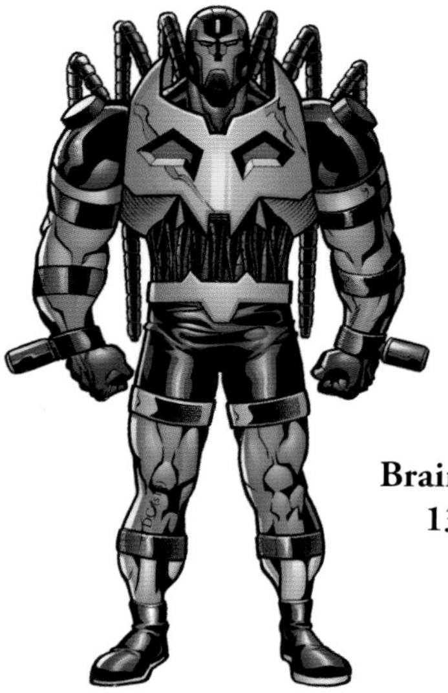

Brainiac 13

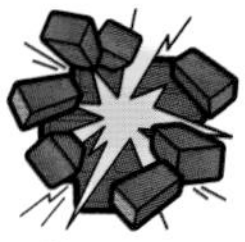

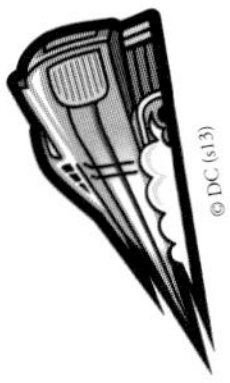

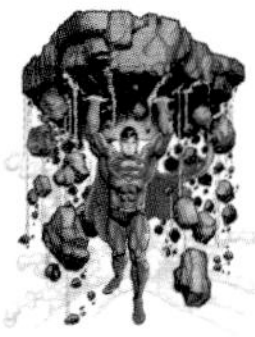

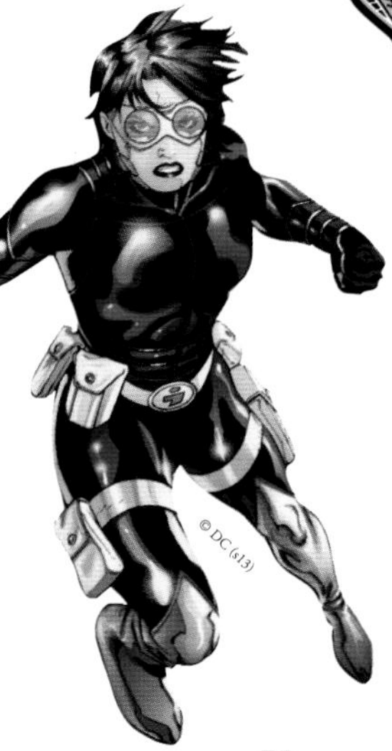

Ursa

Down But Not Out

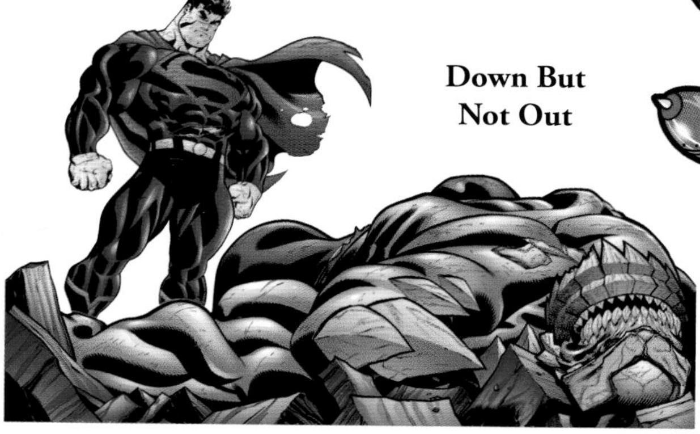

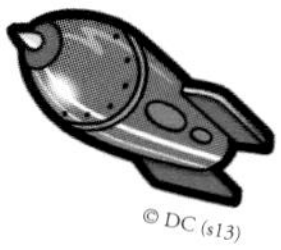

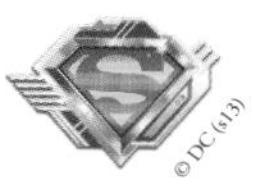

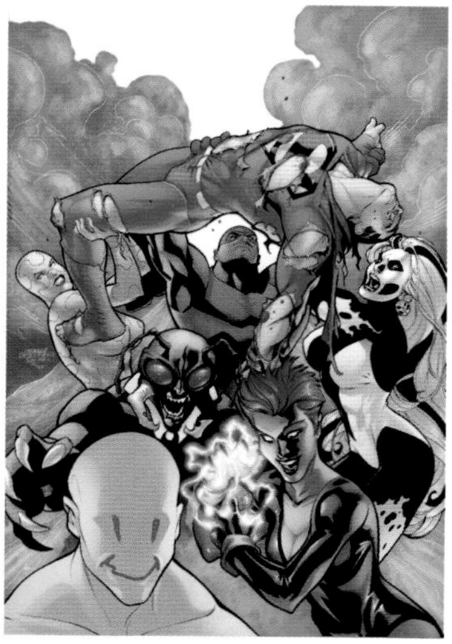

Ganging Up

Stickers

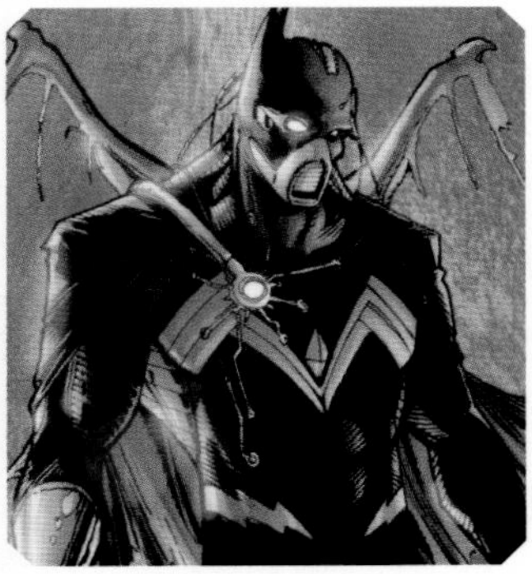

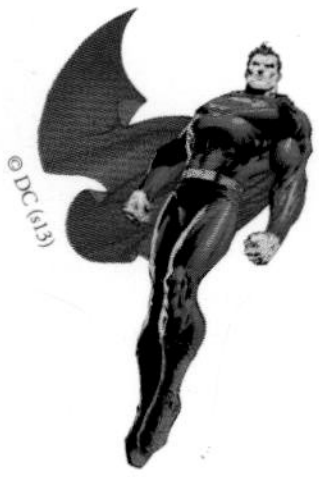

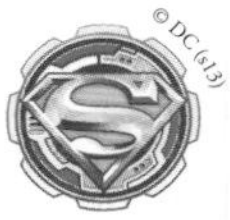

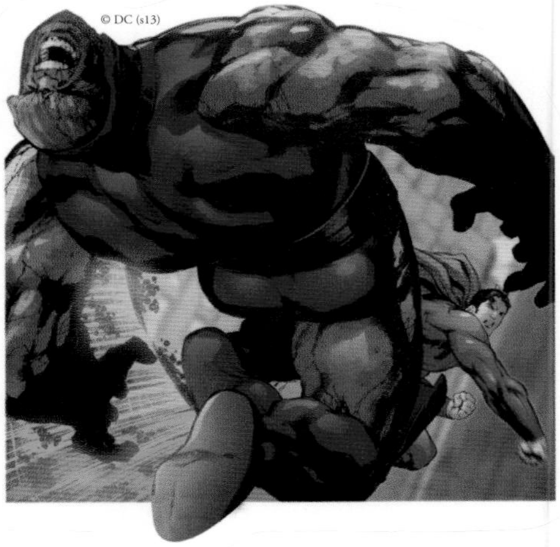

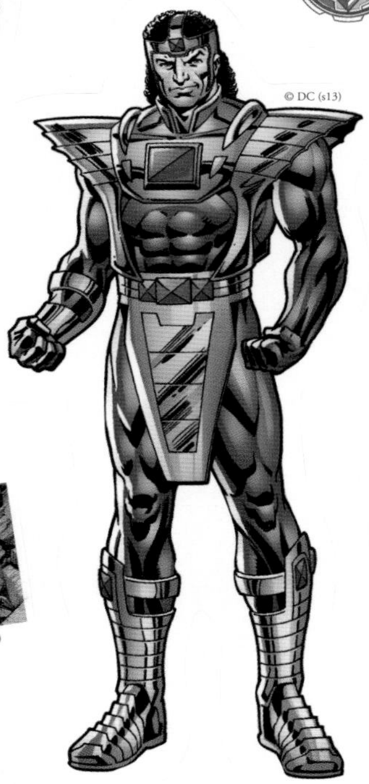

Replikon

Thick Skin

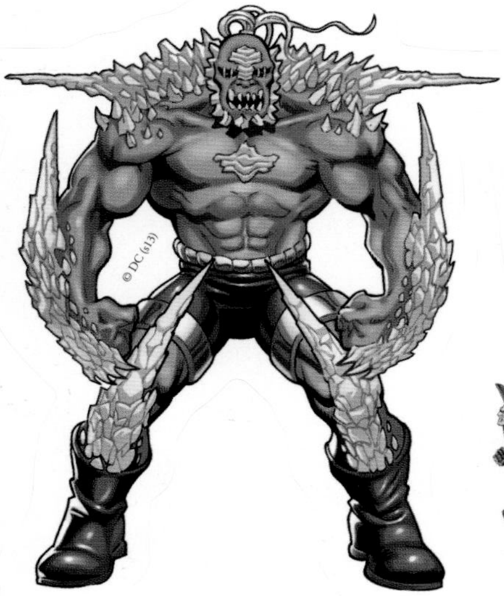

Victory!

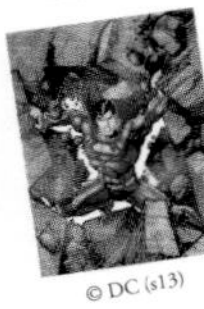

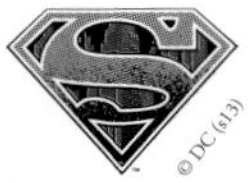

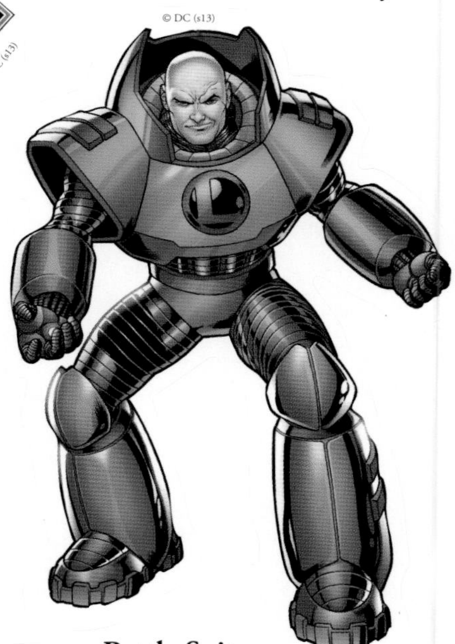

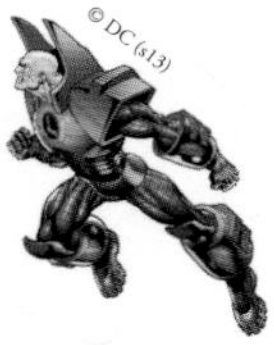

Grayven

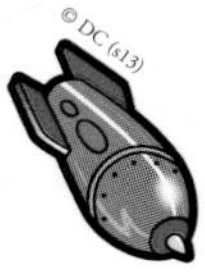

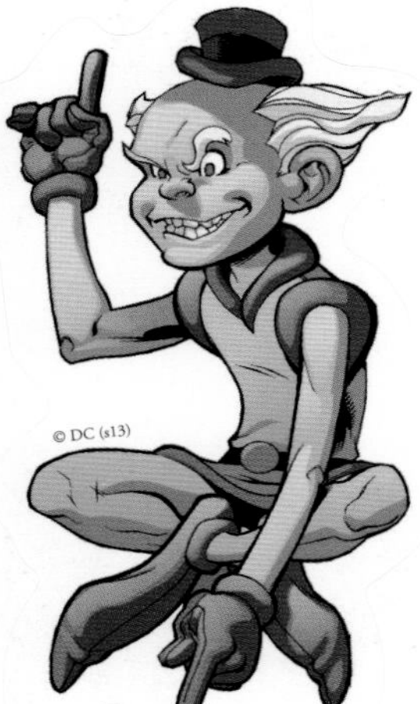

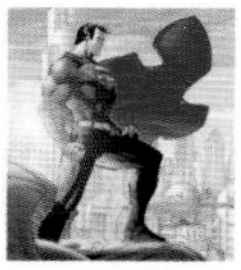

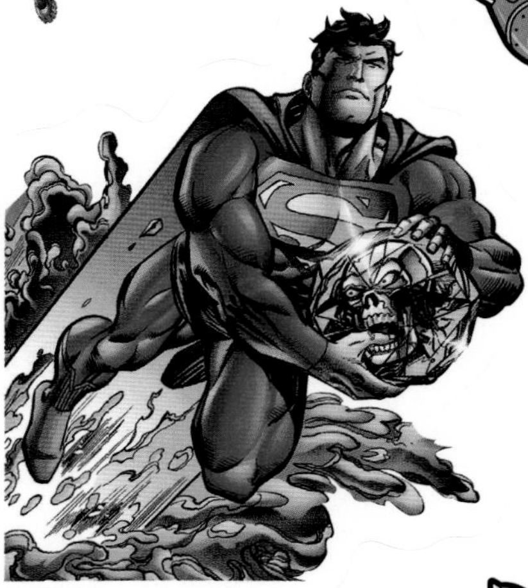

Battle Suit

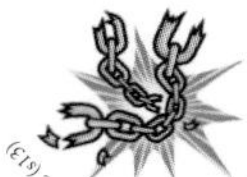

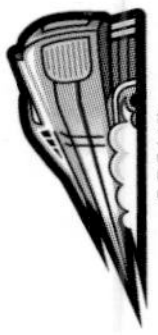

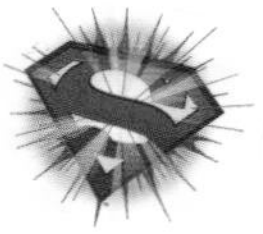

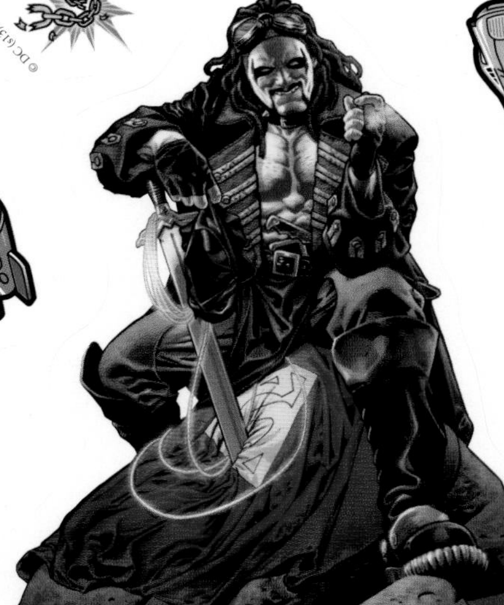

Getting Ahead

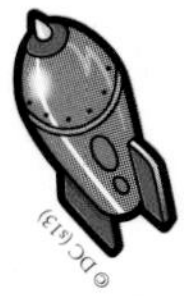

Apokolips

Mr. Mxyzptlk

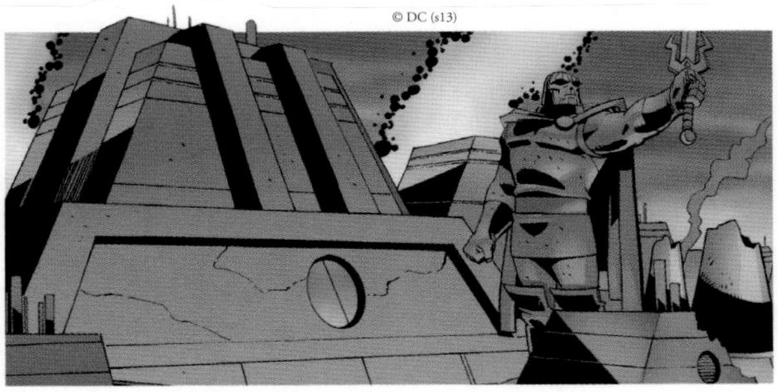

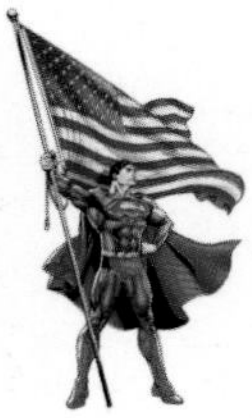

Lobo

Stickers

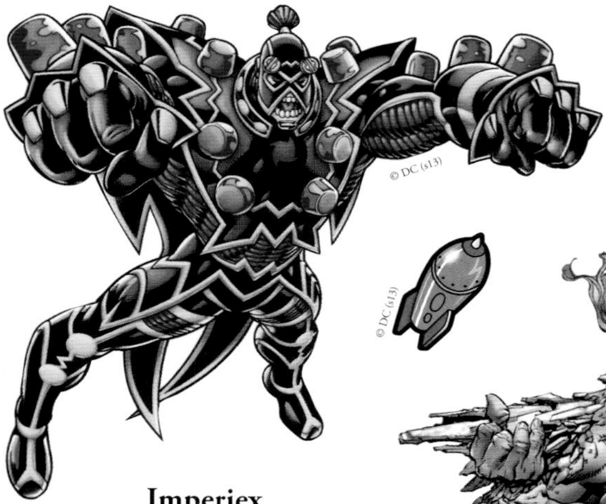

Imperiex

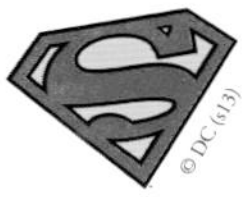

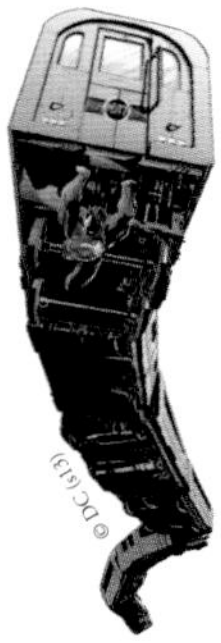

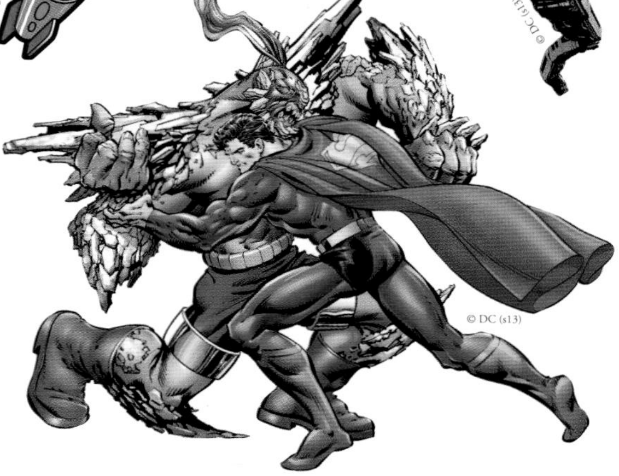

Not Dead Yet

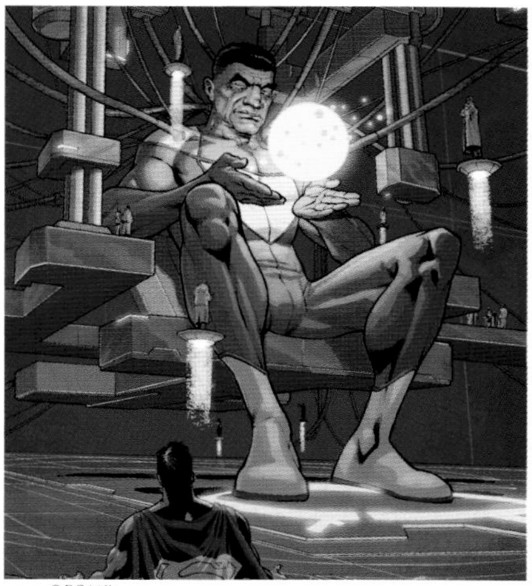

Bruno Mannheim

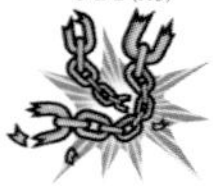

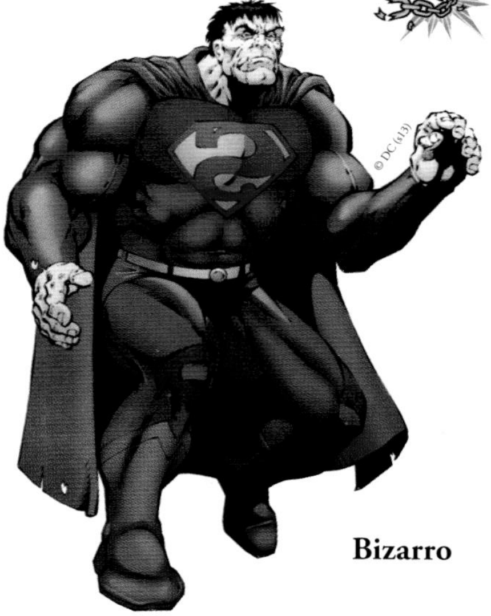

Bizarro

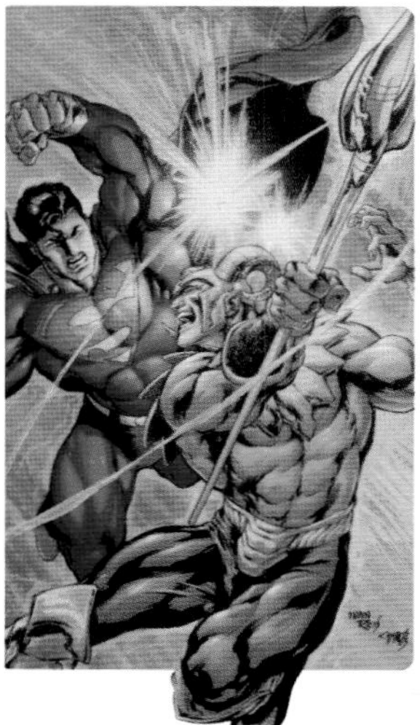

Future Foe

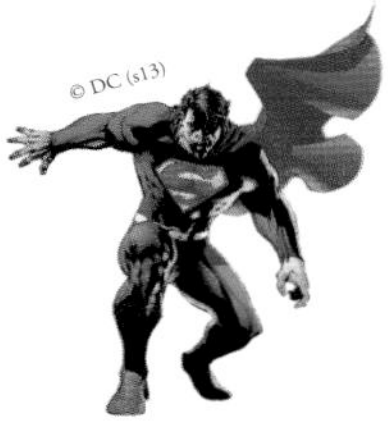

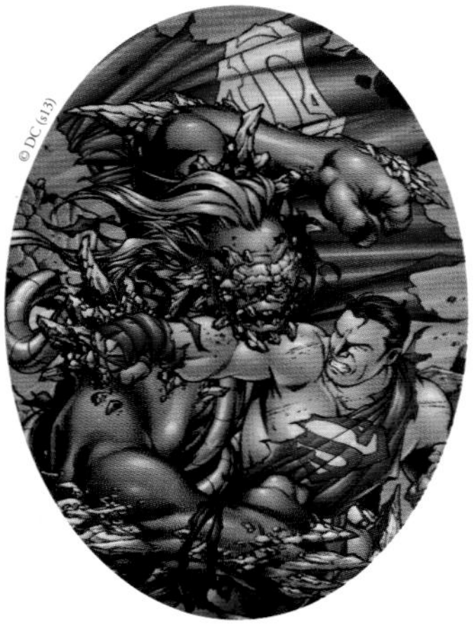

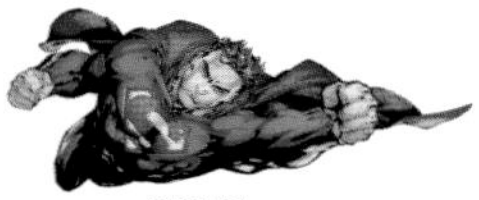

Deadly Battle

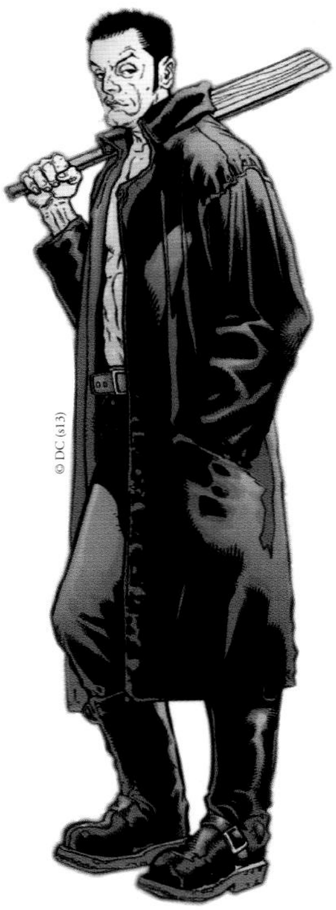

Manchester Black

Revenge Squad

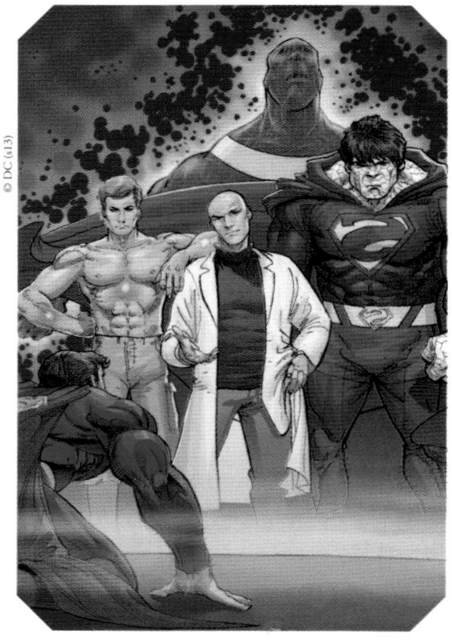

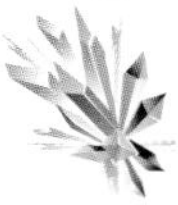

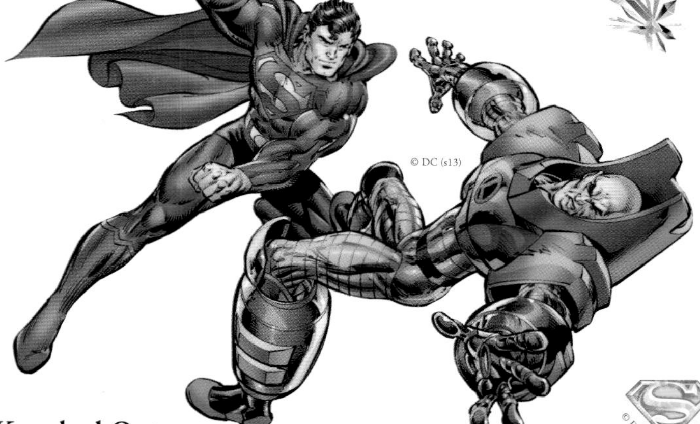

Knocked Out

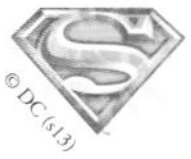

Stickers

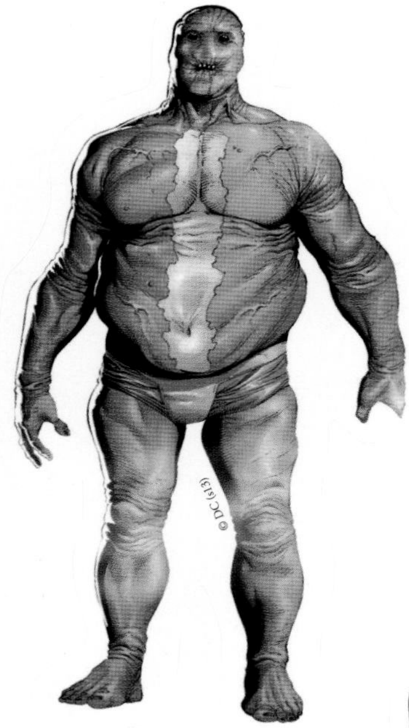

Greedy

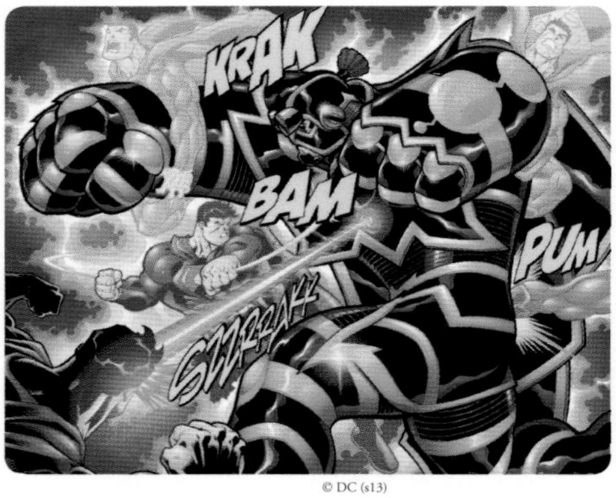
KRAK
BAM
PUM
SZZRAKK

Odd Teamup

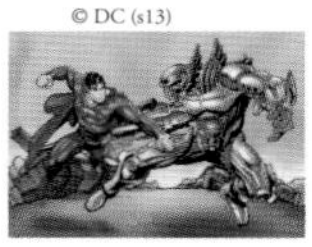

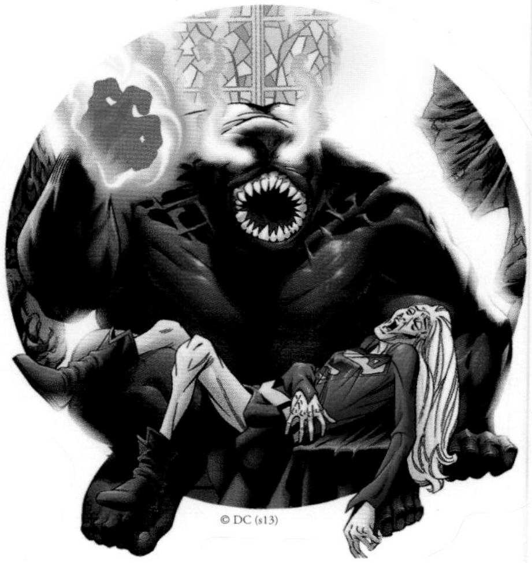

Warming Up

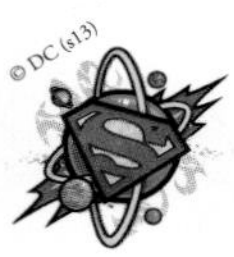

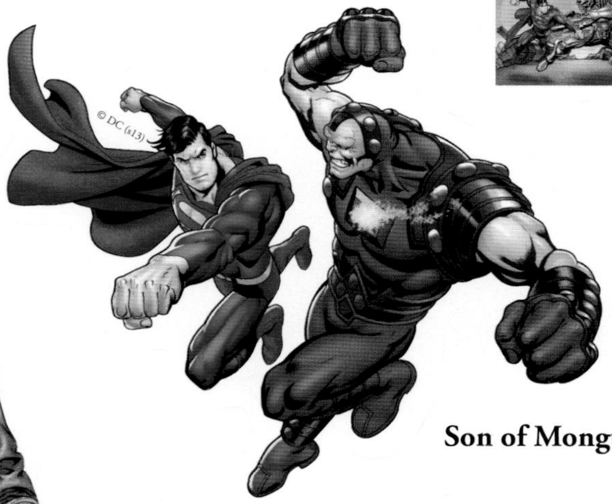

Son of Mongul

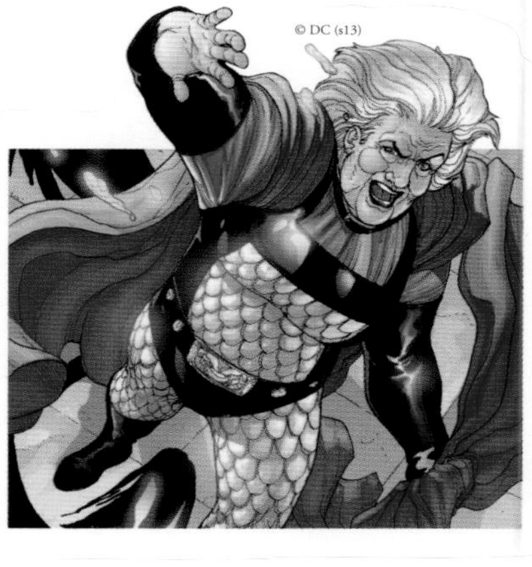

Granny Goodness

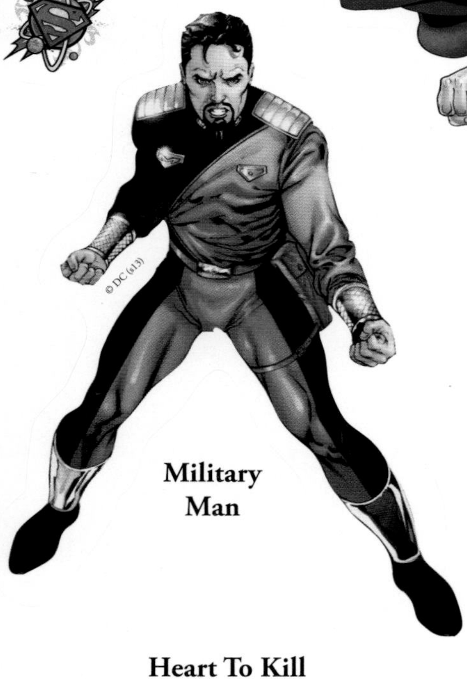

Military Man

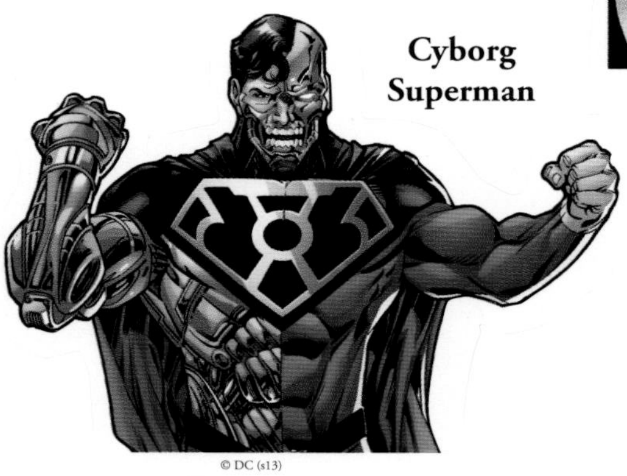

Cyborg Superman

Heart To Kill

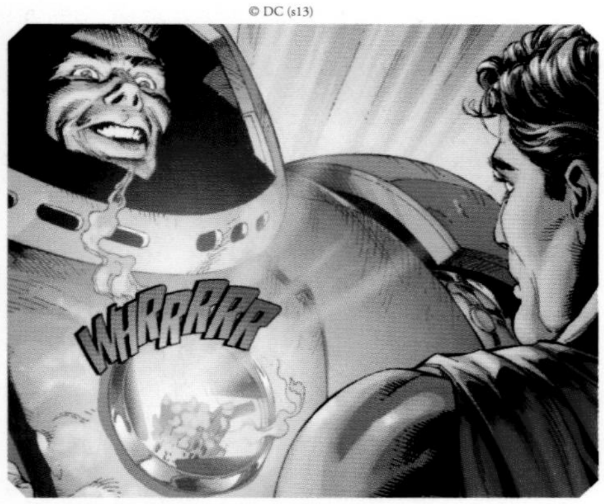
WHRRRRR

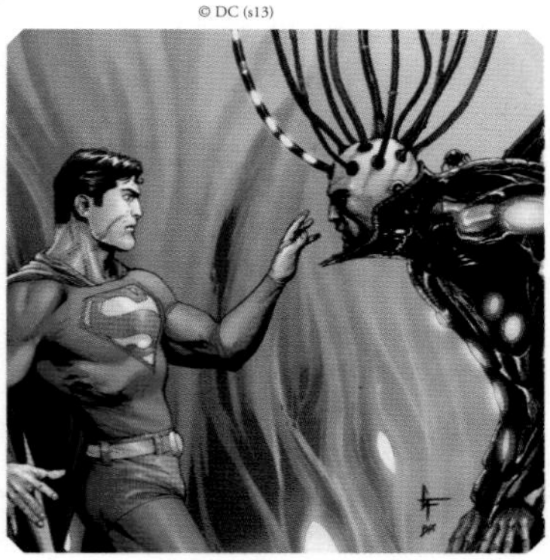

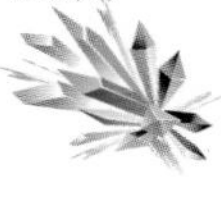

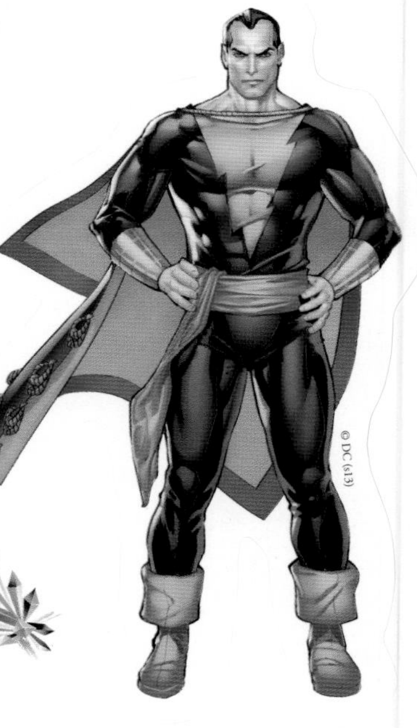

Ultimate Prize

Black Adam

Stickers

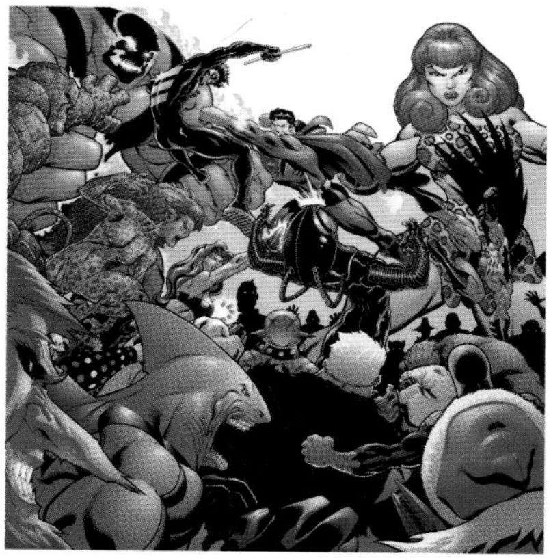

Against the Odds

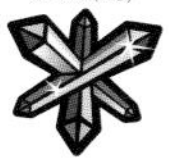

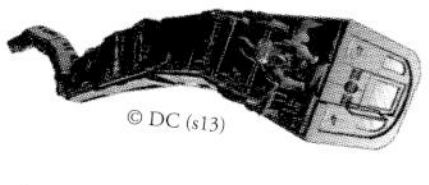

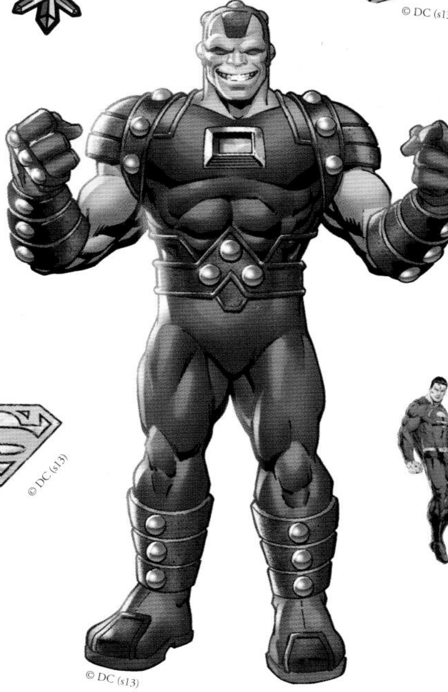

Mongul

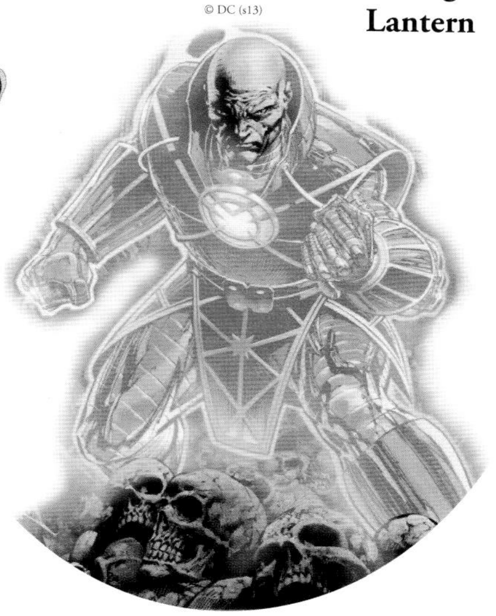

Orange Lantern

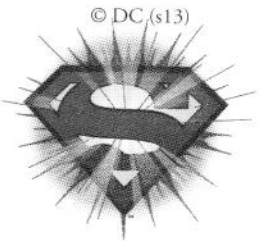

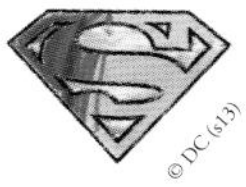

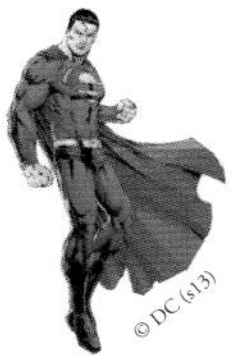

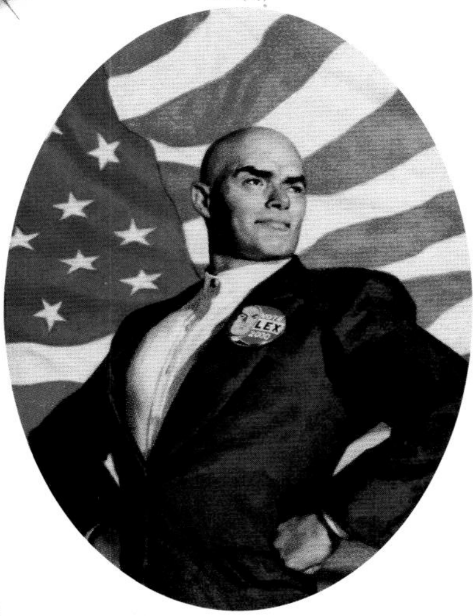

President Luthor

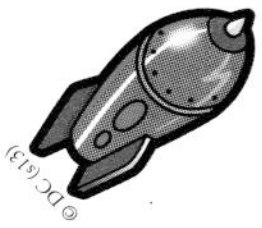

Atomic Skull

Auctioneer

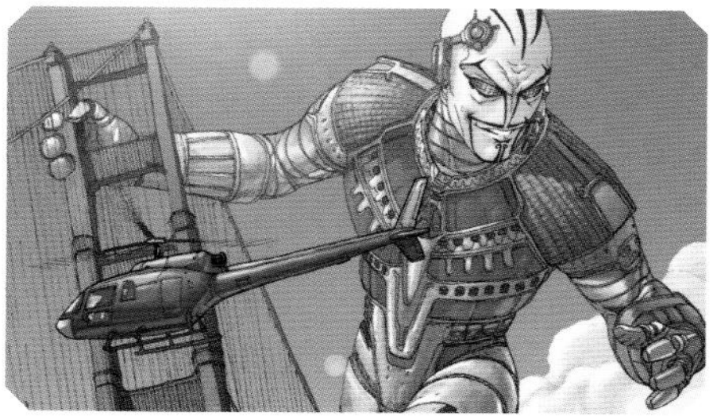

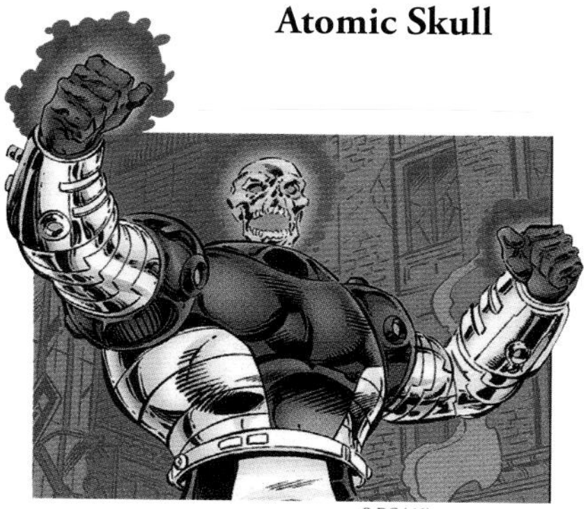

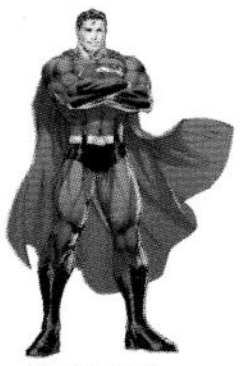

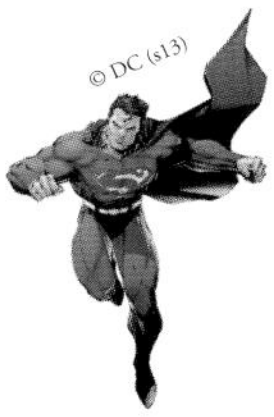

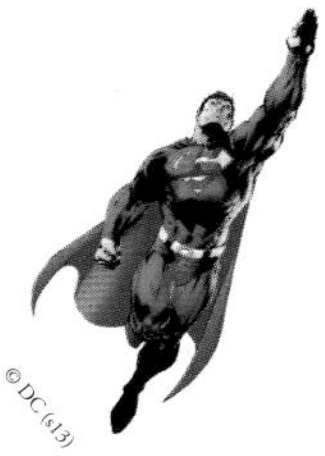

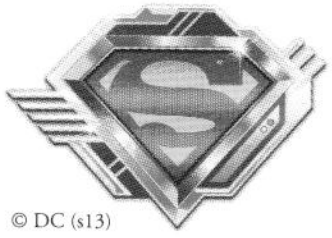

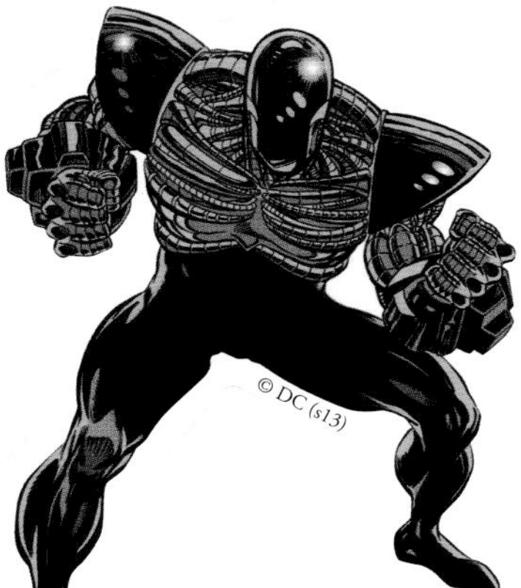

Conduit

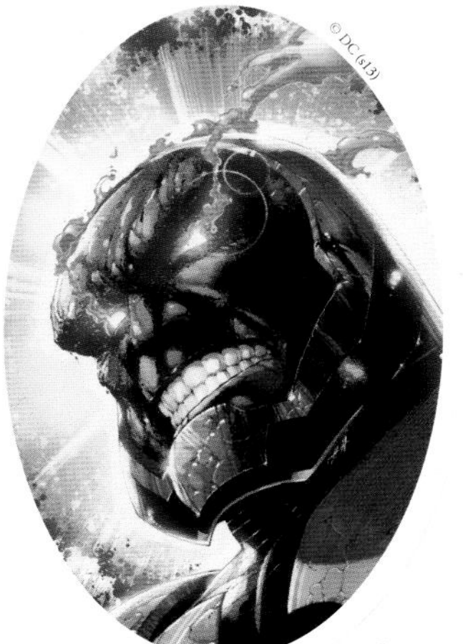

Omega Beams

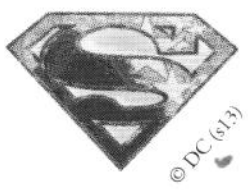

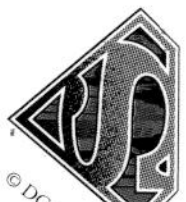

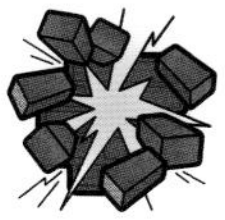

Power Thief

Stickers

H’el

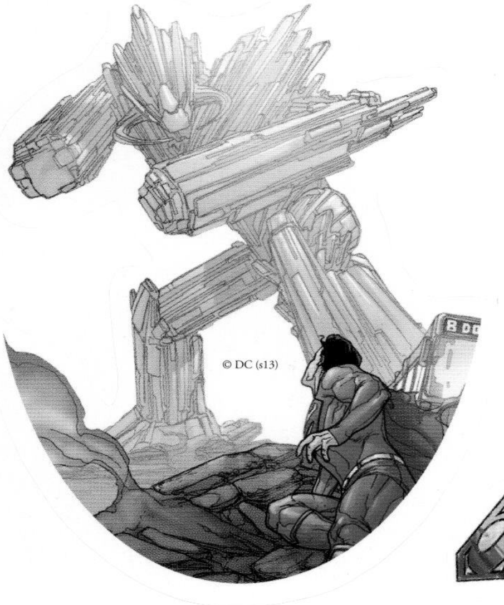
© DC (s13)

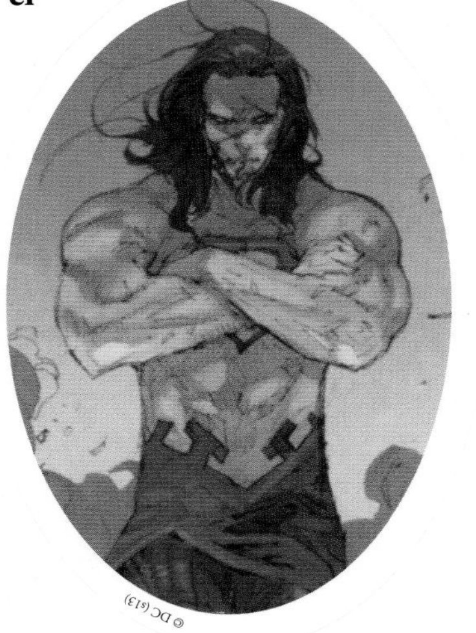
© DC (s13)

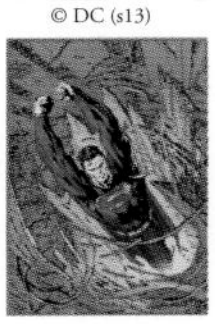
© DC (s13)

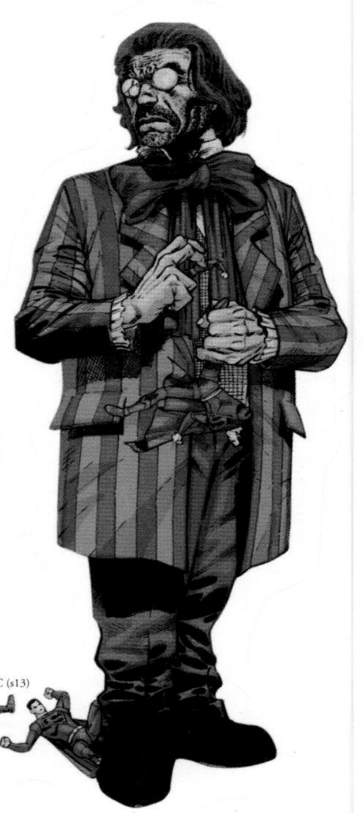

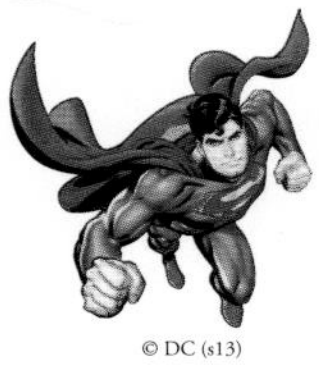
© DC (s13)

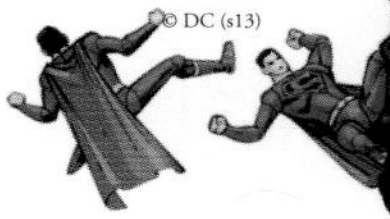
© DC (s13)

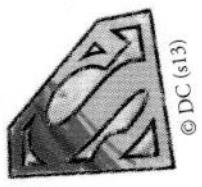
© DC (s13)

Nice Try

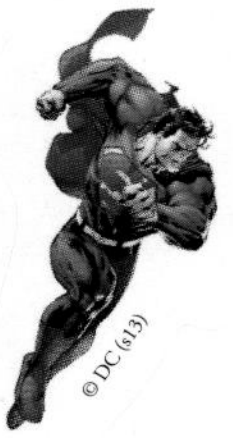
© DC (s13)

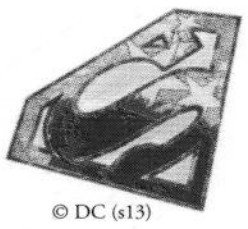
© DC (s13)

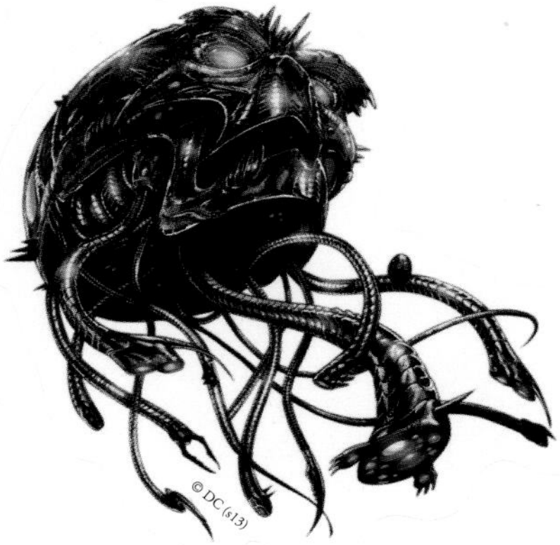
© DC (s13)

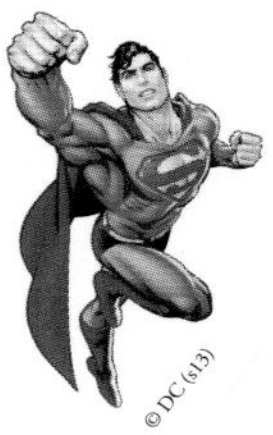
© DC (s13)

Toyman

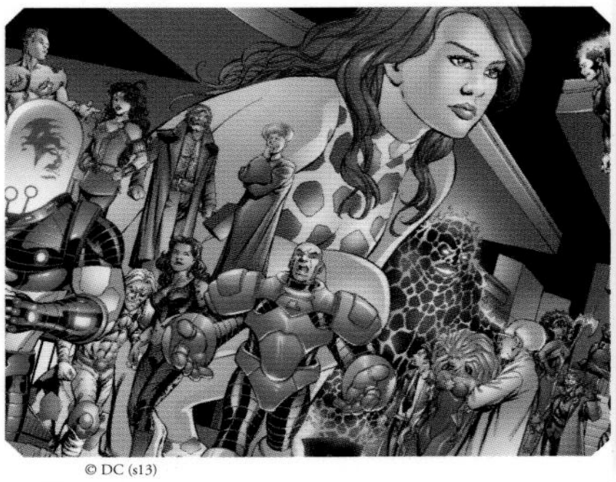
© DC (s13)

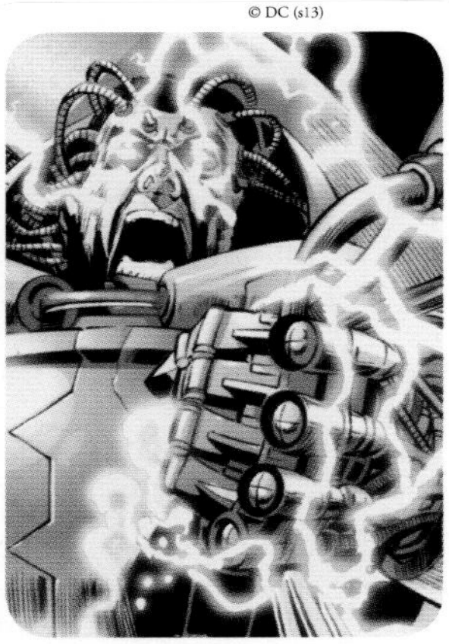
© DC (s13)

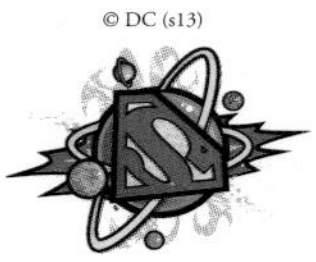
© DC (s13)

Skull Ship

Injustice League

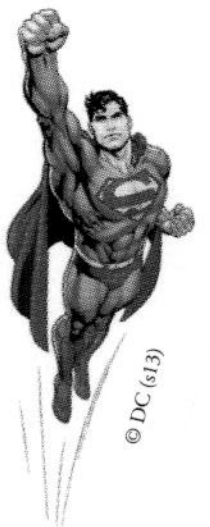
© DC (s13)

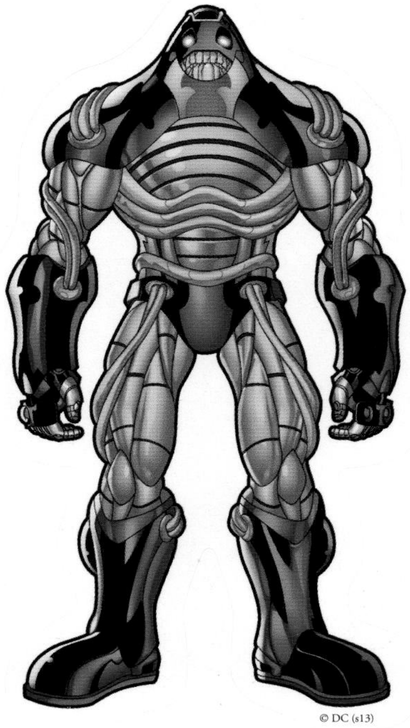
© DC (s13)

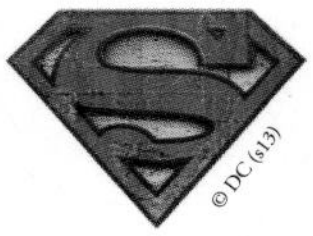
© DC (s13)

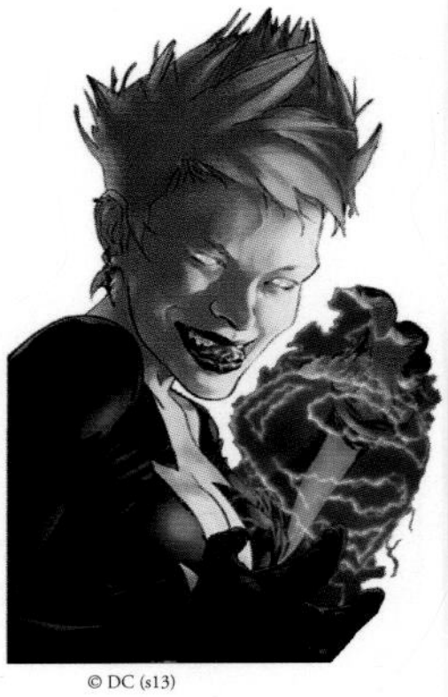
© DC (s13)

New Man

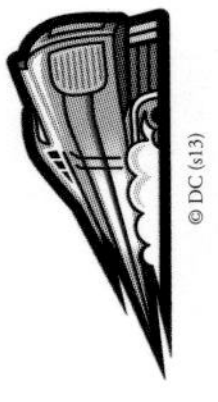
© DC (s13)

Livewire

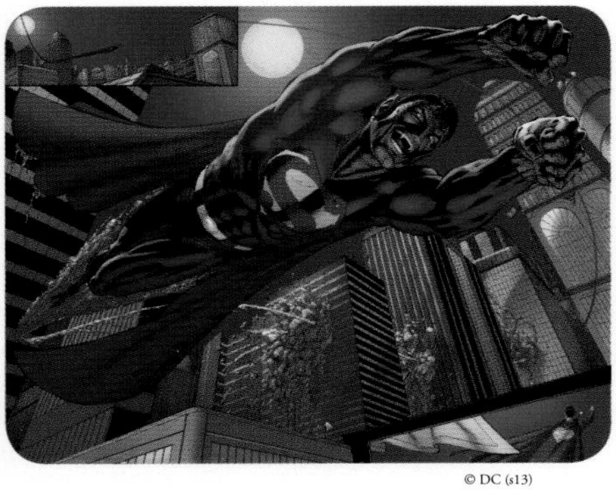
© DC (s13)

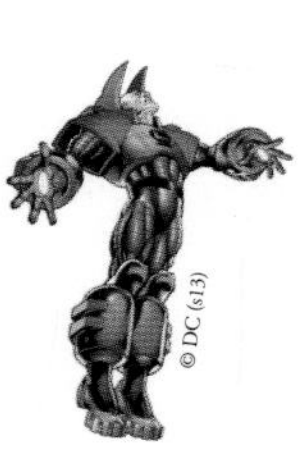
© DC (s13)

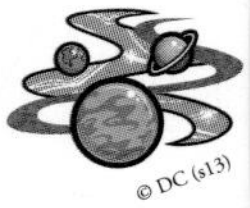
© DC (s13)

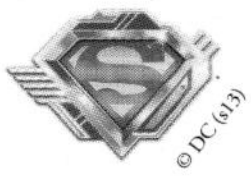
© DC (s13)

Eclipso

Anti-Monitor

Stickers

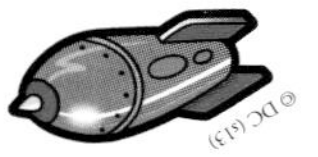

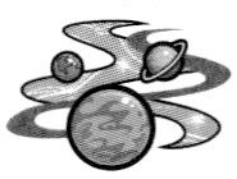

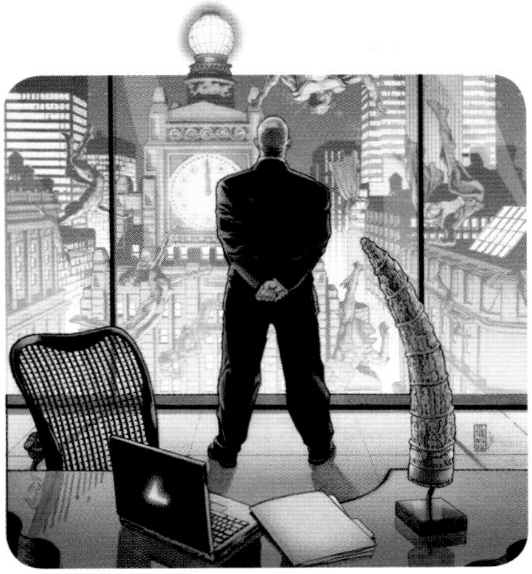

Infinity, Inc.

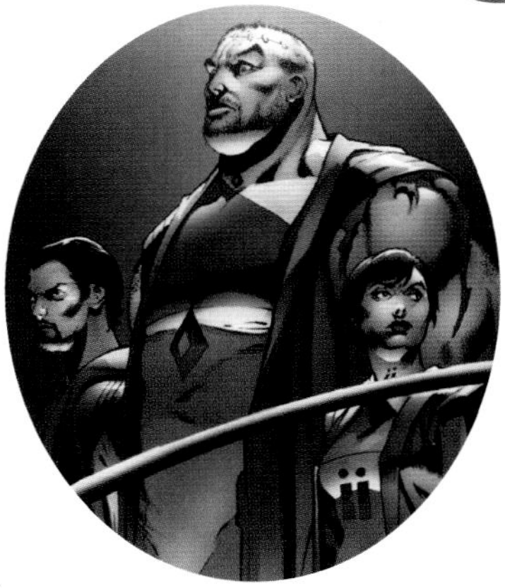

Phantom Zone

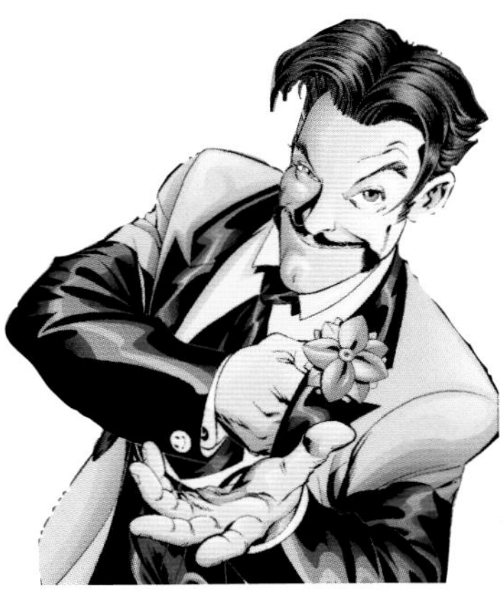

Prankster

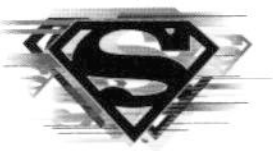

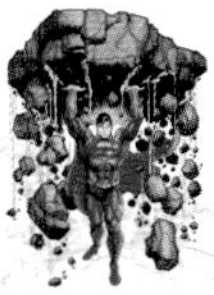

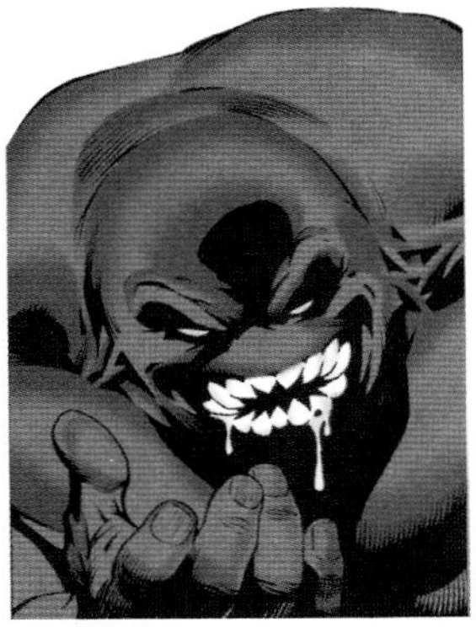

Monster Looks

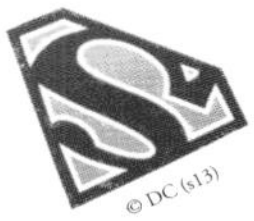

Deadly Powers

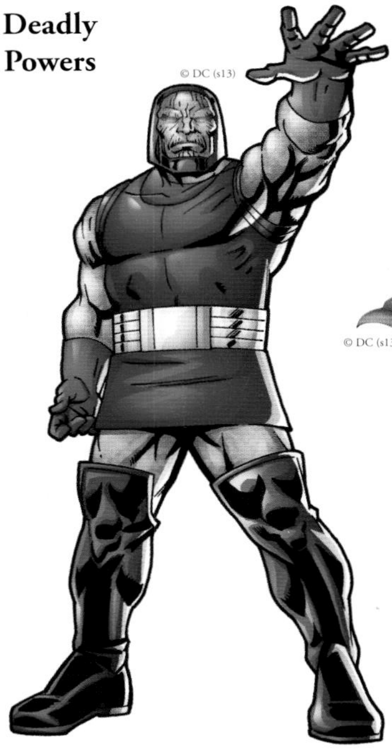

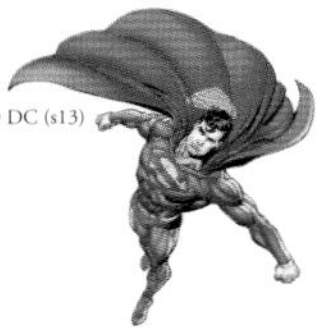

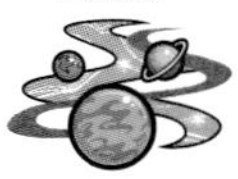

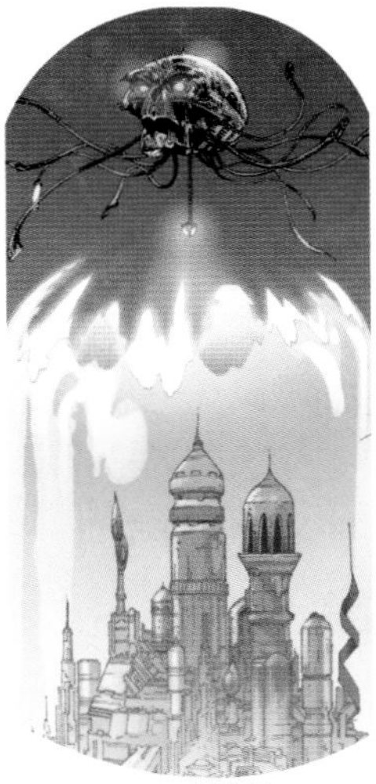

Collector of Worlds

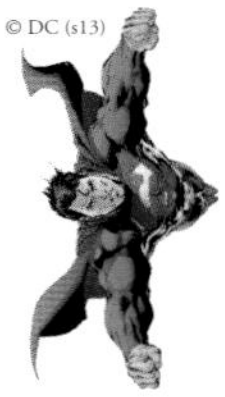

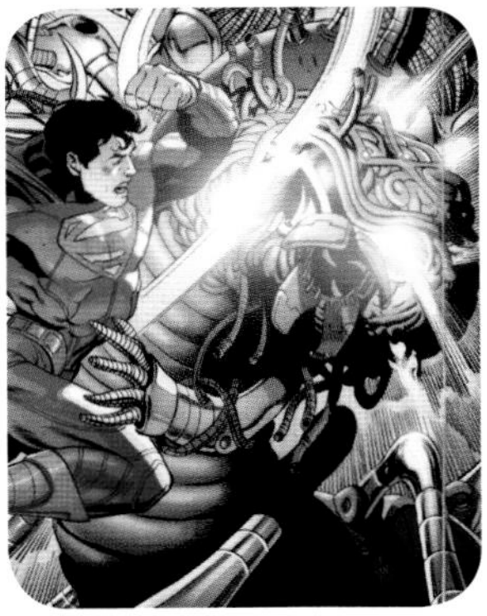

Brain Power

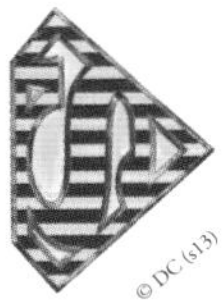

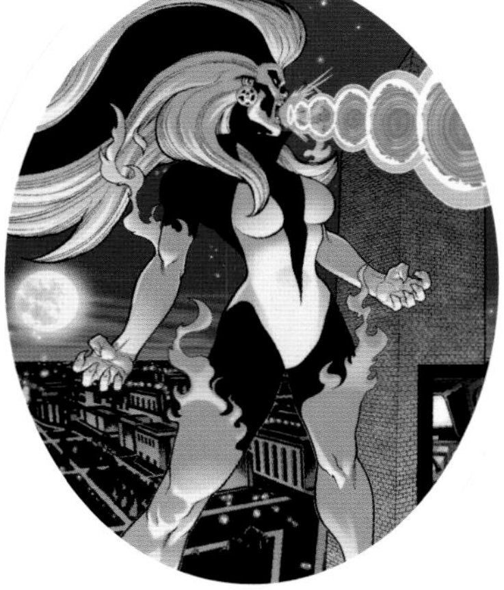

Silver Banshee

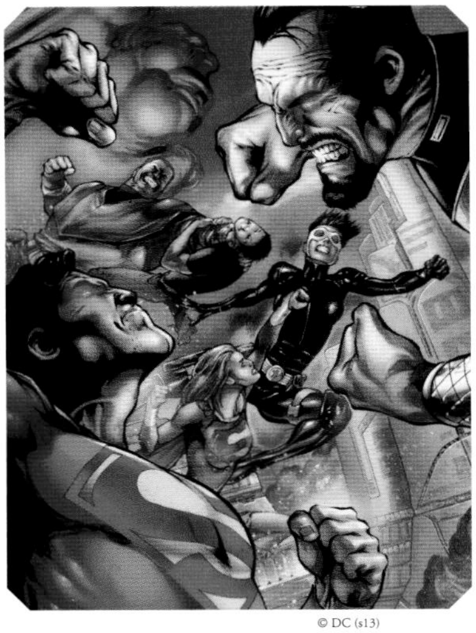

Dangerous Foe

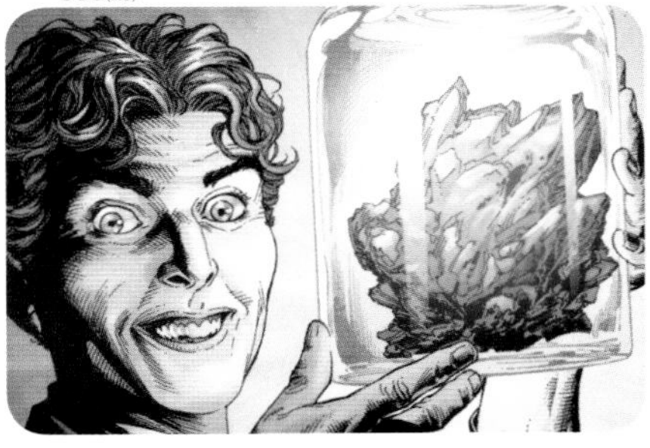

Damaged Child

Stickers

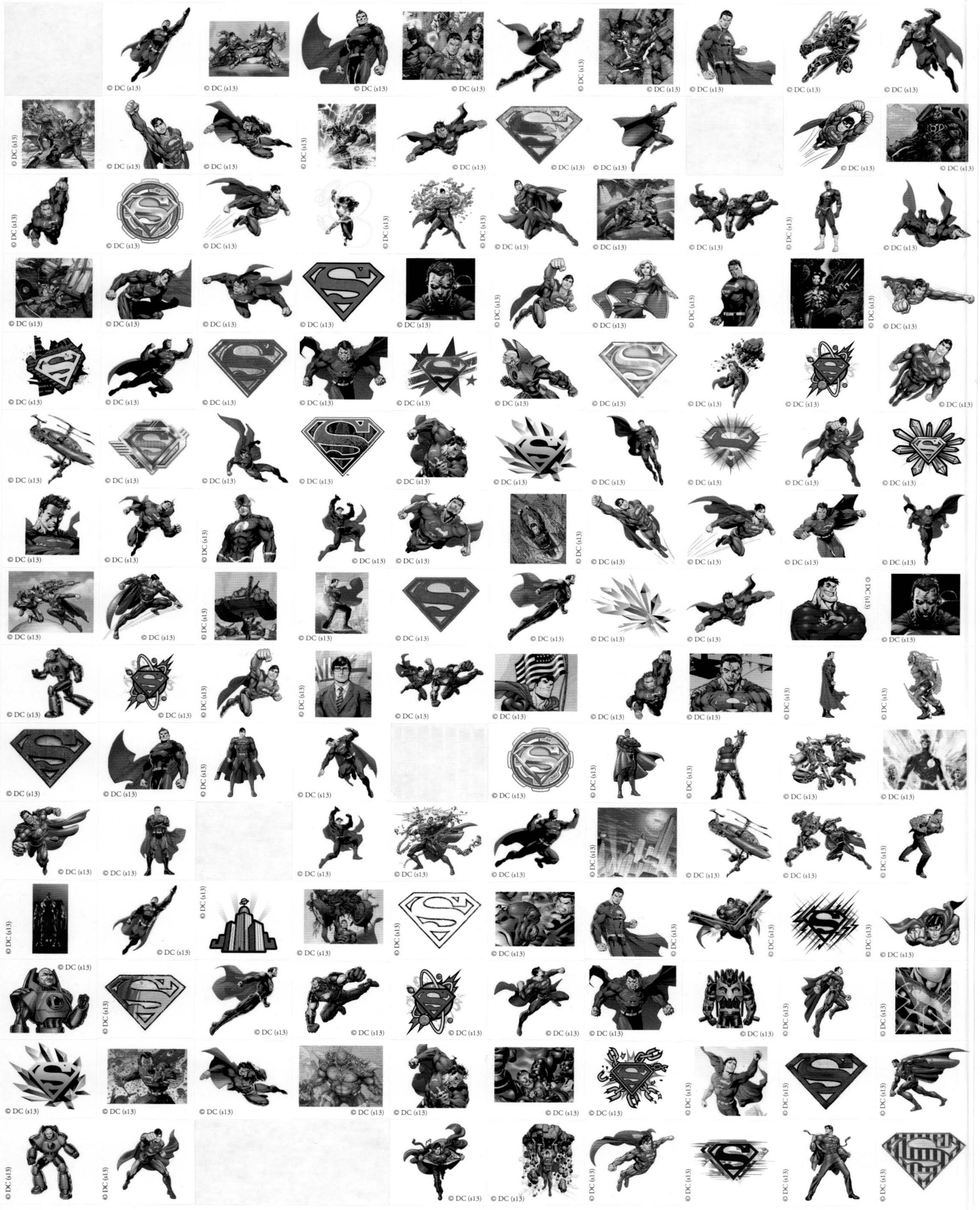
© DC (s13)

Stickers

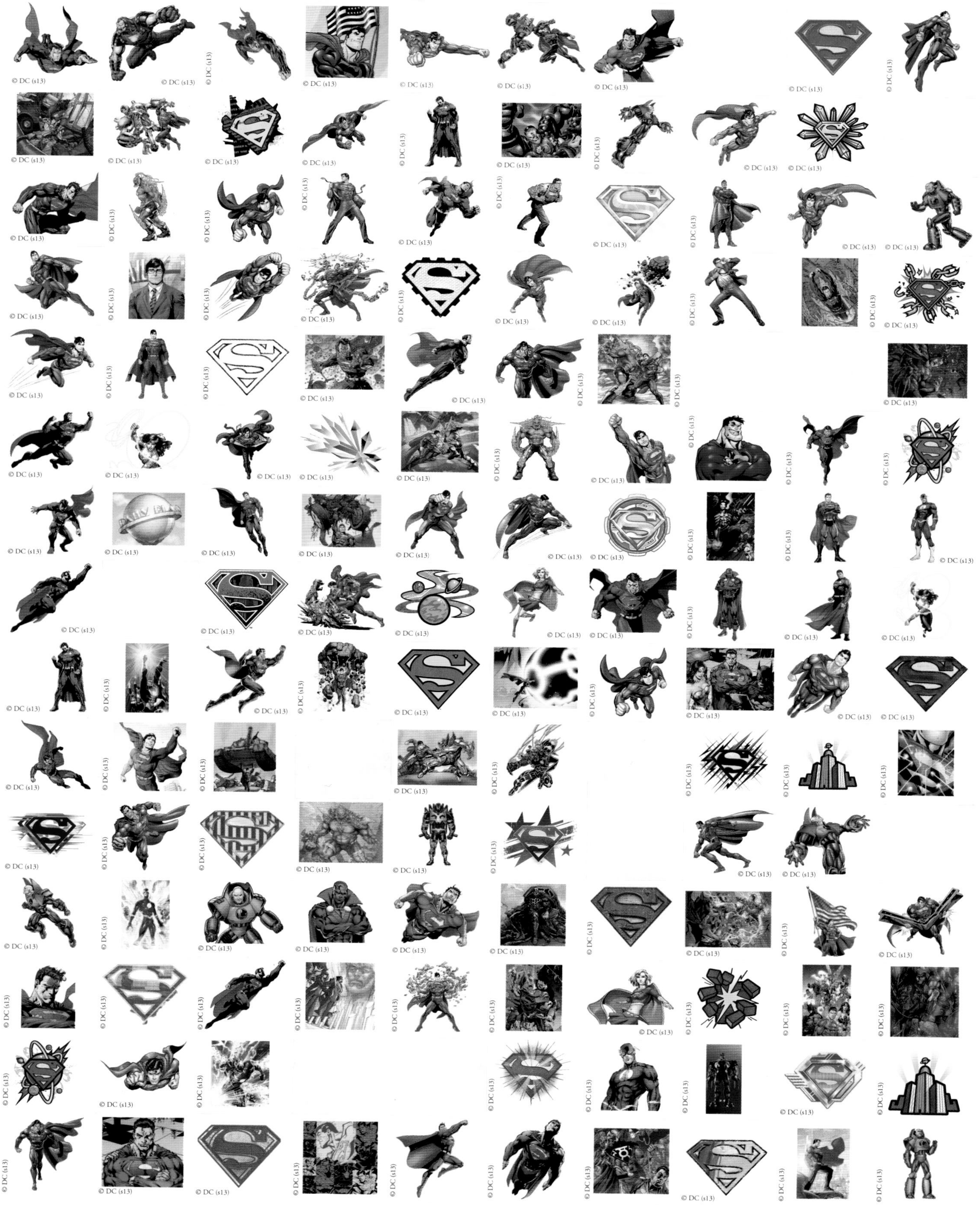
© DC (s13)

Extra Stickers

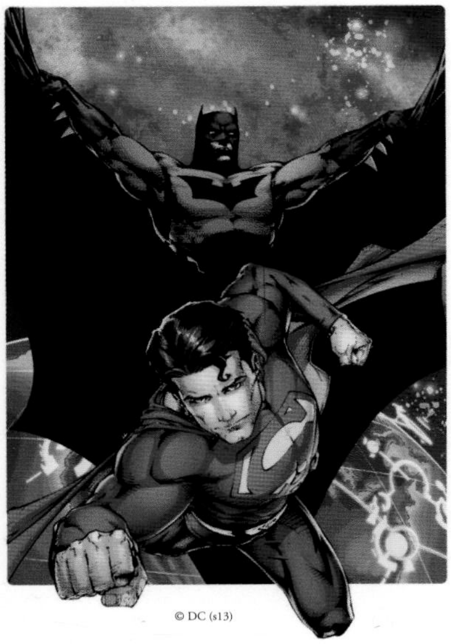
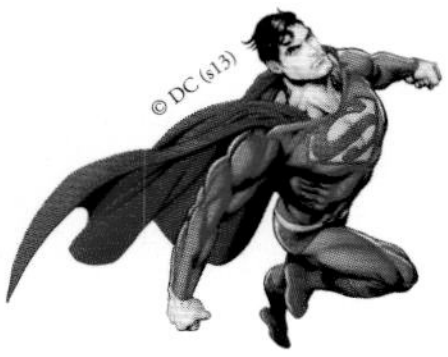
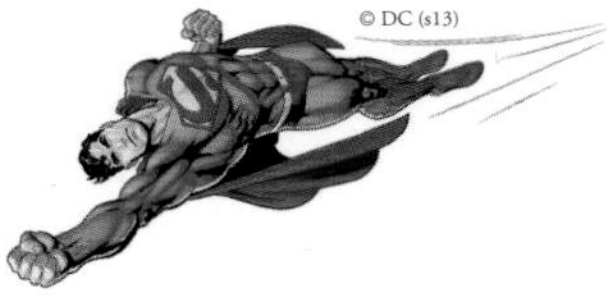
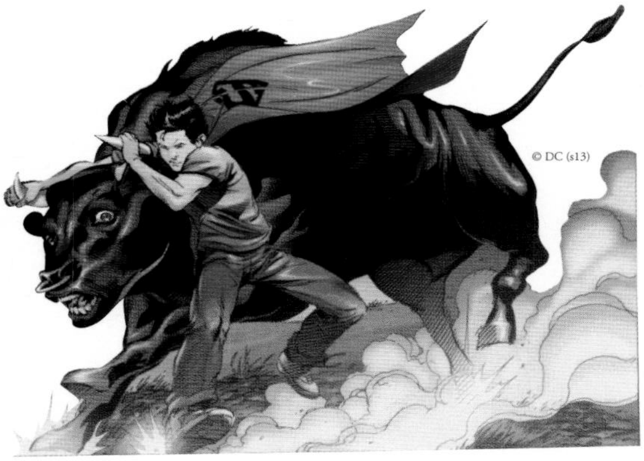
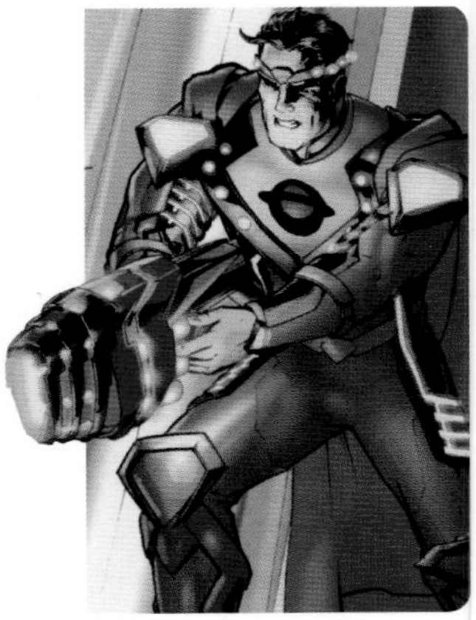
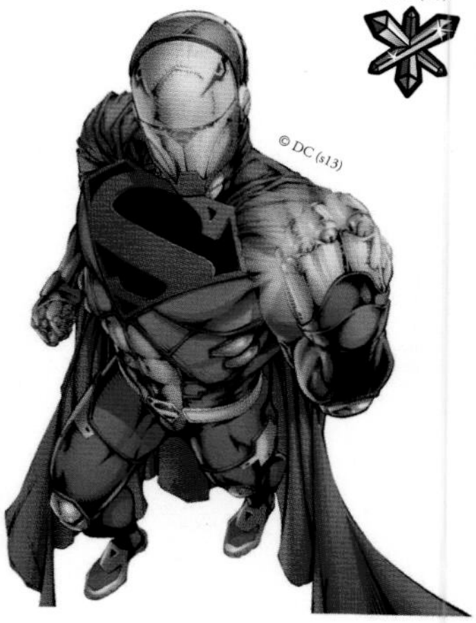
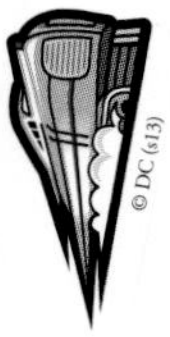
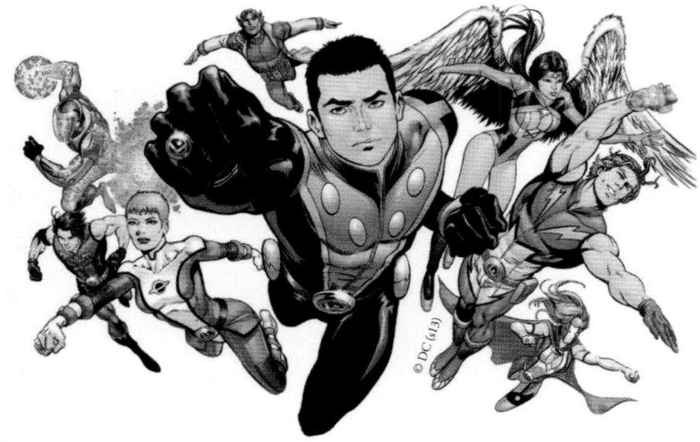
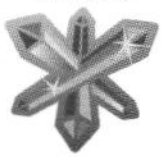
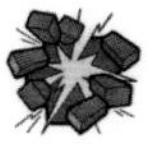
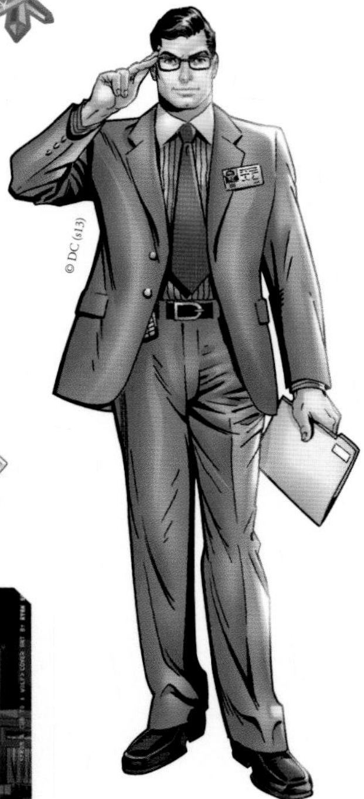
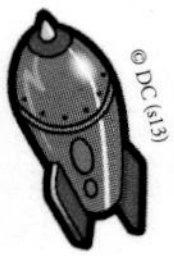
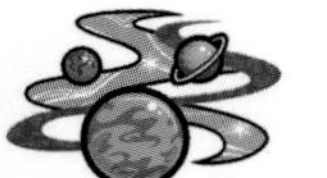
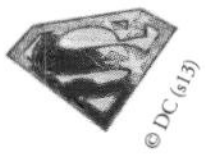
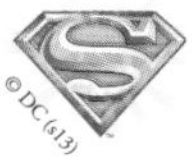
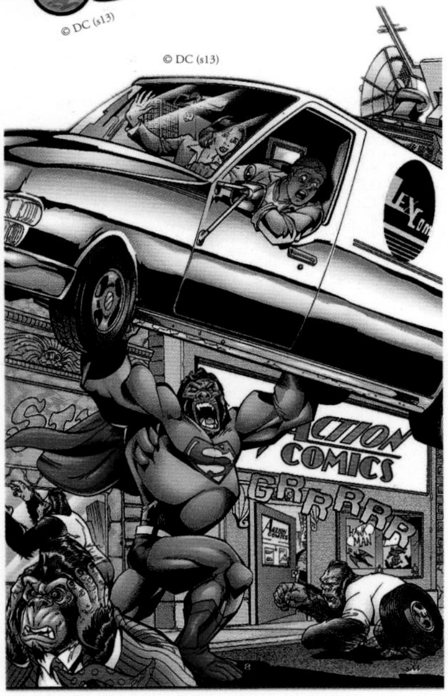
ACTION
COMICS
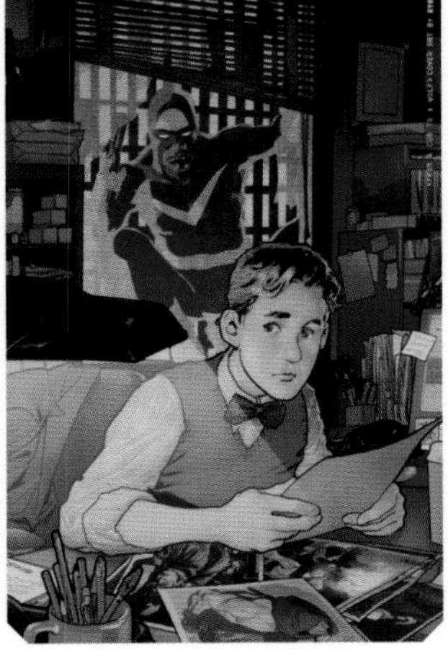
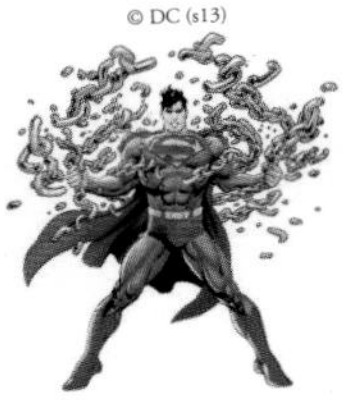
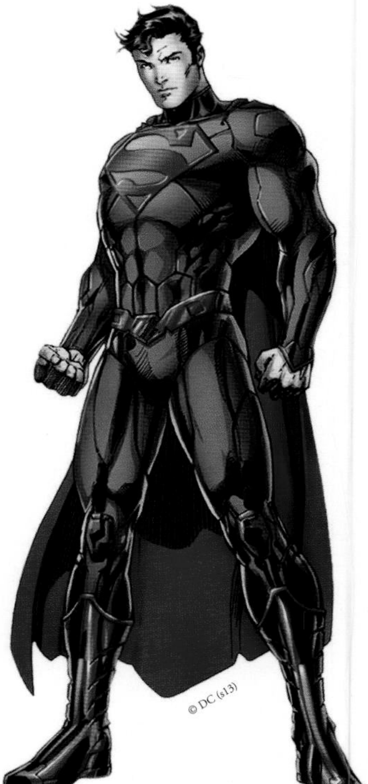

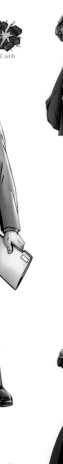

Stickers

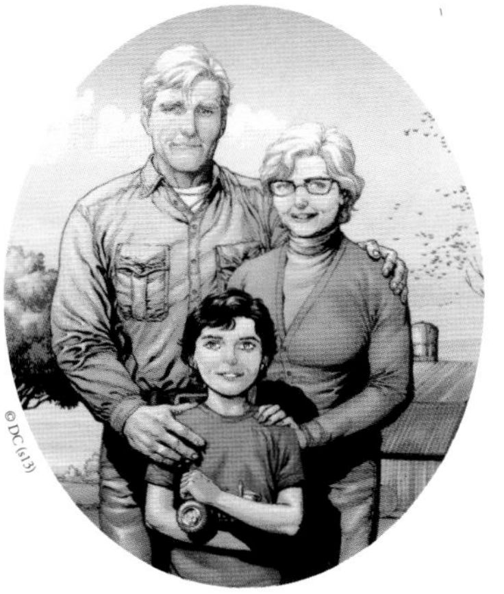

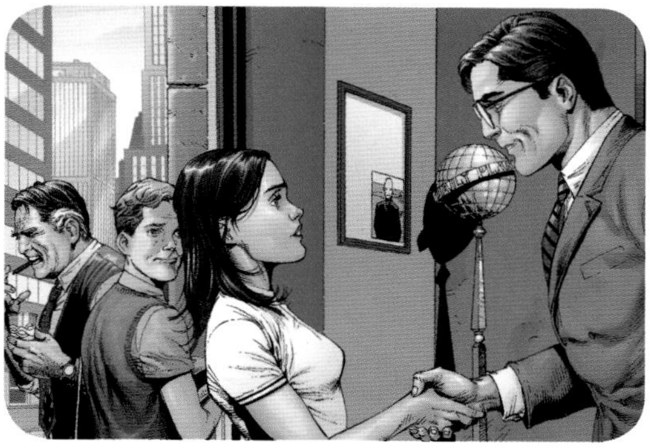

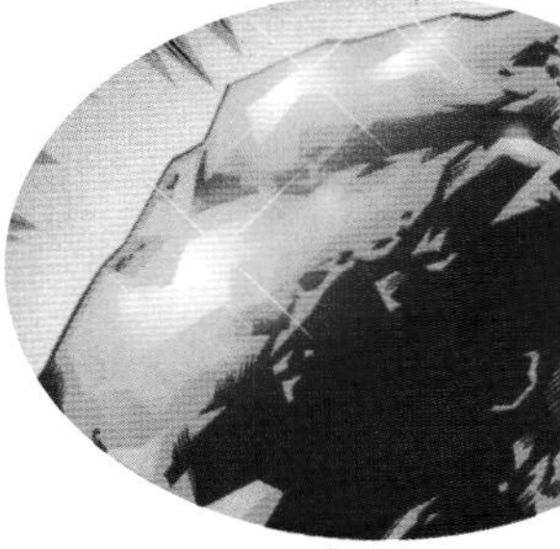

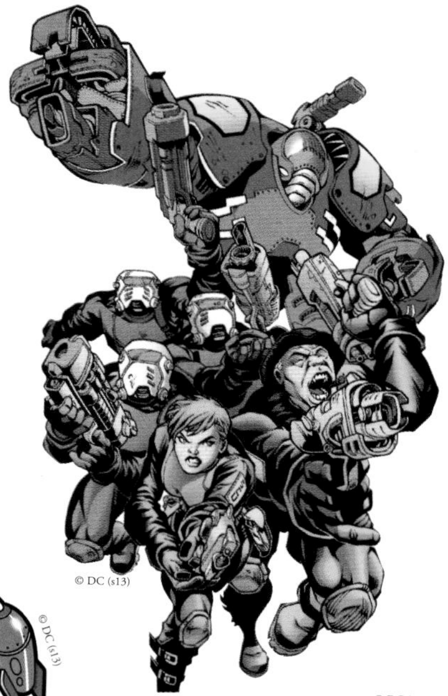

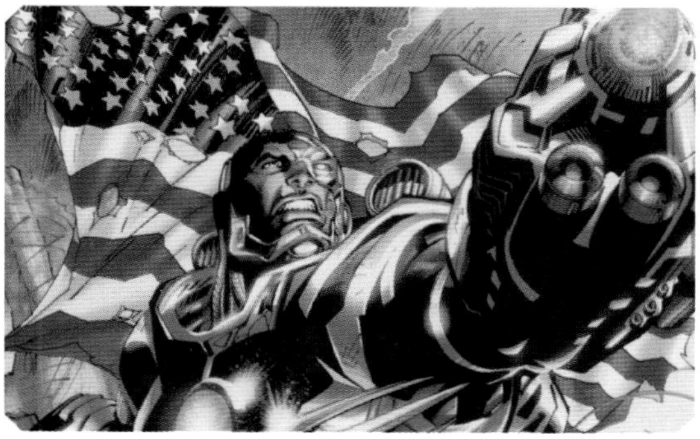

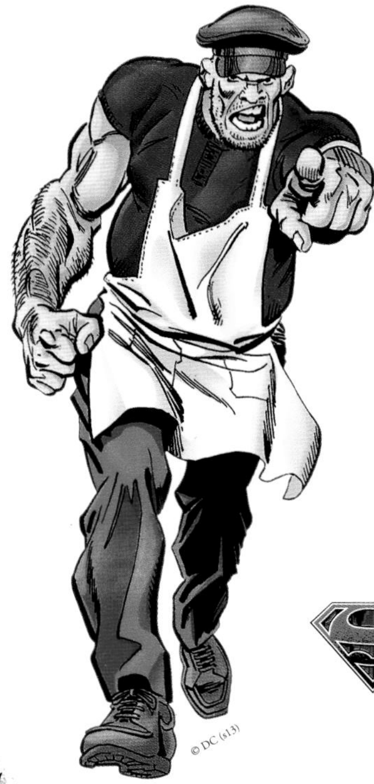

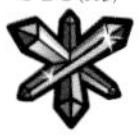

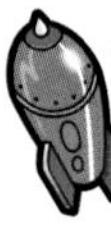

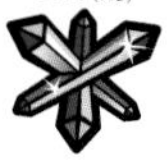

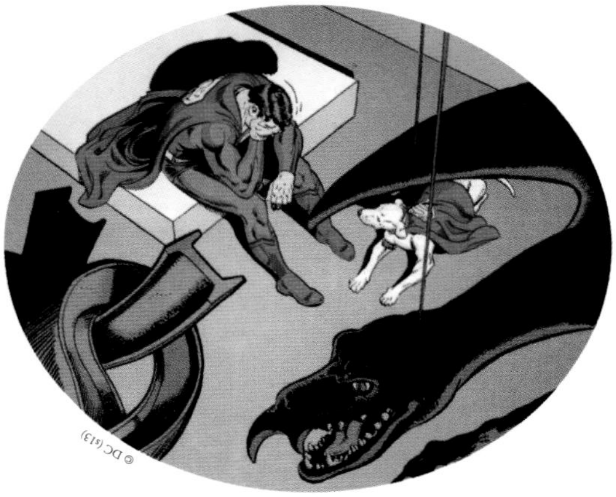

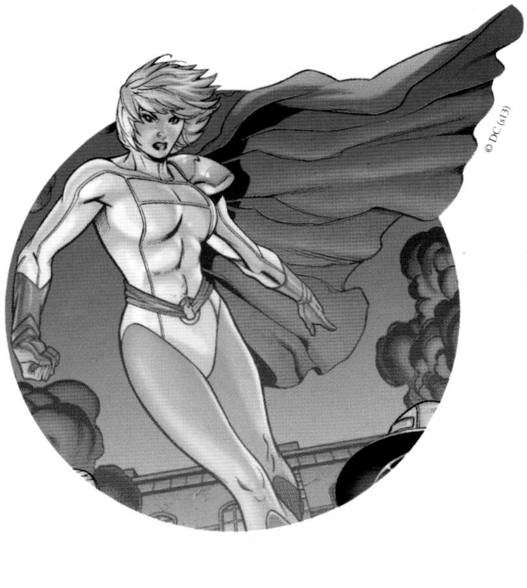

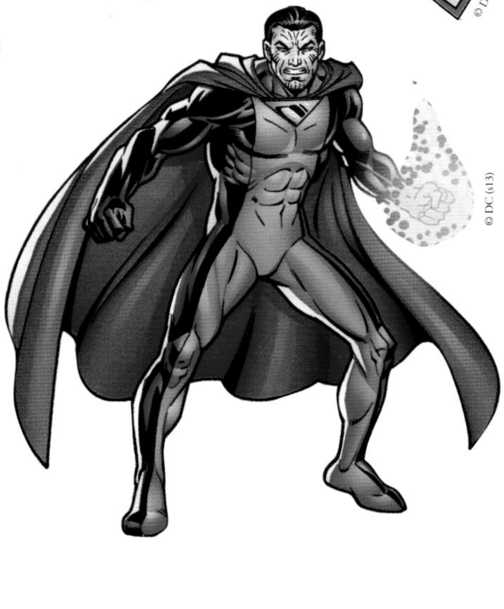

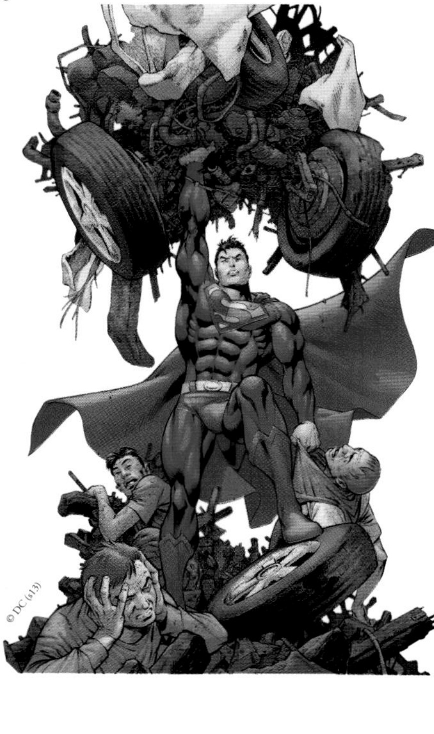

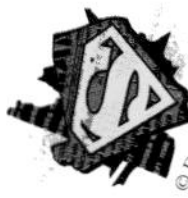

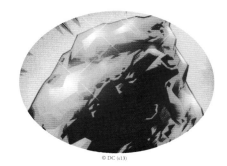

Extra Stickers

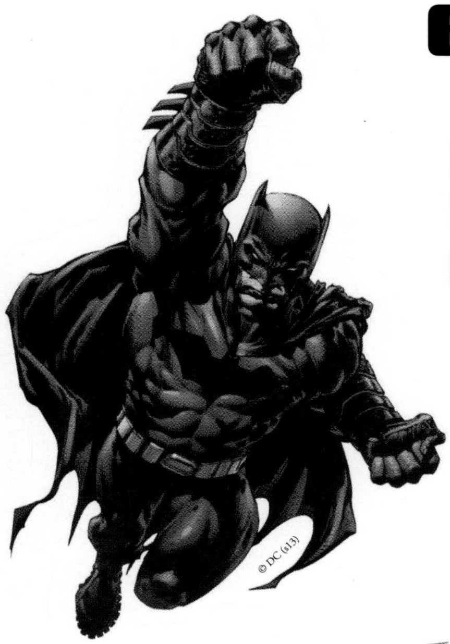

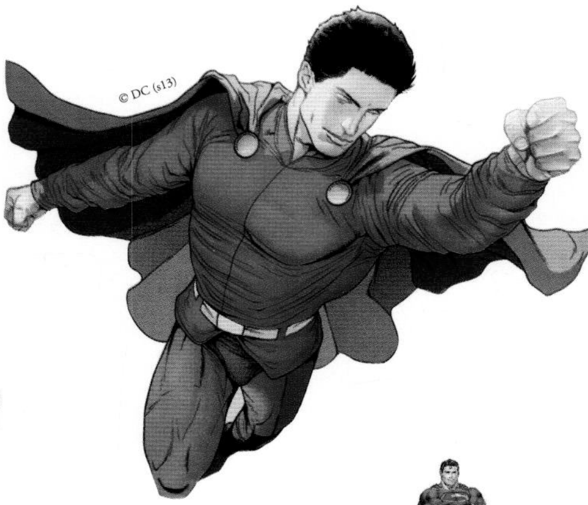

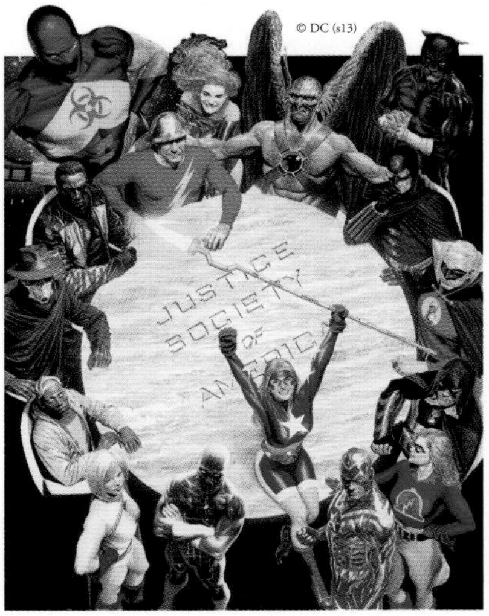

JUSTICE
SOCIETY
OF
AMERICA

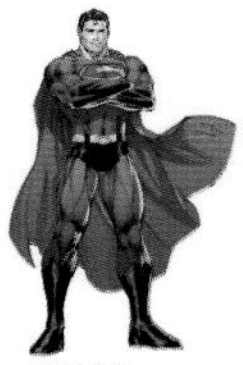

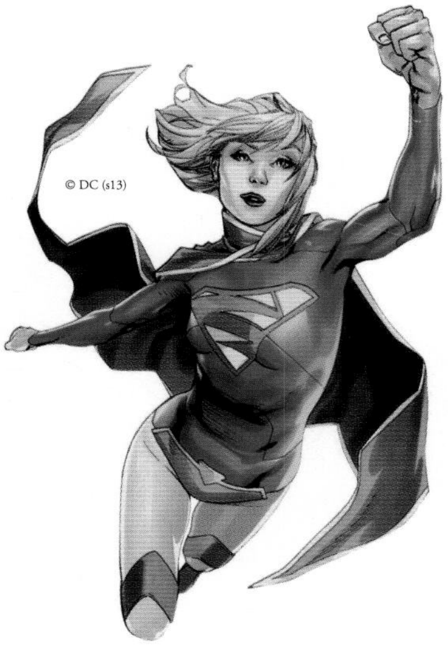

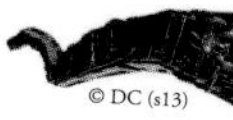

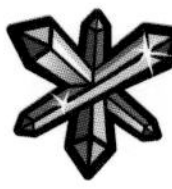

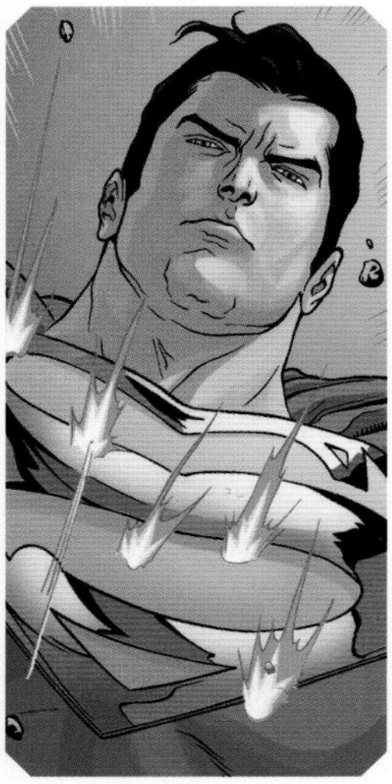

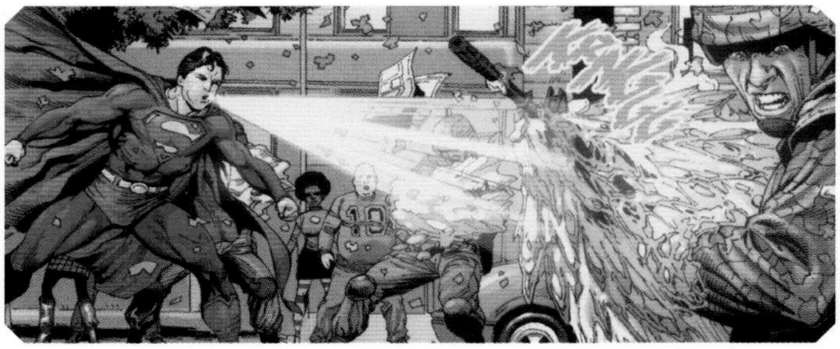

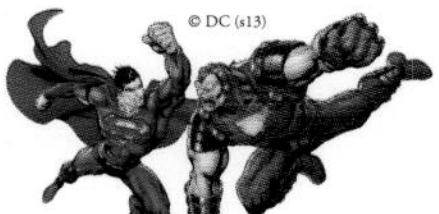

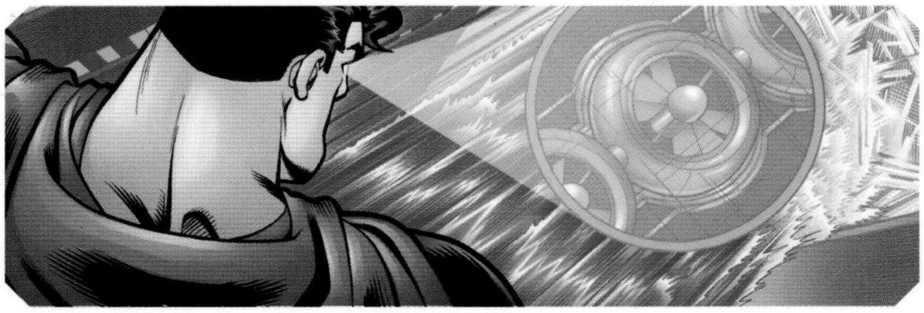

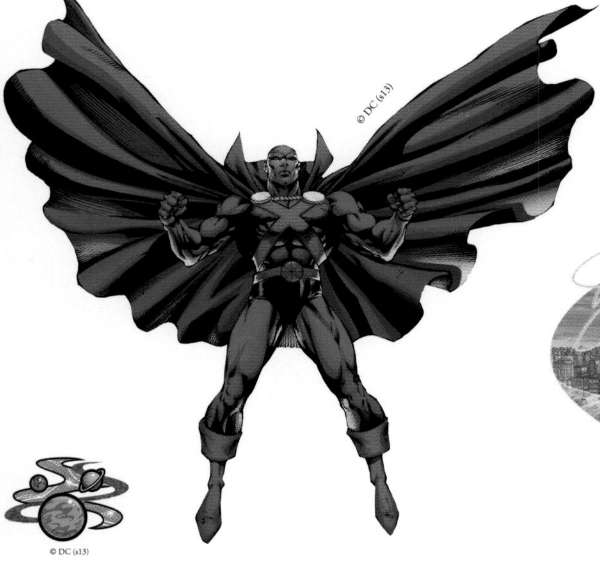

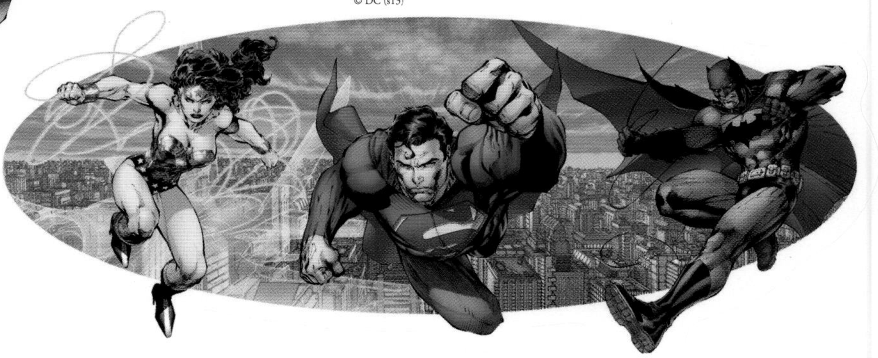

Extra Stickers

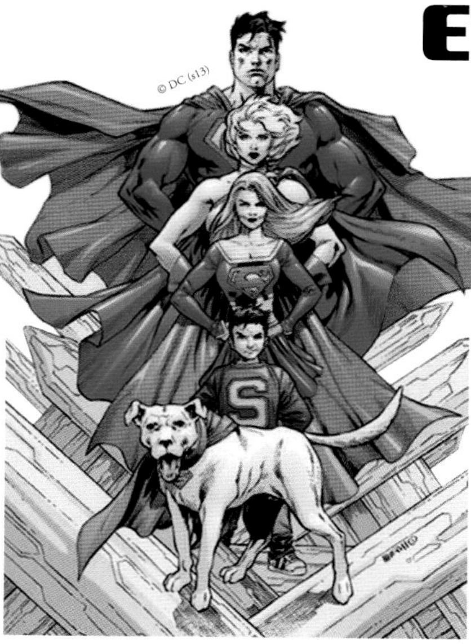

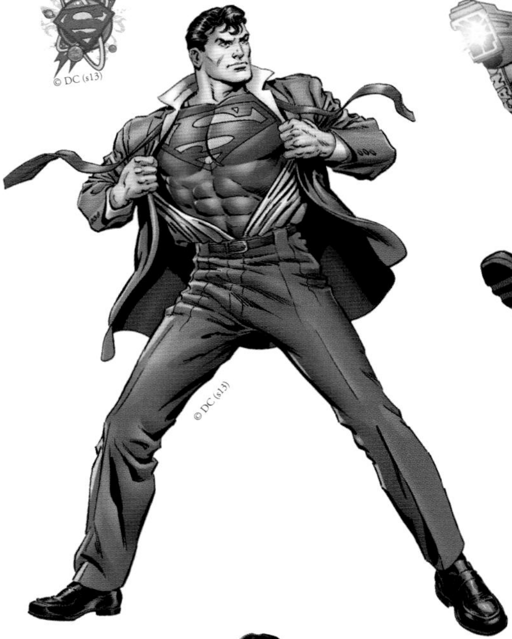

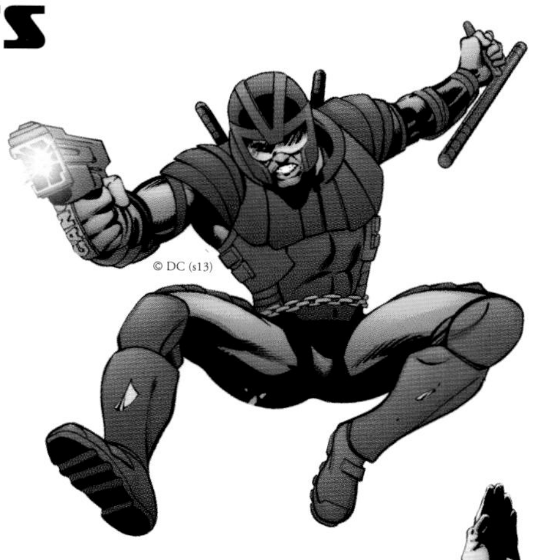

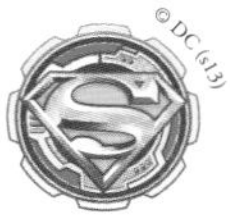

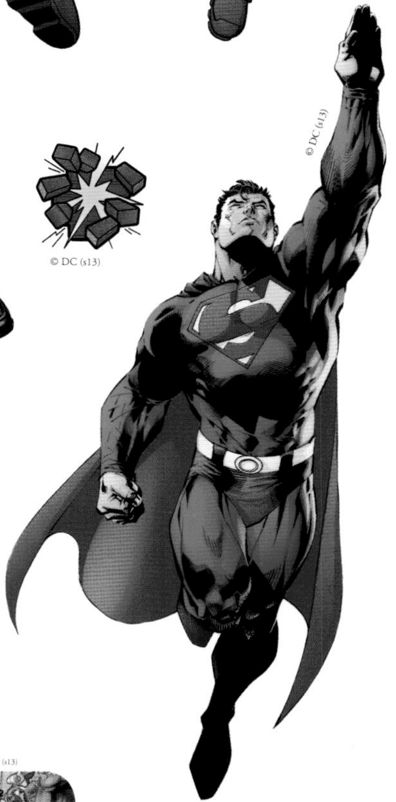

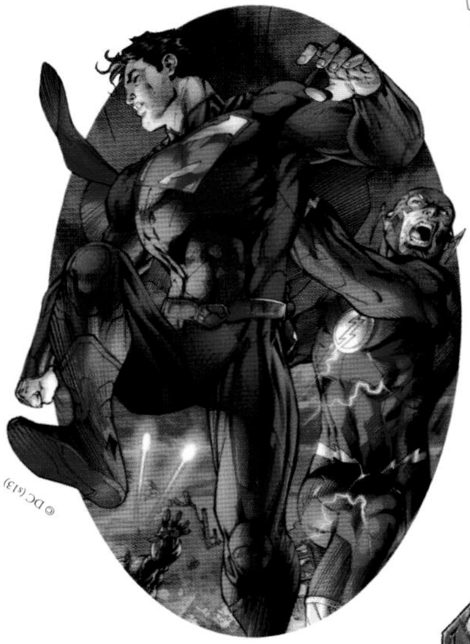

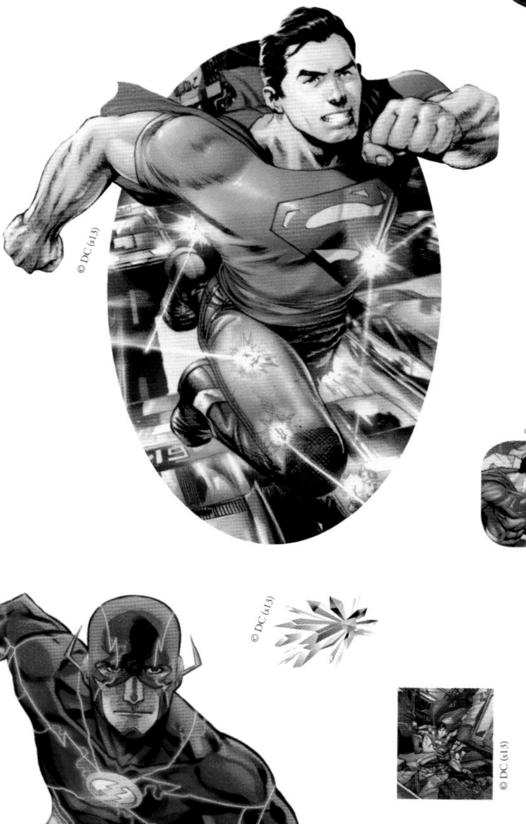

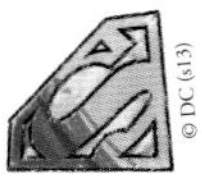

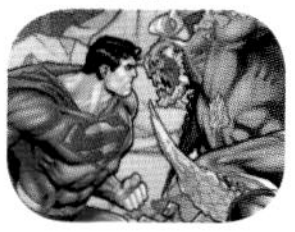

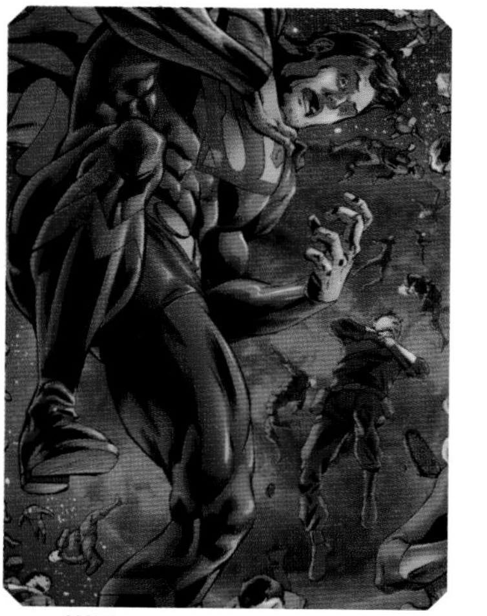

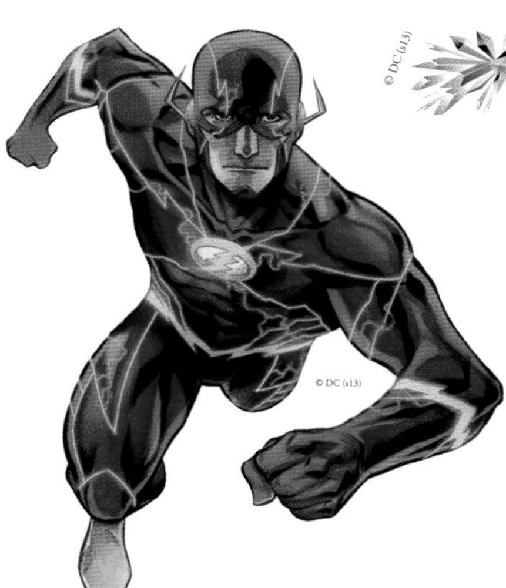

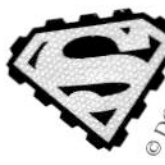

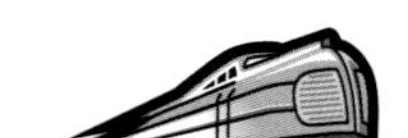

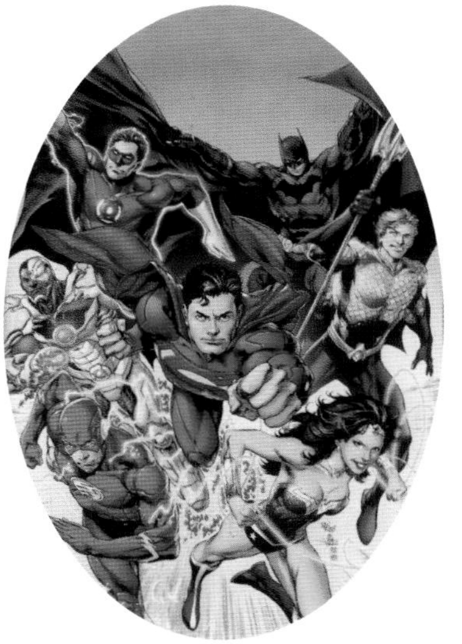

Extra Stickers

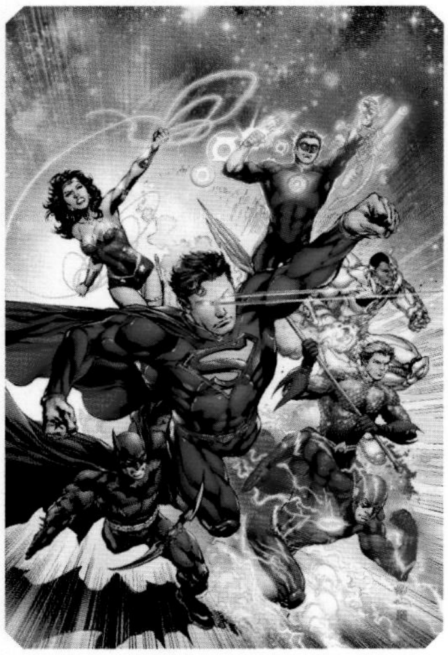

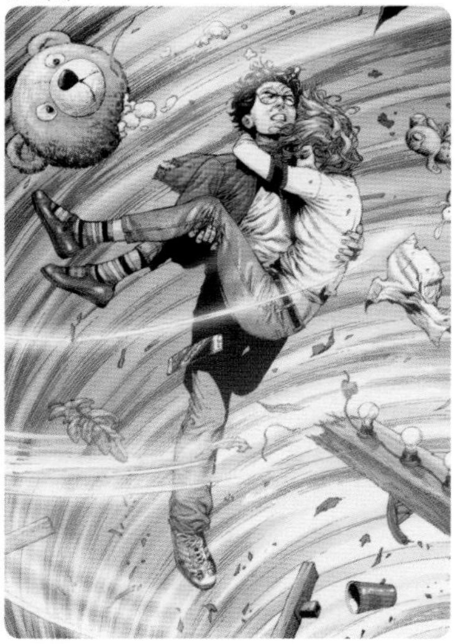

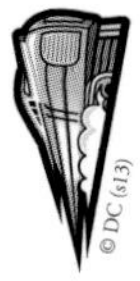

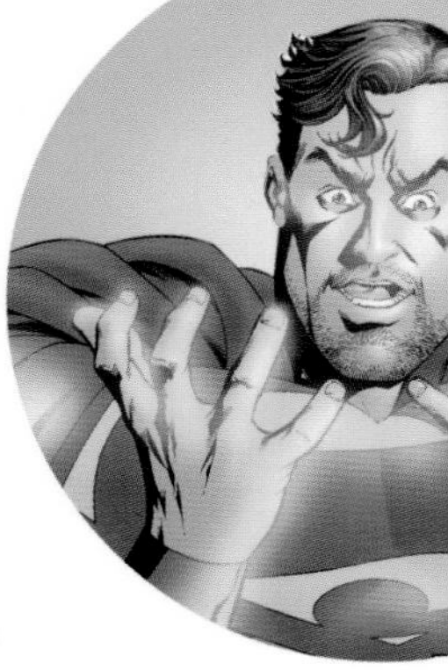

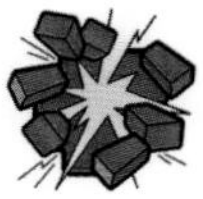

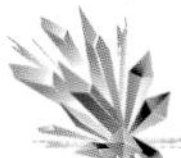

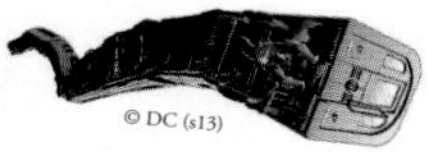

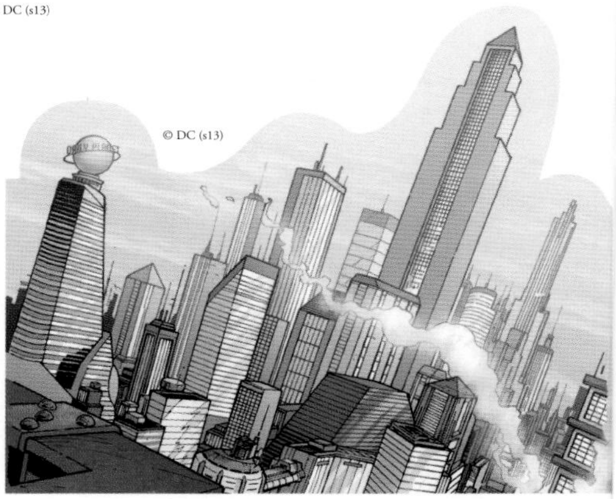

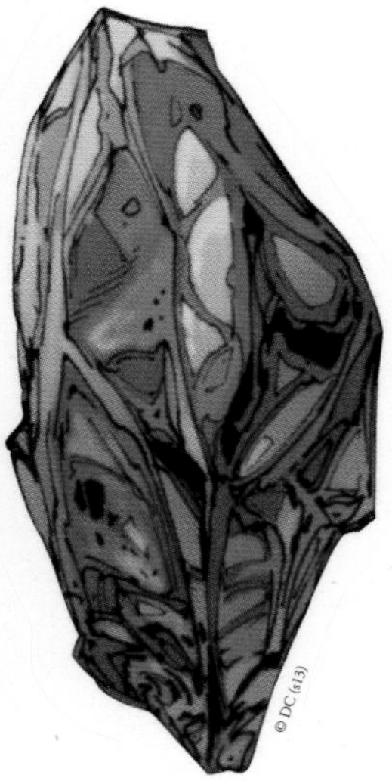

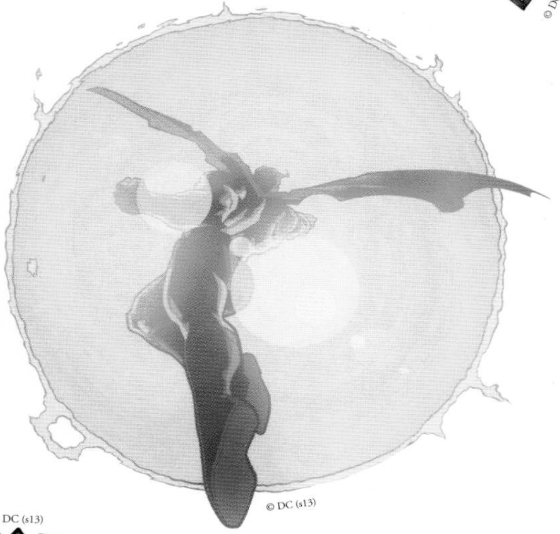

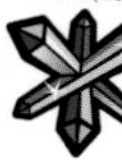

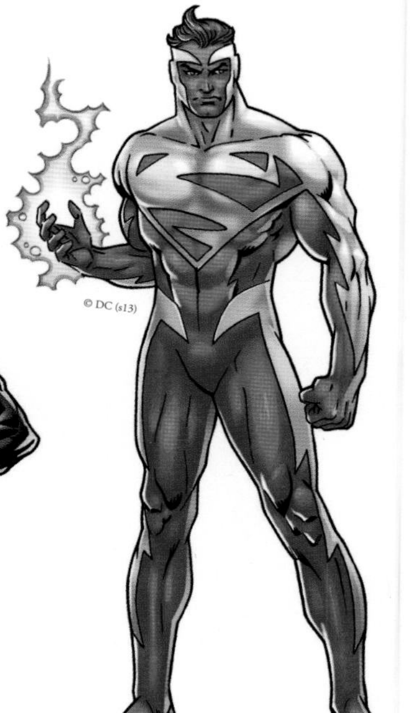

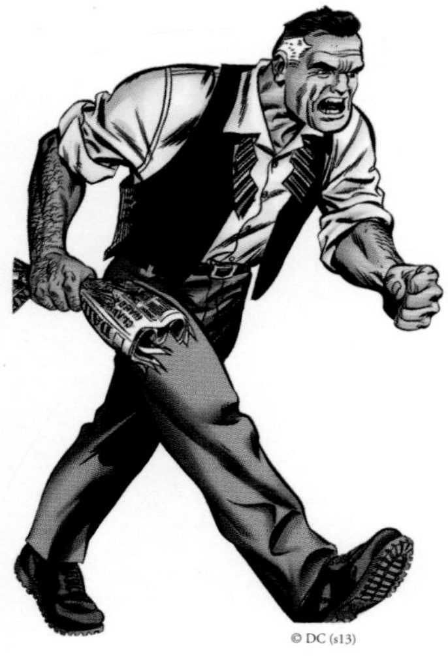

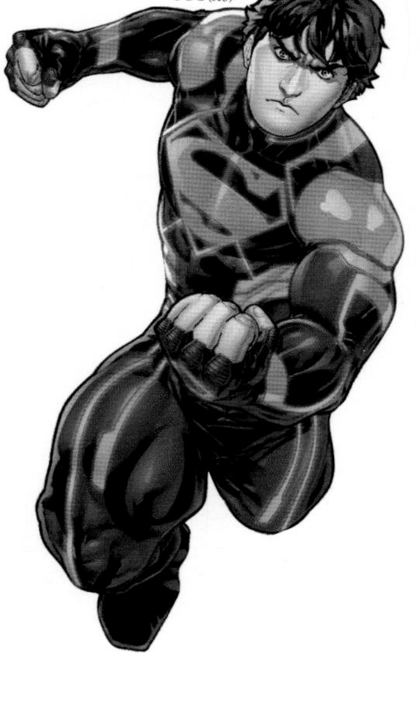

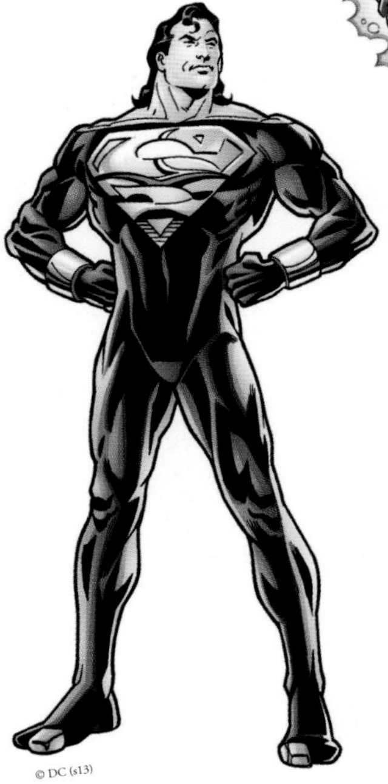

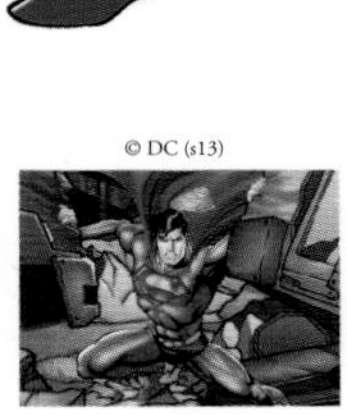

Extra Stickers

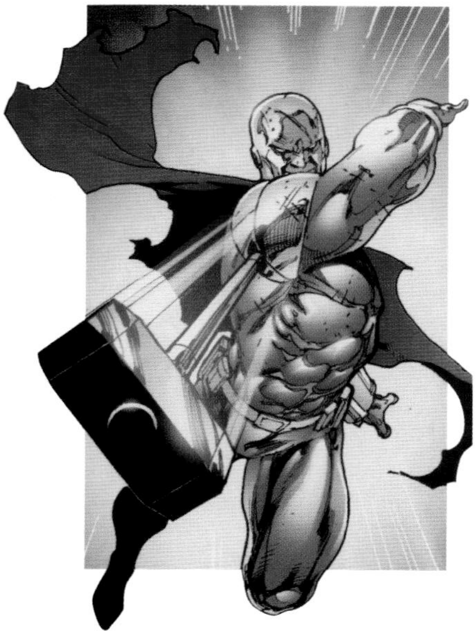

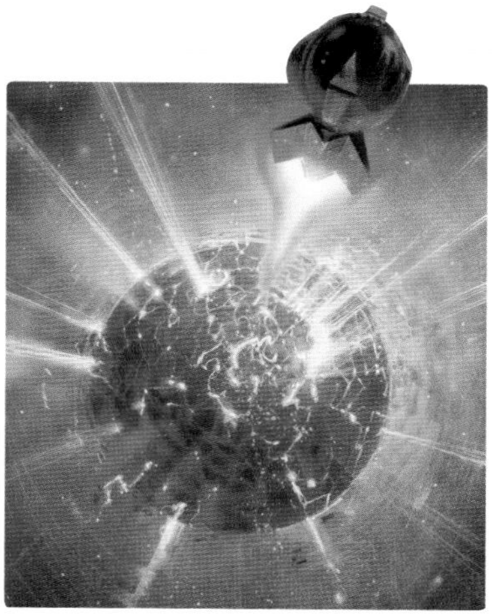

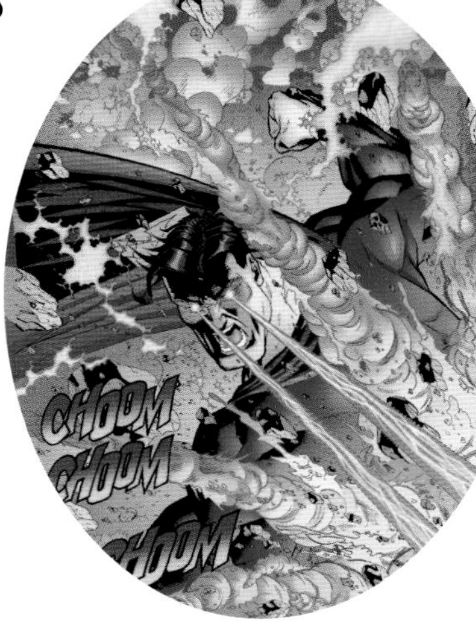
CHOOM
CHOOM
CHOOM

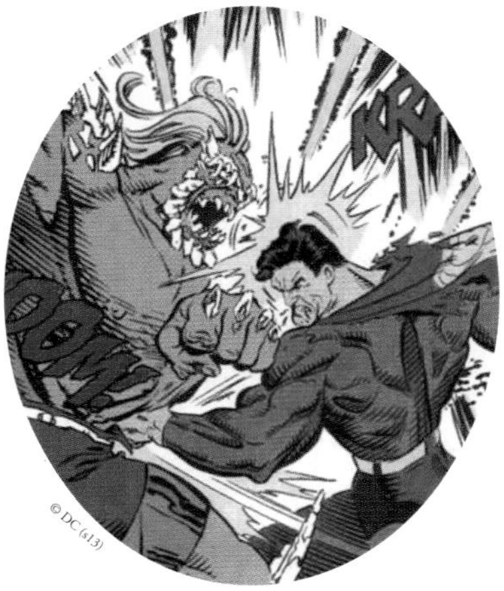

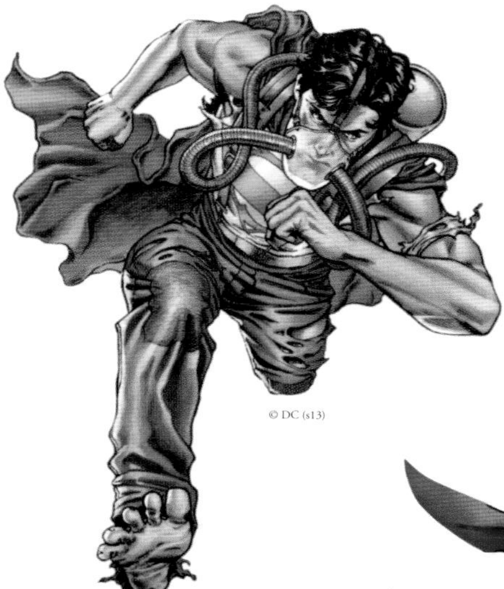

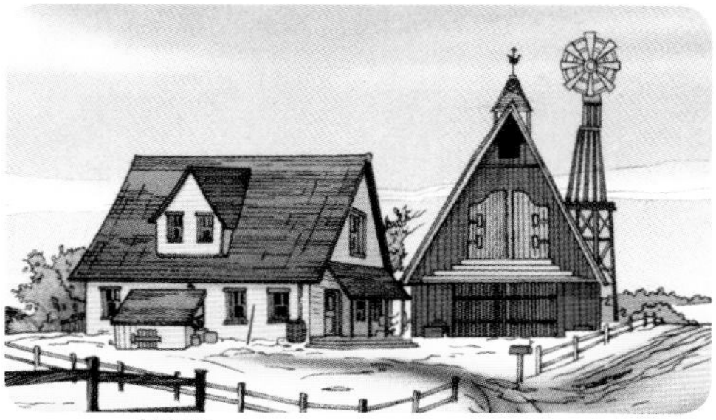

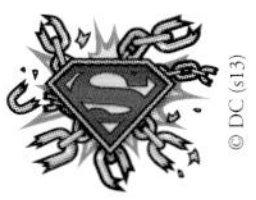

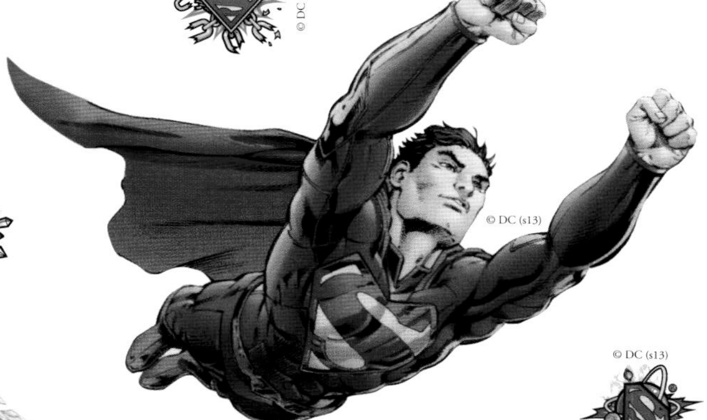

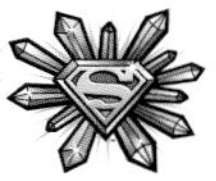

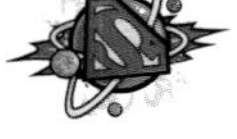

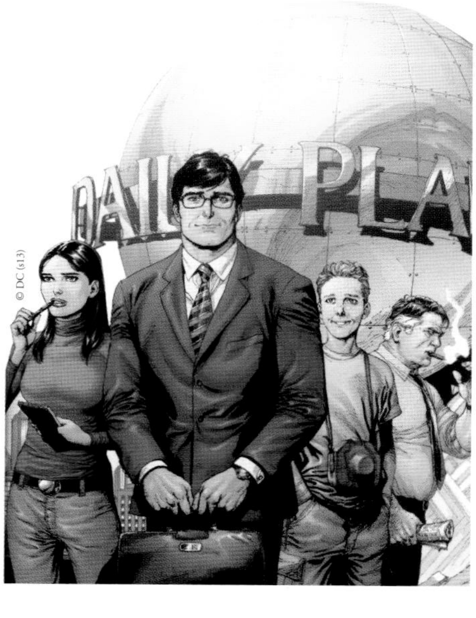

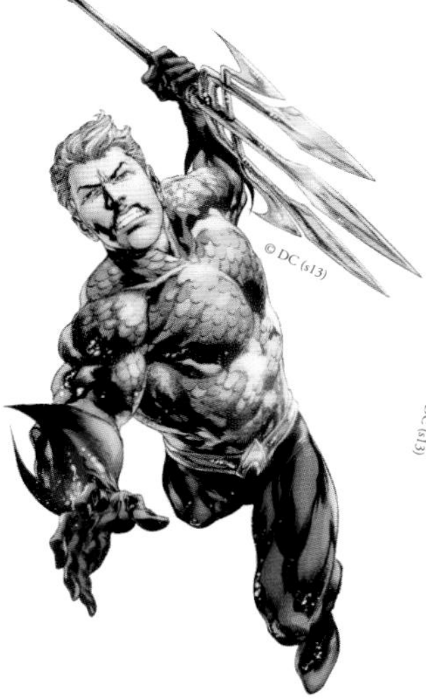

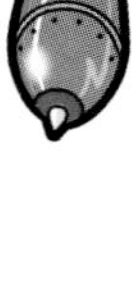

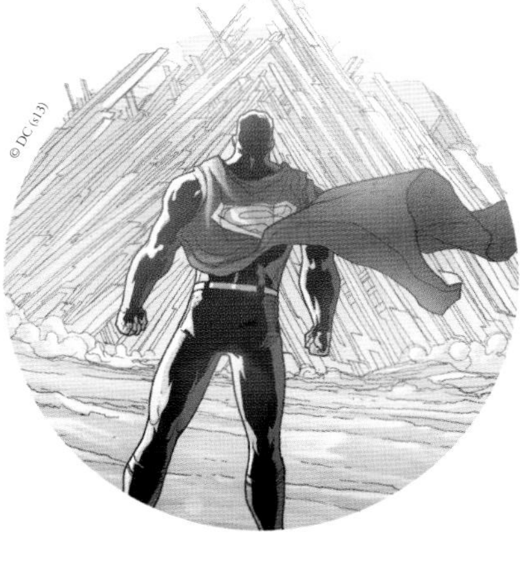

Extra Stickers

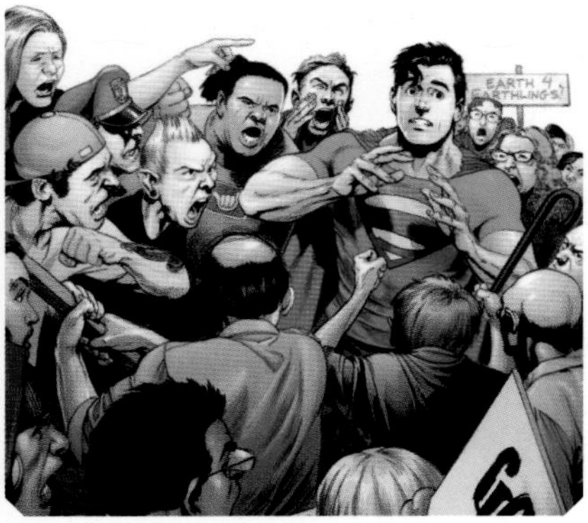

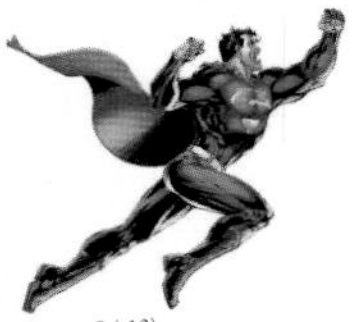

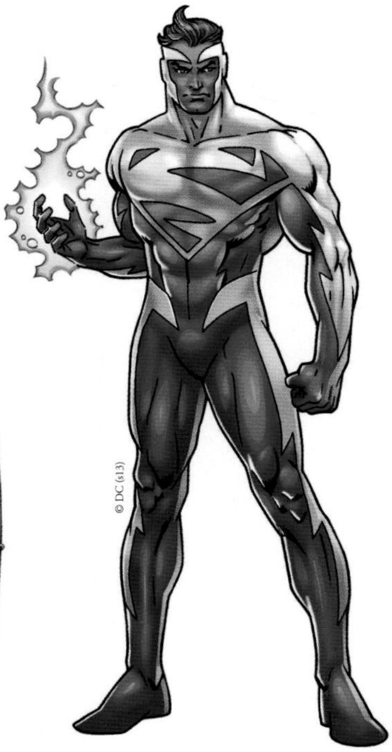

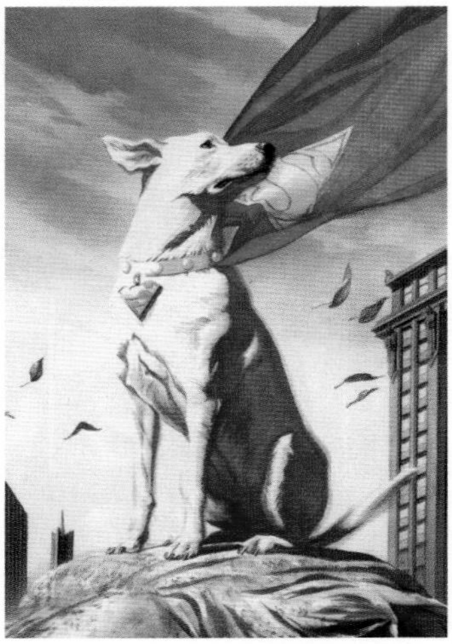

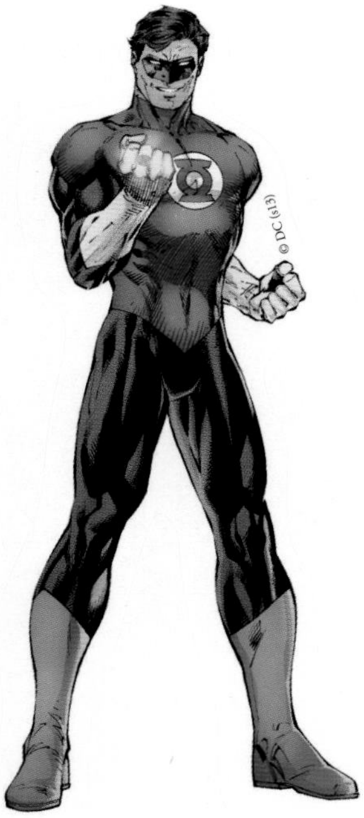

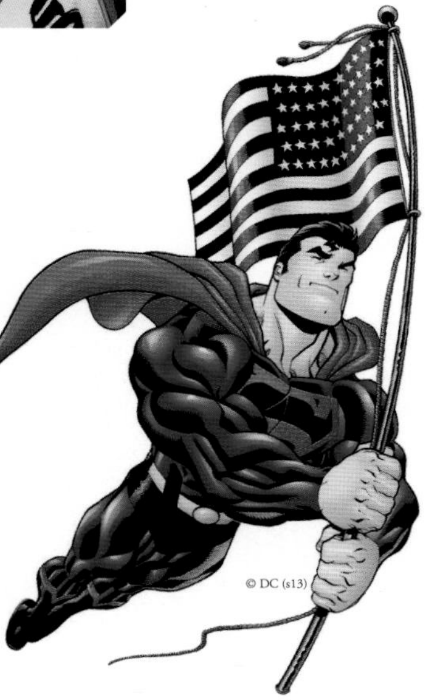

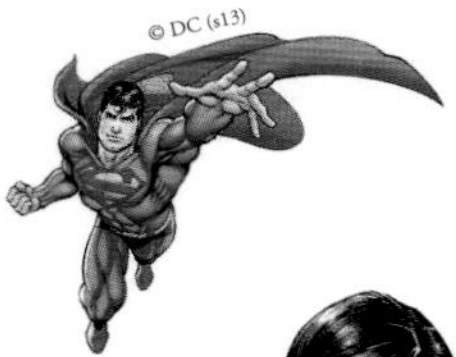

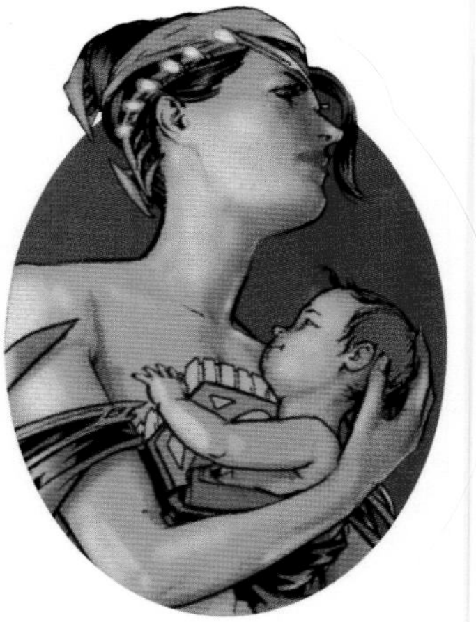

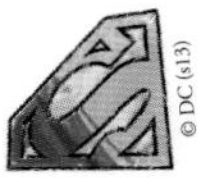

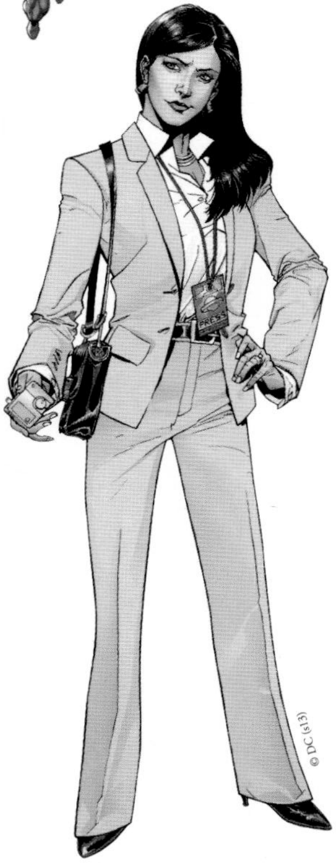

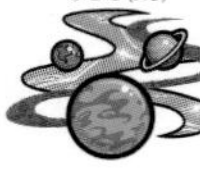

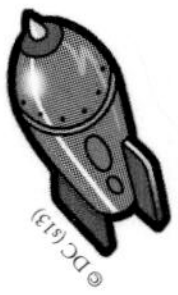

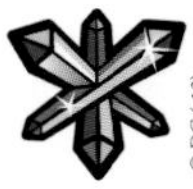

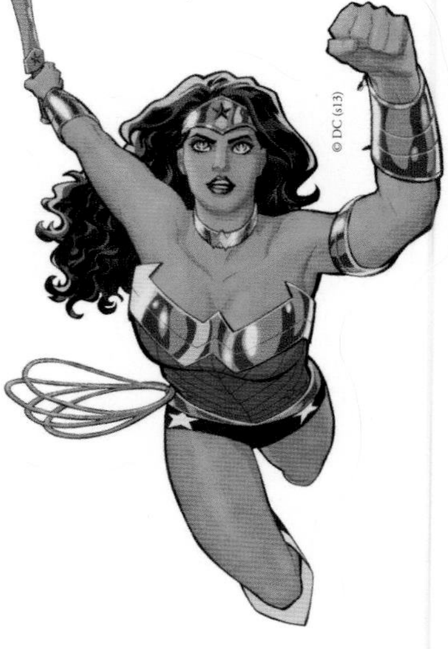

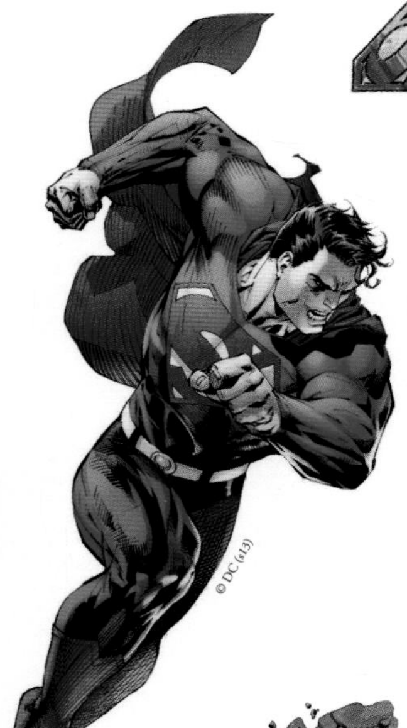

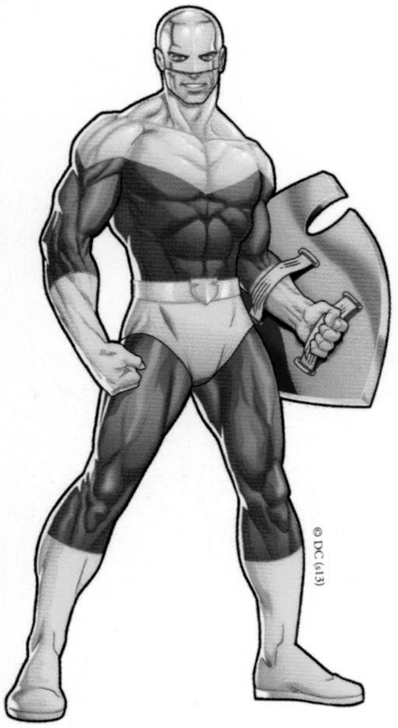

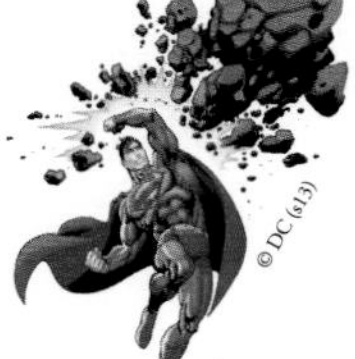

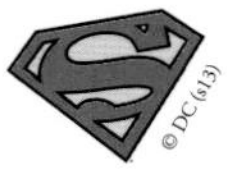

Extra Stickers

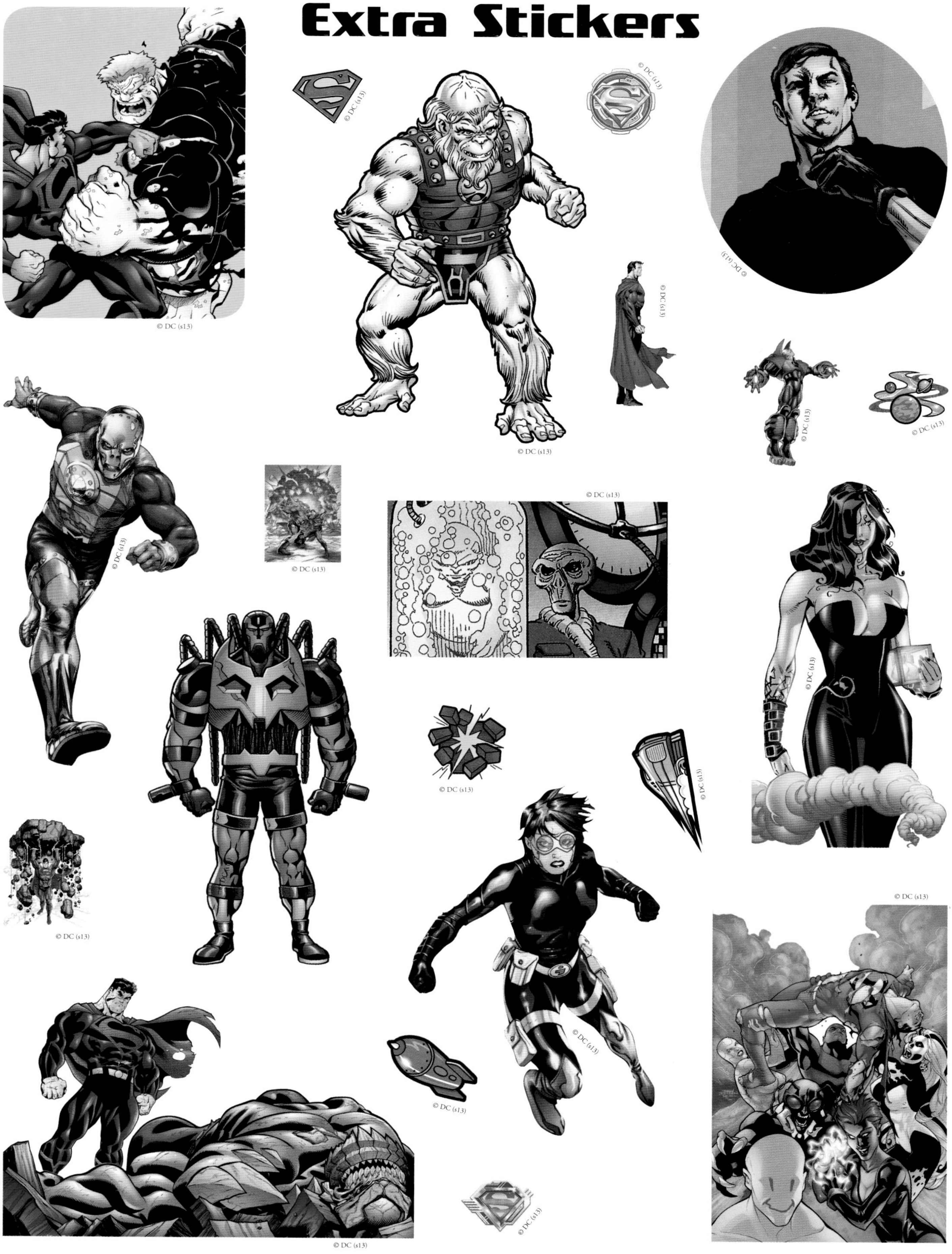

Extra Stickers

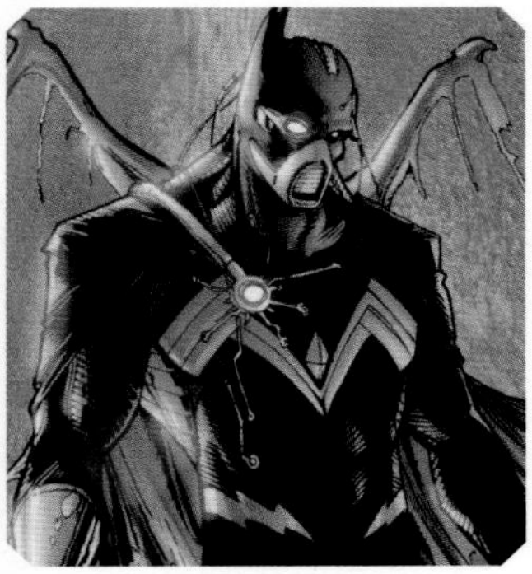

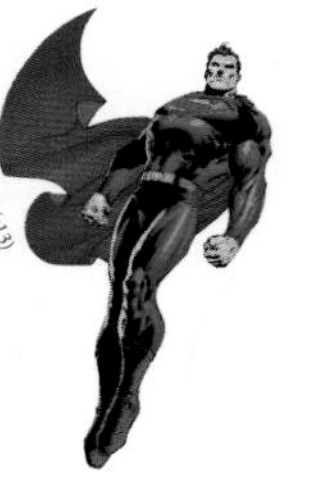

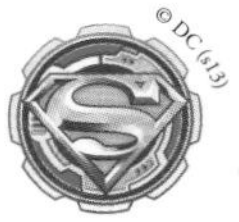

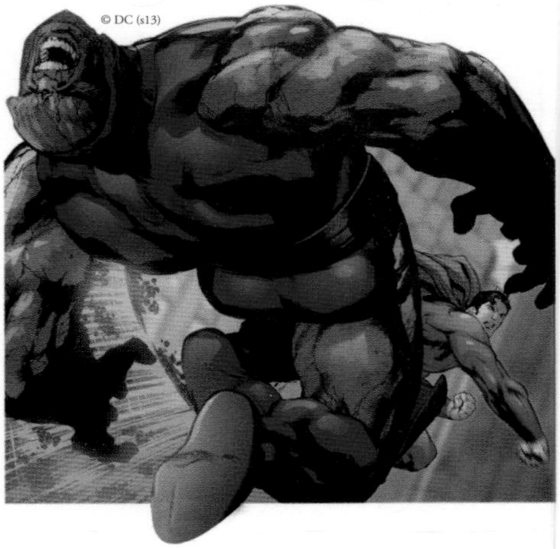

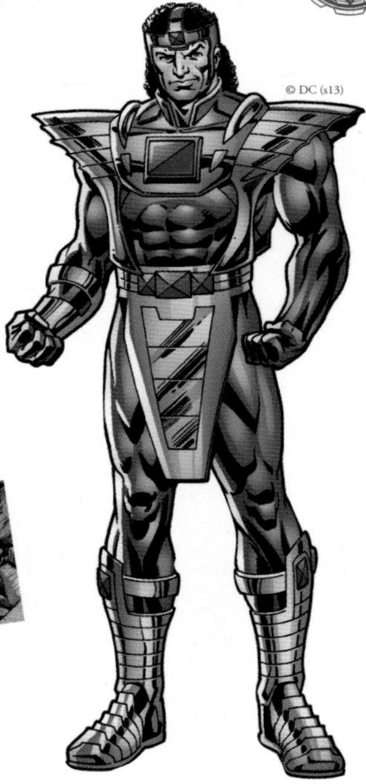

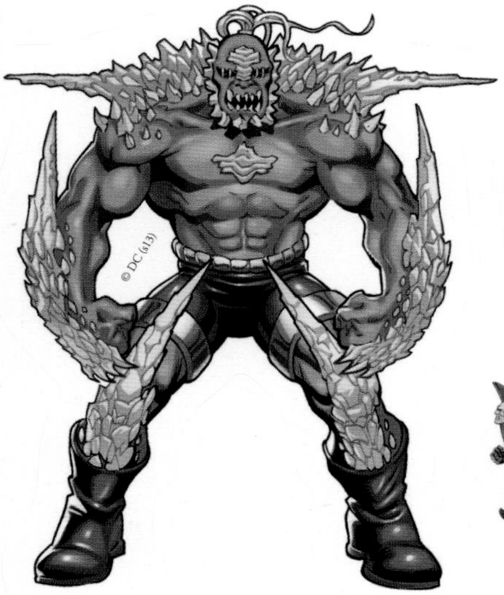

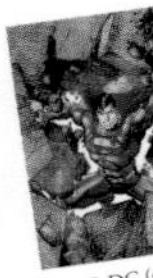

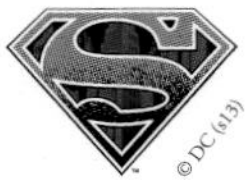

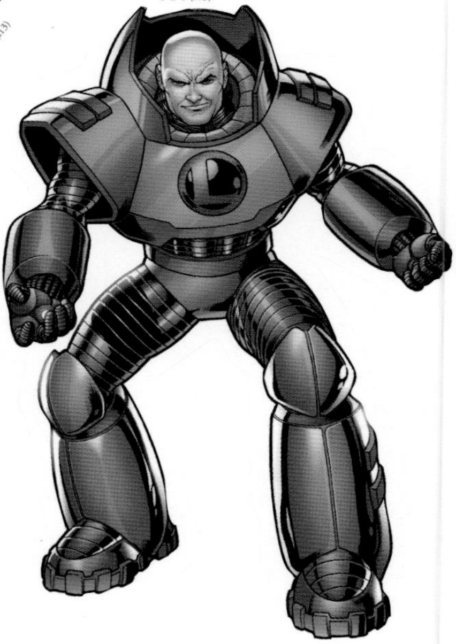

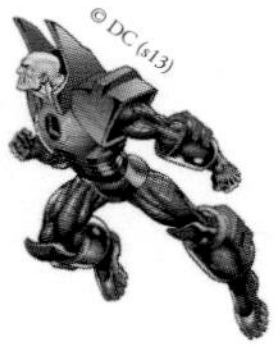

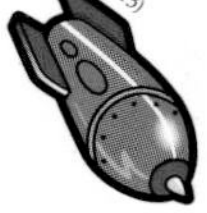

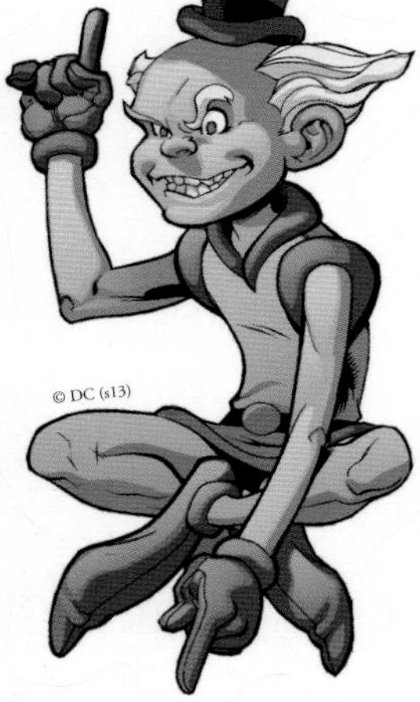

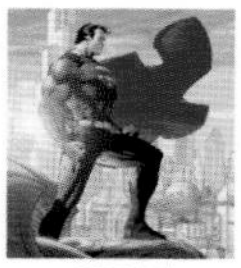

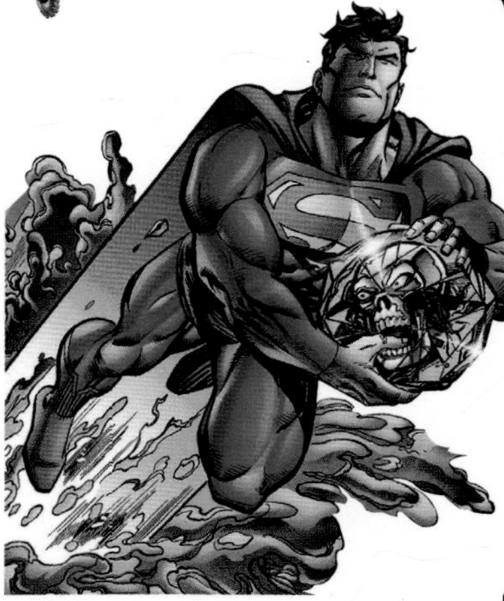

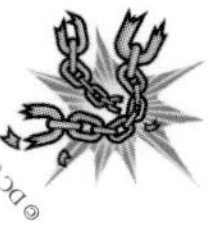

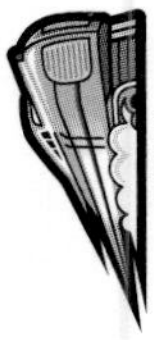

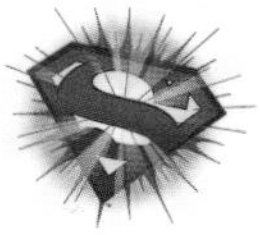

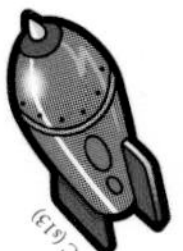

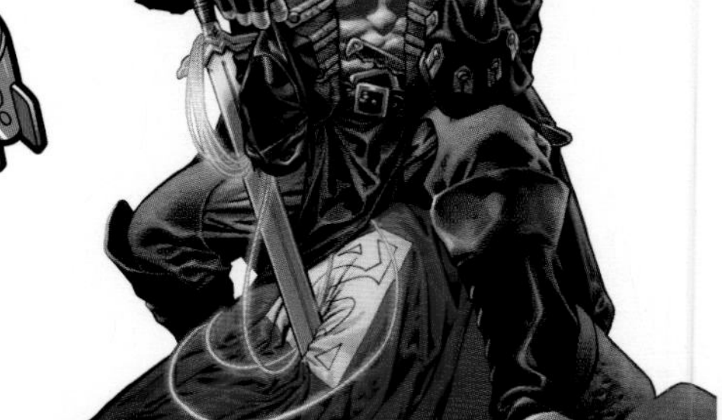

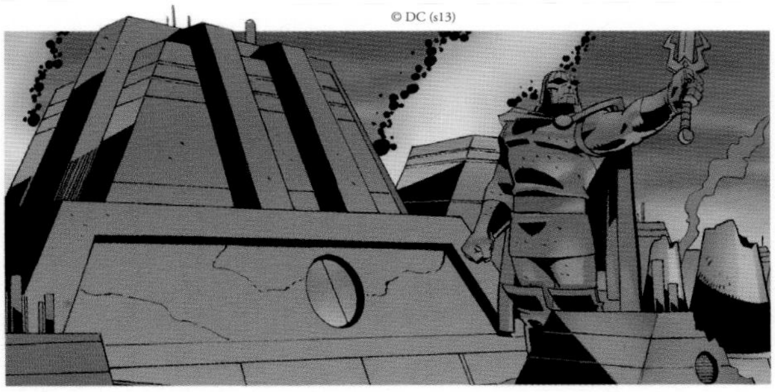

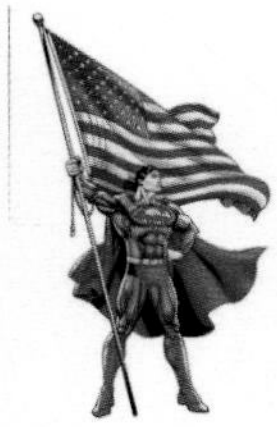

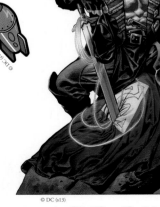

Extra Stickers

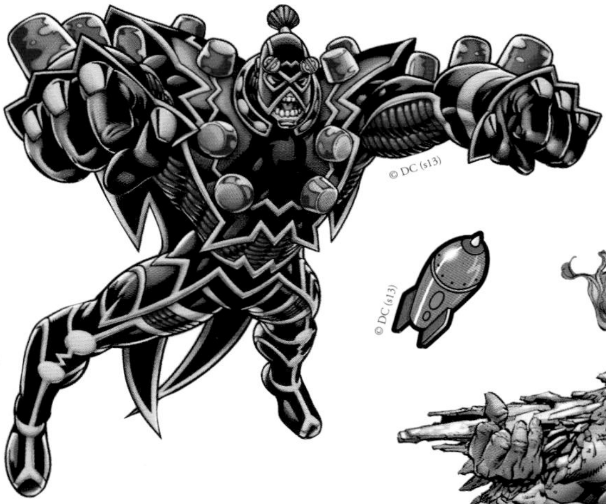

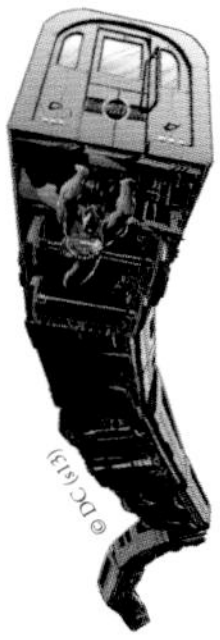

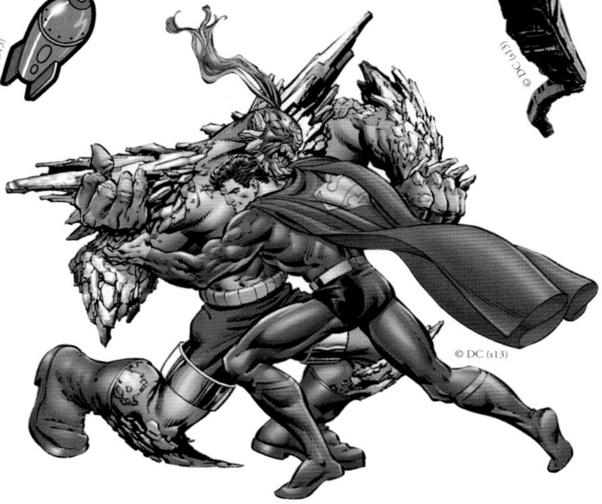

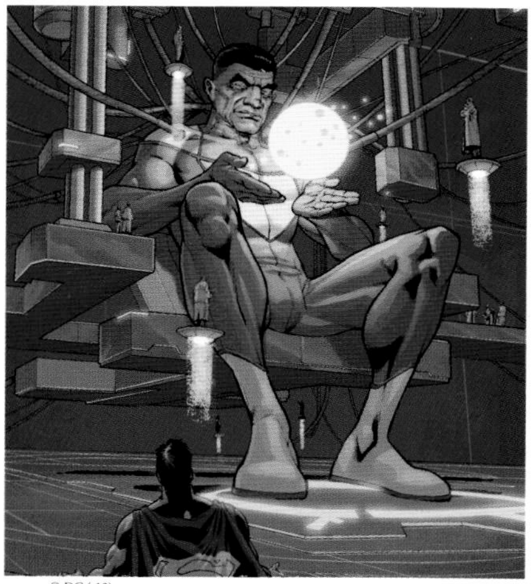

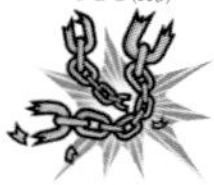

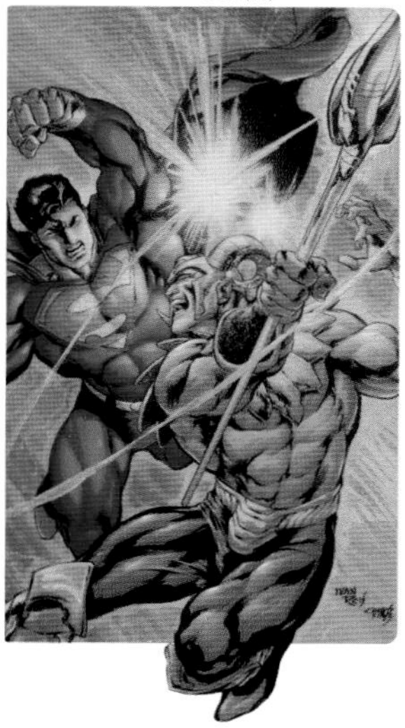

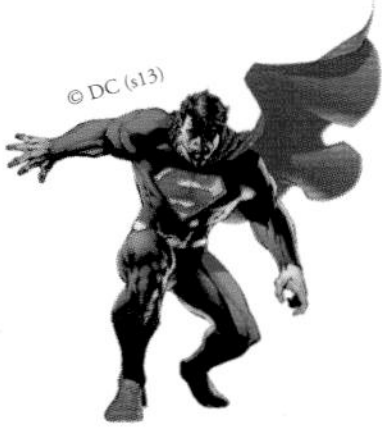

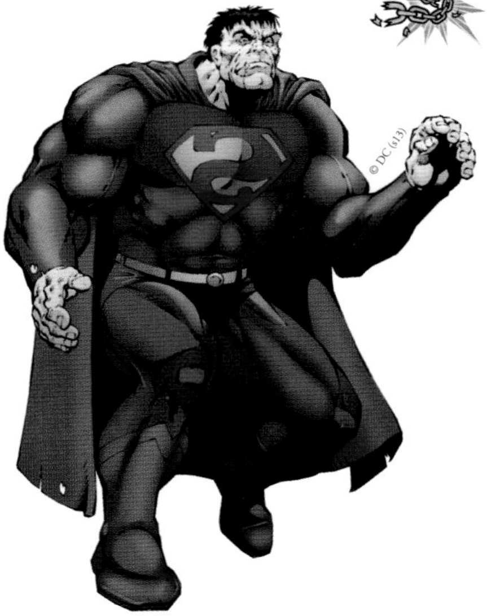

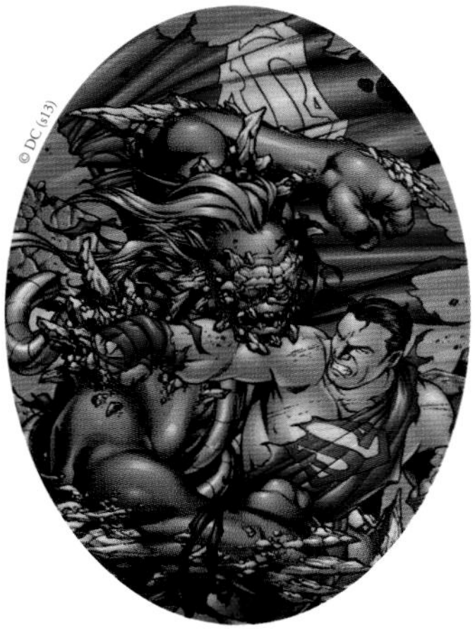

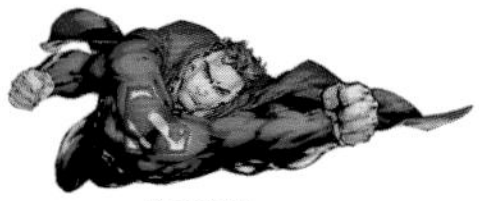

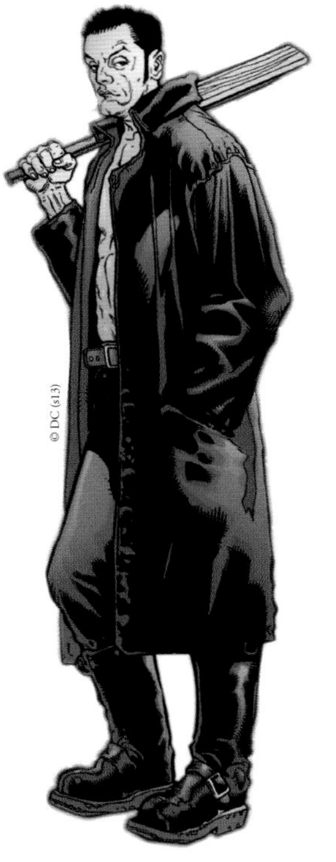

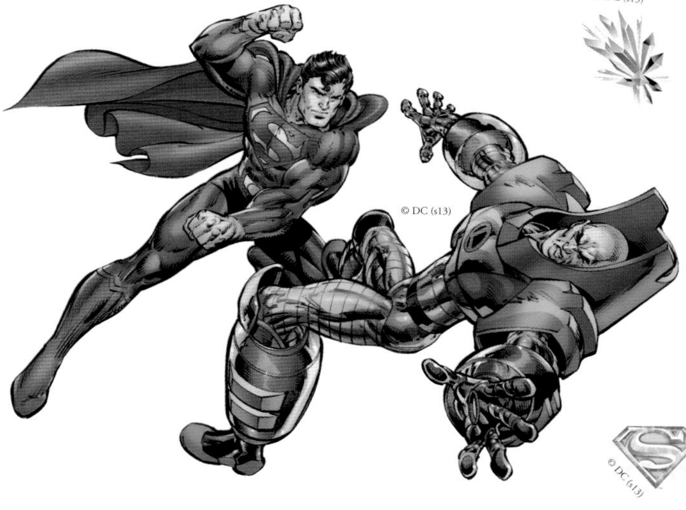

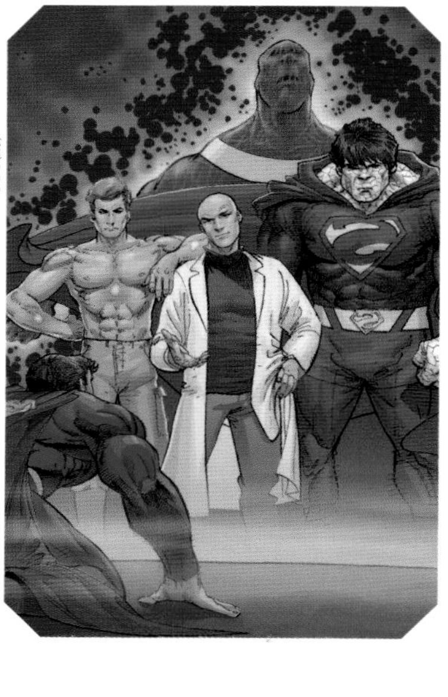

Extra Stickers

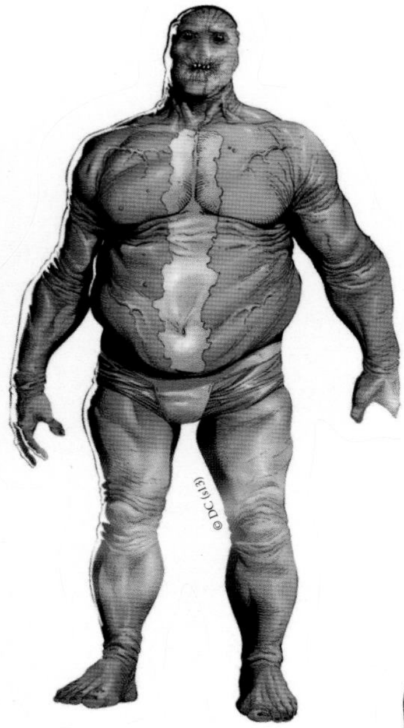

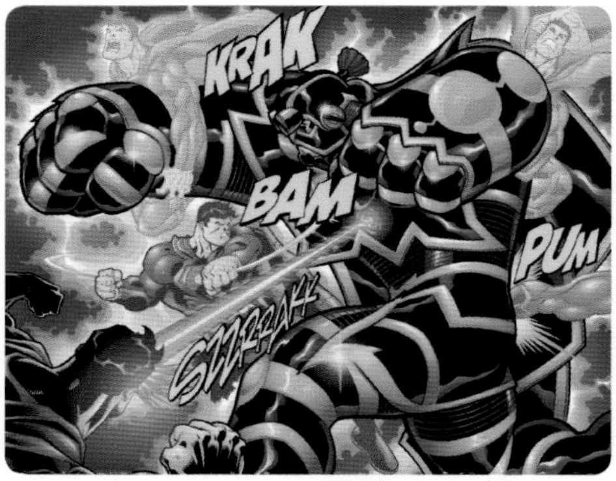

KRAK
BAM
PUM

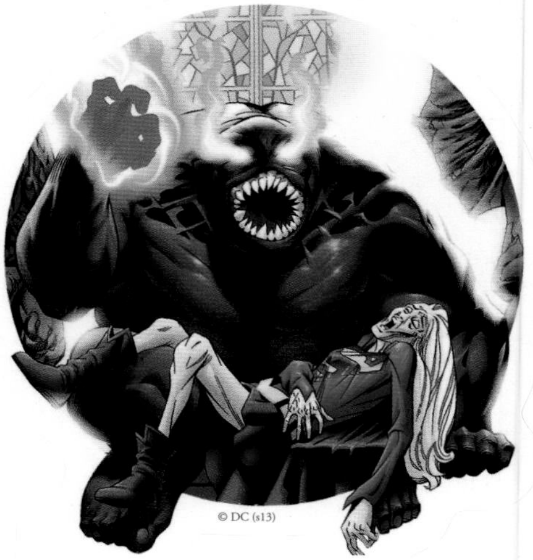

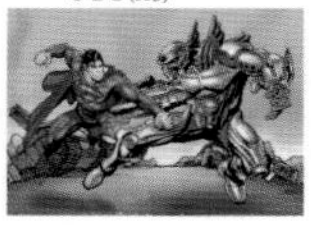

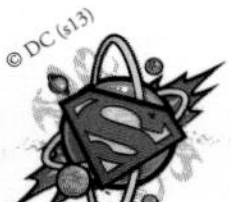

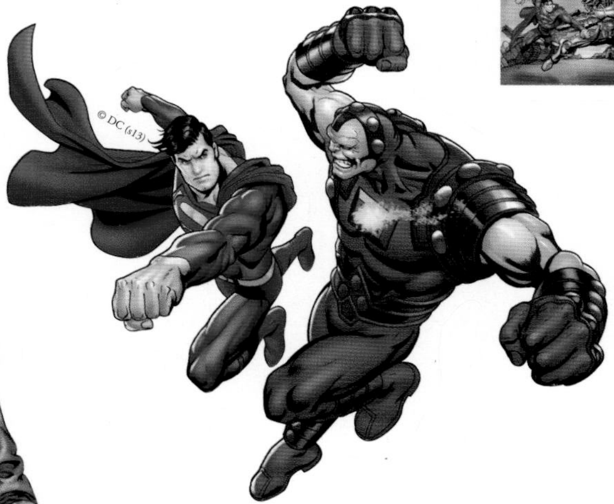

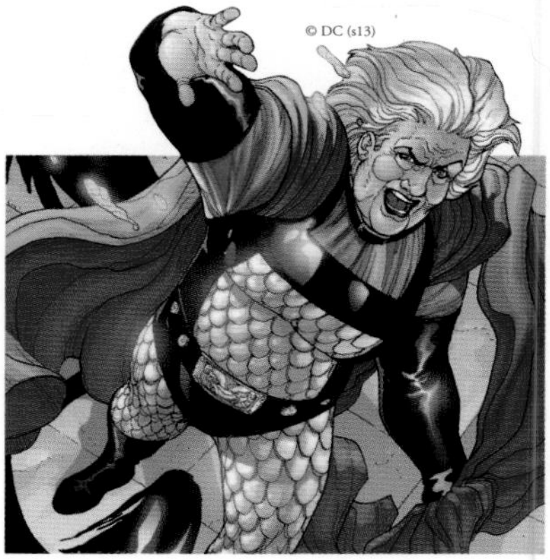

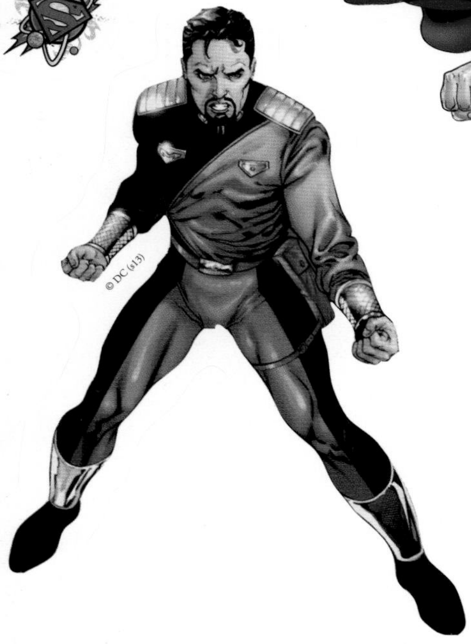

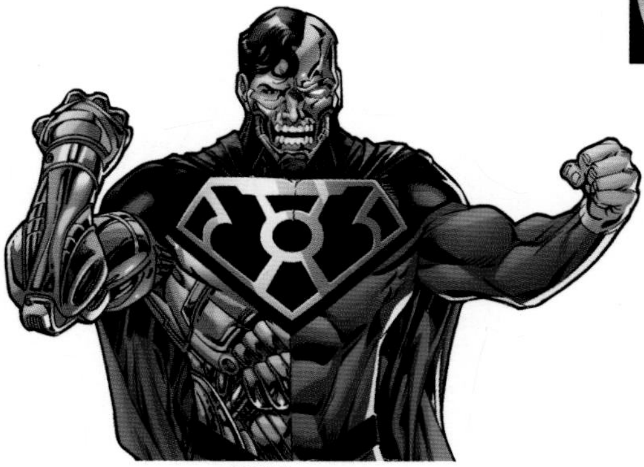

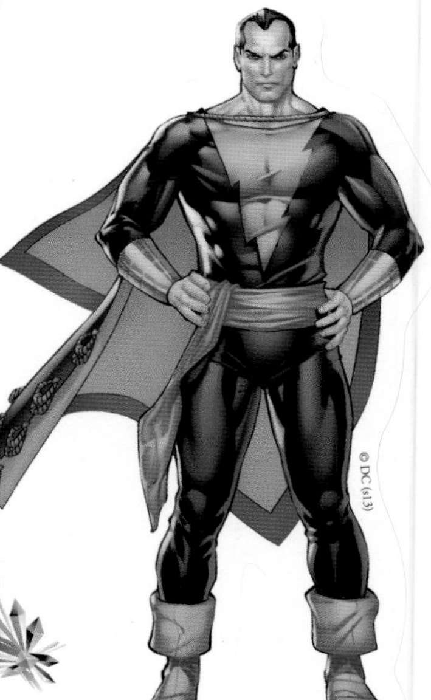

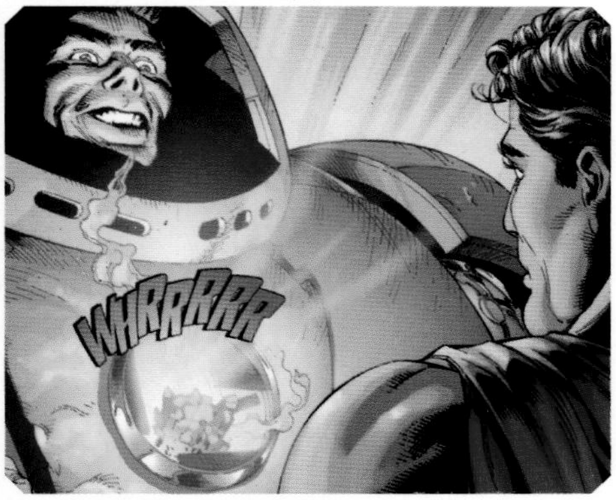

WHRRRRR

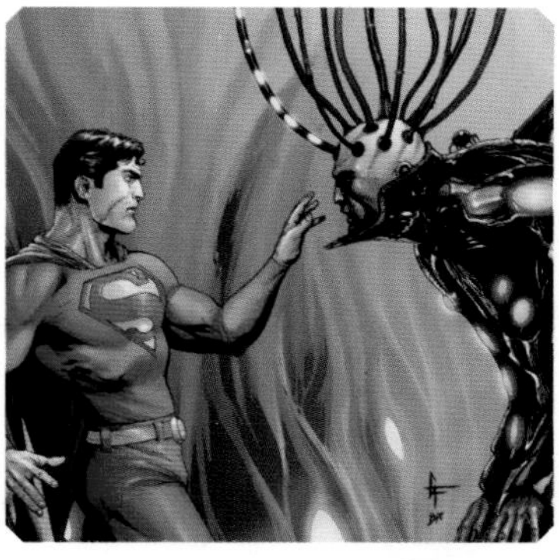

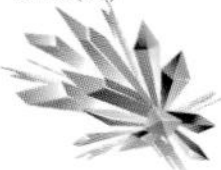

Extra Stic

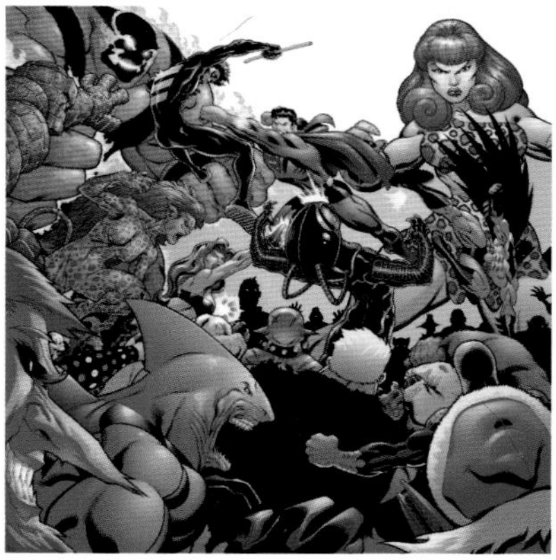

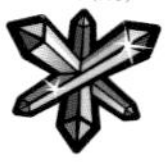

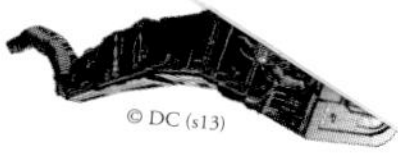

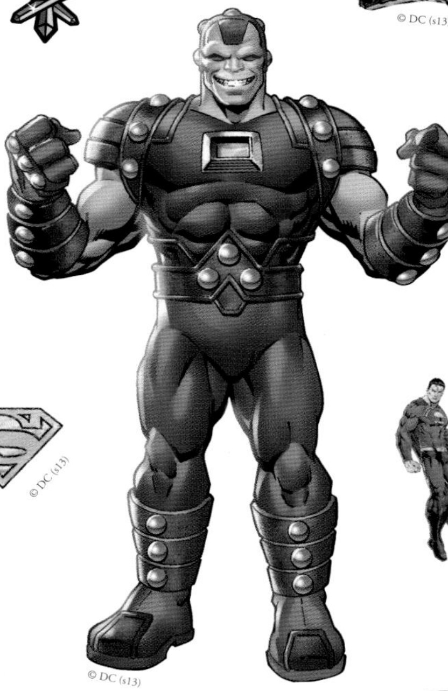

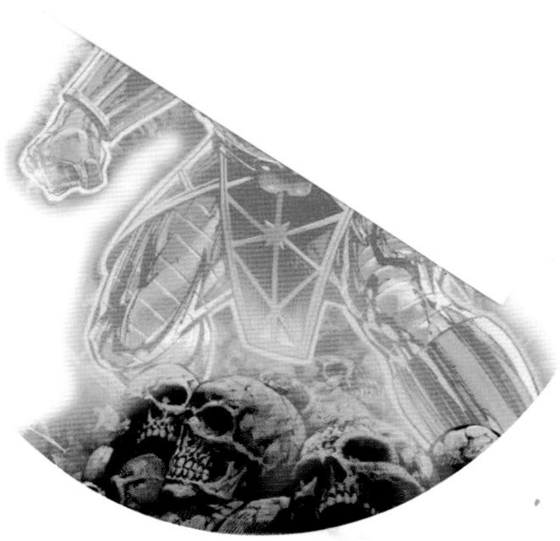

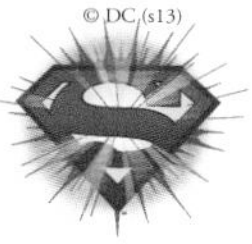

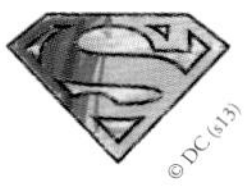

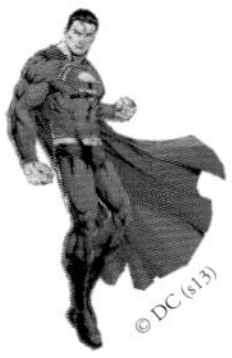

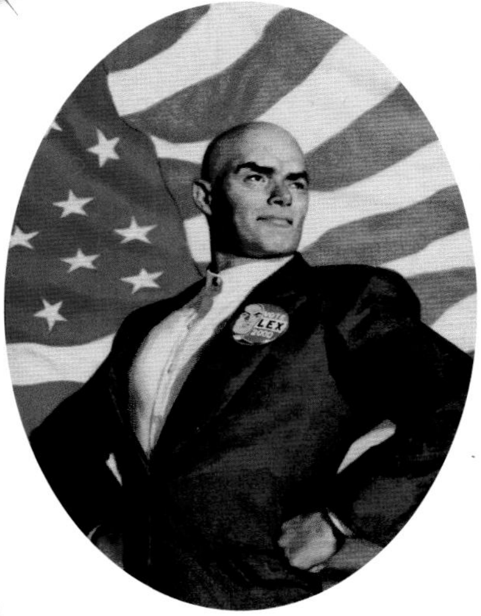

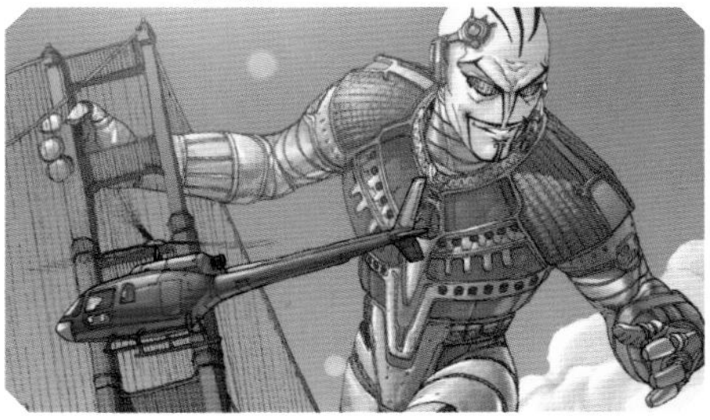

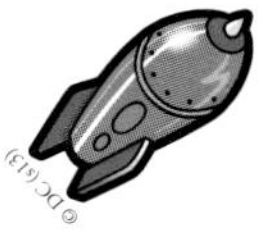

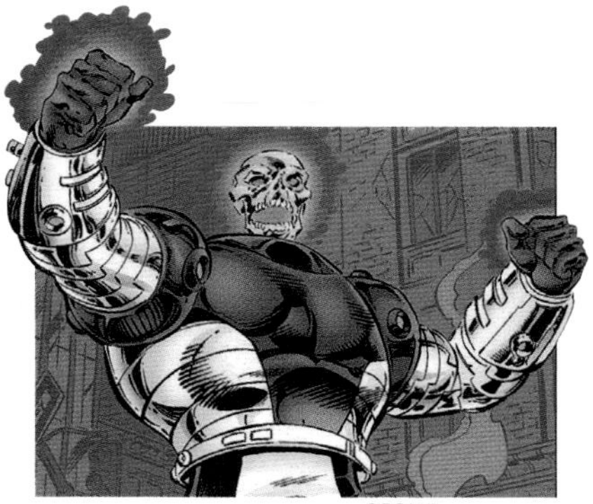

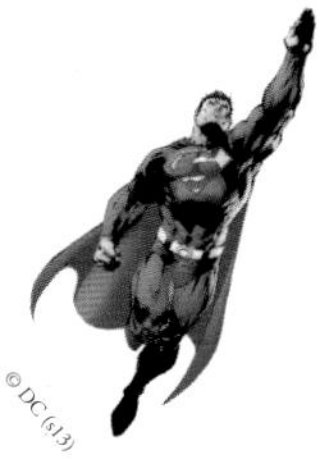

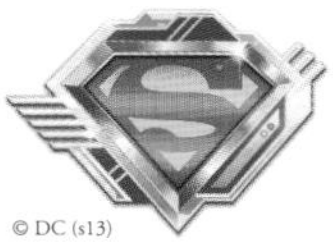

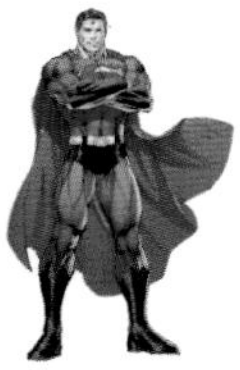

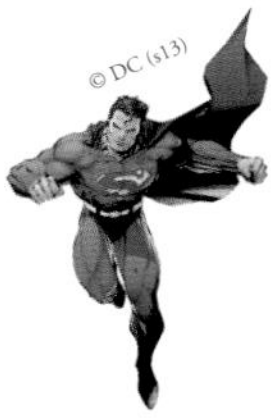

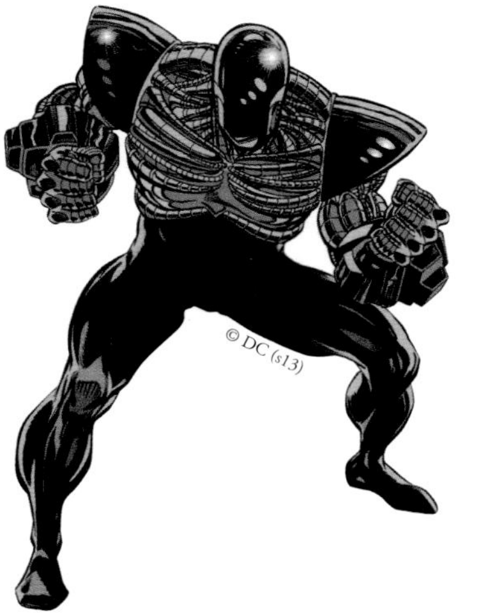

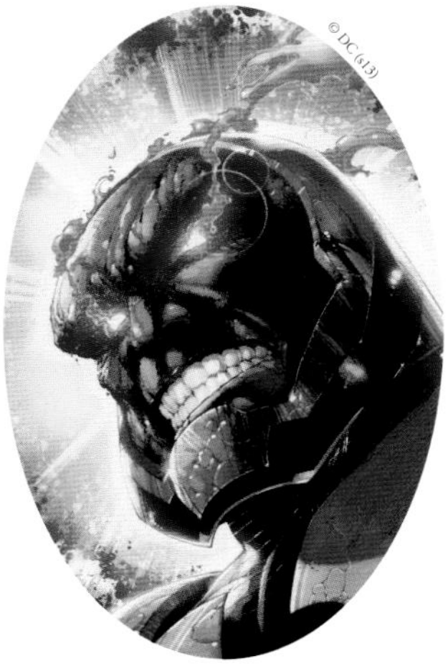

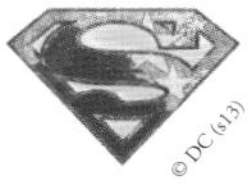

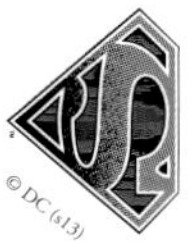

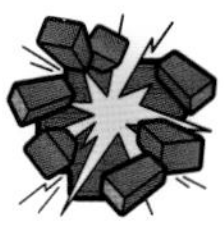

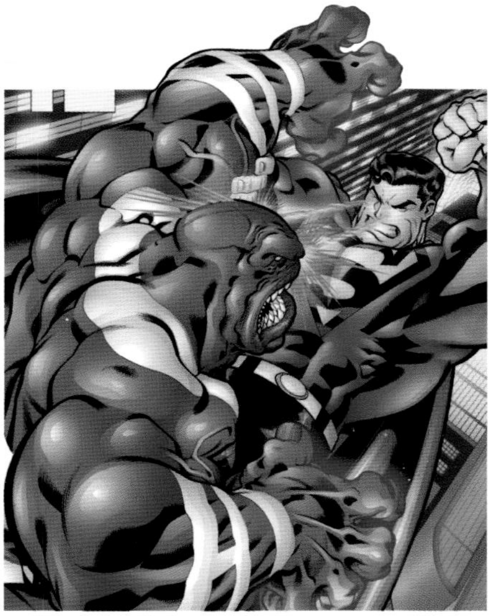

Extra Stickers

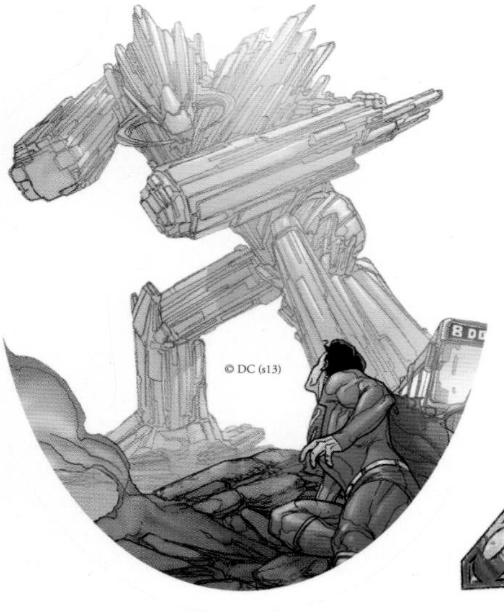
© DC (s13)
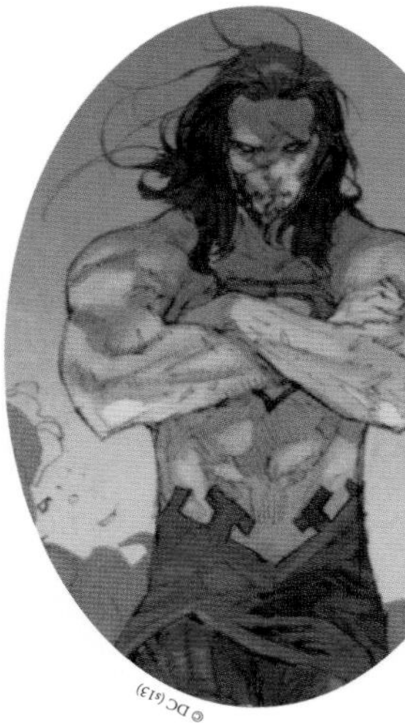
© DC (s13)
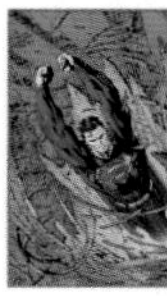
© DC (s13)
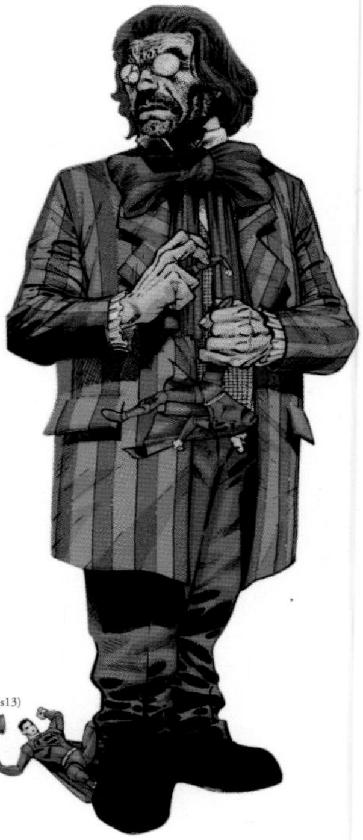
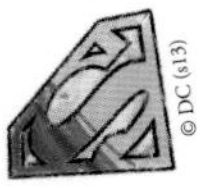
© DC (s13)
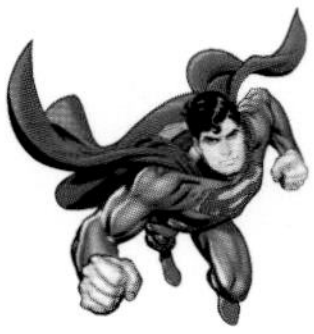
© DC (s13)
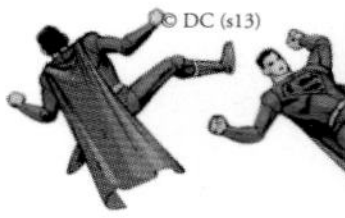
© DC (s13)
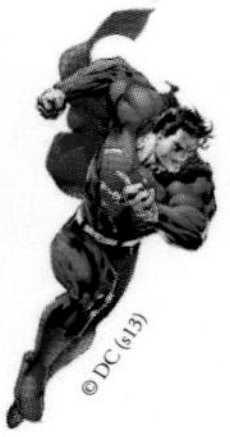
© DC (s13)
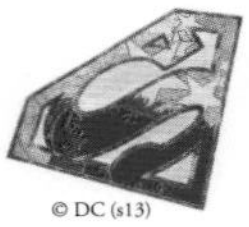
© DC (s13)
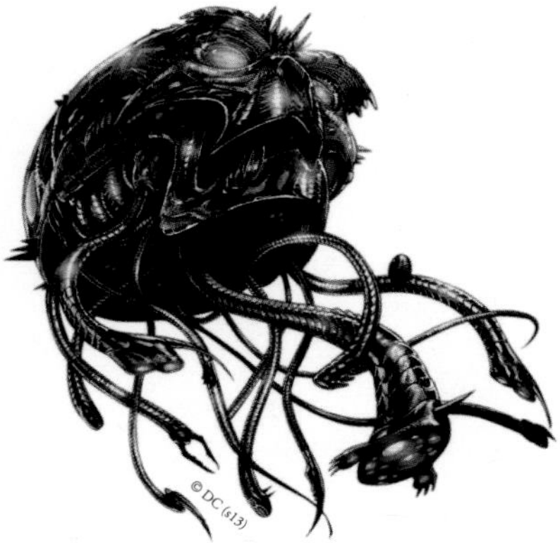
© DC (s13)
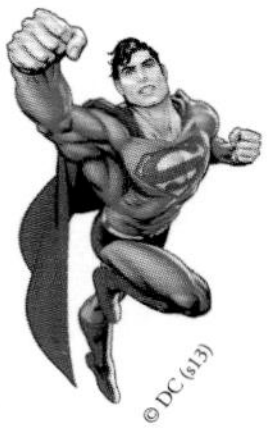
© DC (s13)
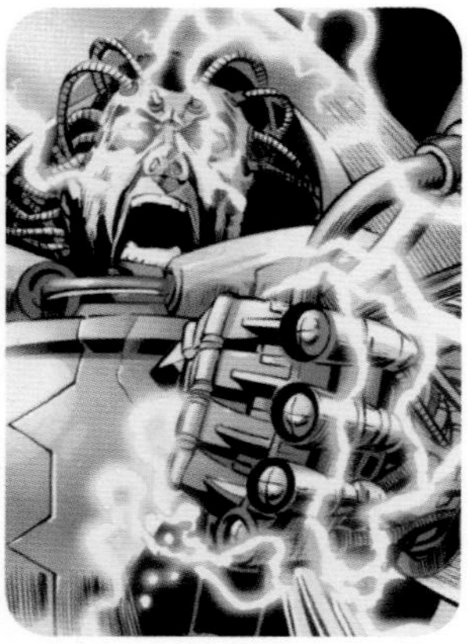
© DC (s13)
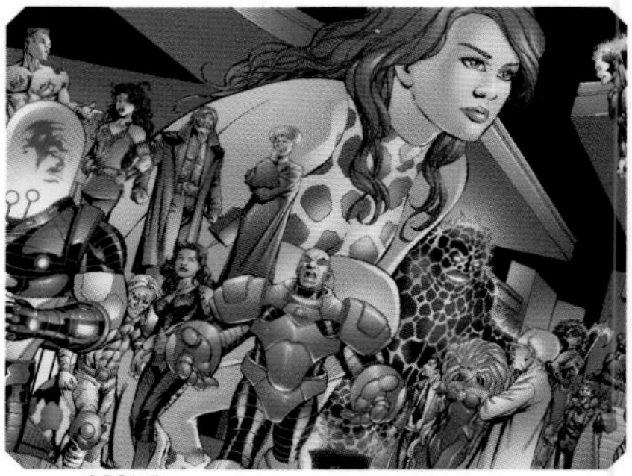
© DC (s13)
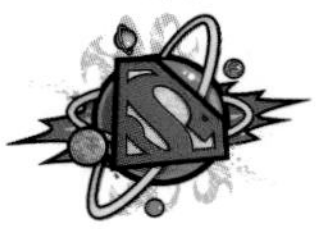
© DC (s13)
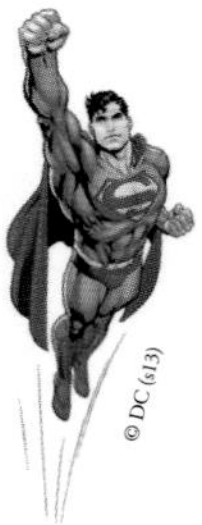
© DC (s13)
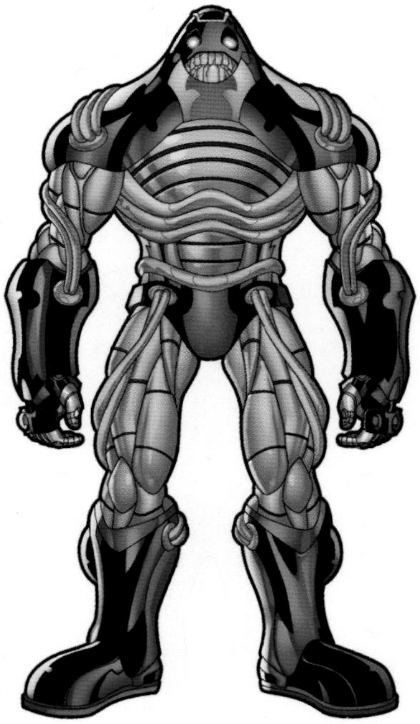
© DC (s13)
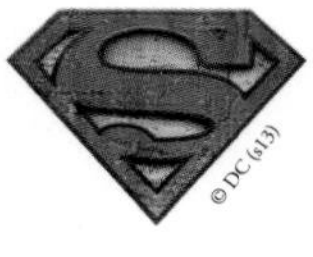
© DC (s13)
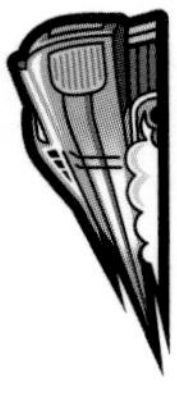
© DC (s13)
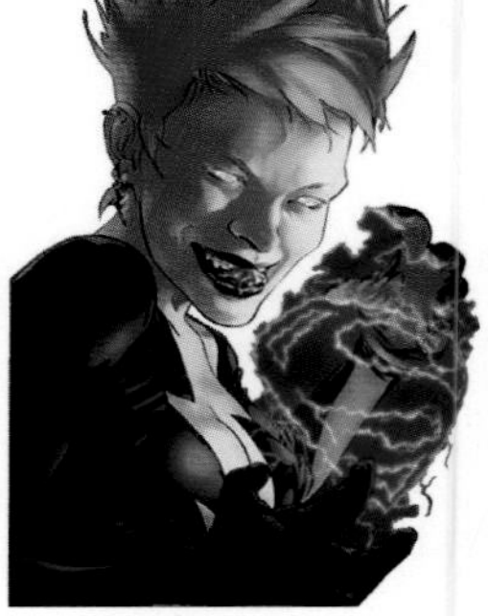
© DC (s13)
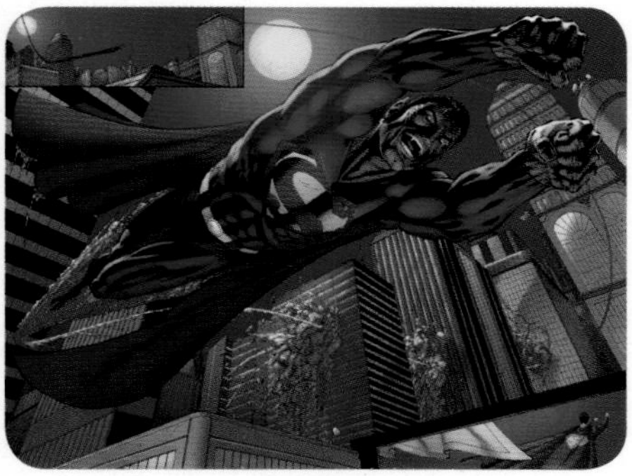
© DC (s13)
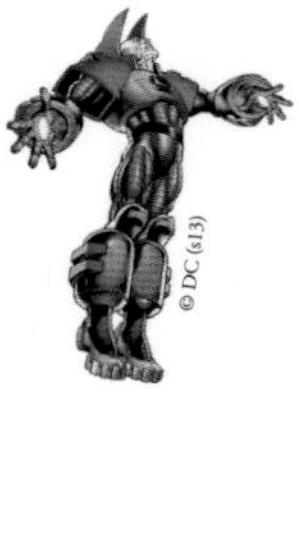
© DC (s13)
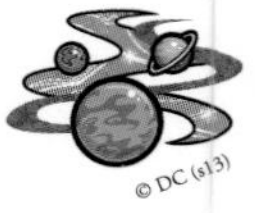
© DC (s13)
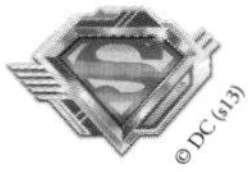
© DC (s13)

Extra Stickers

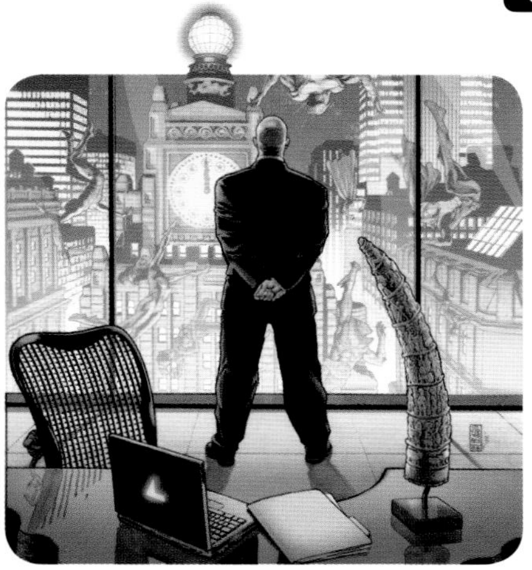

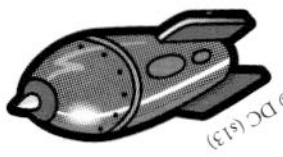

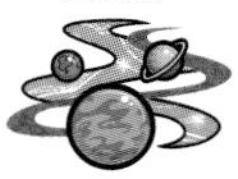

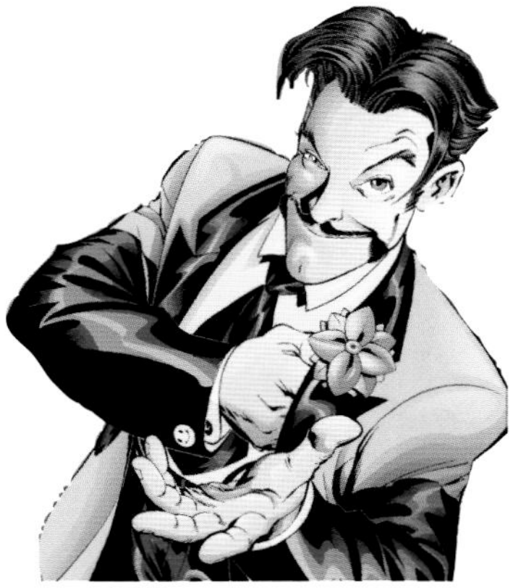

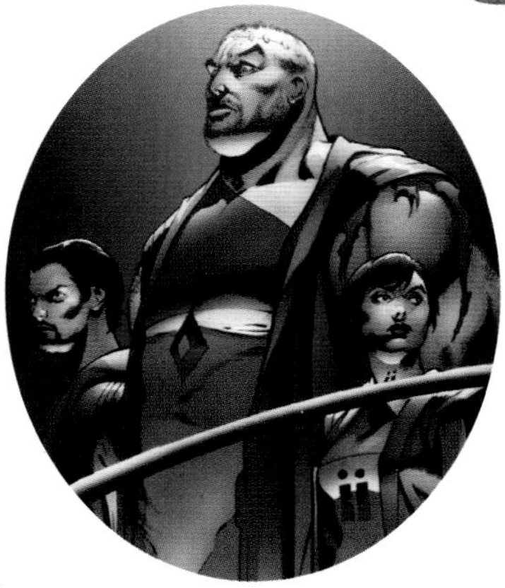

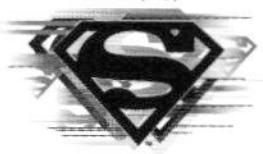

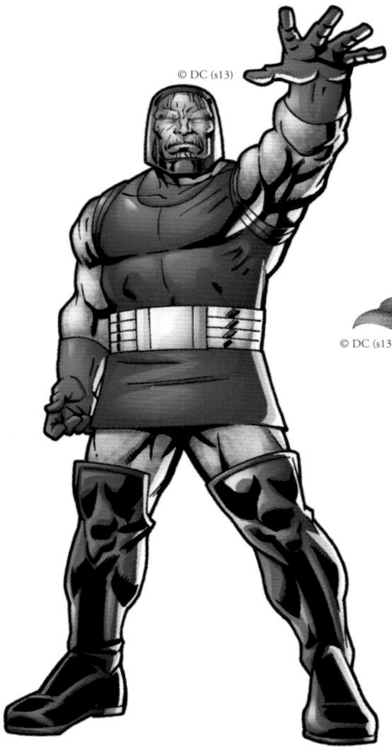

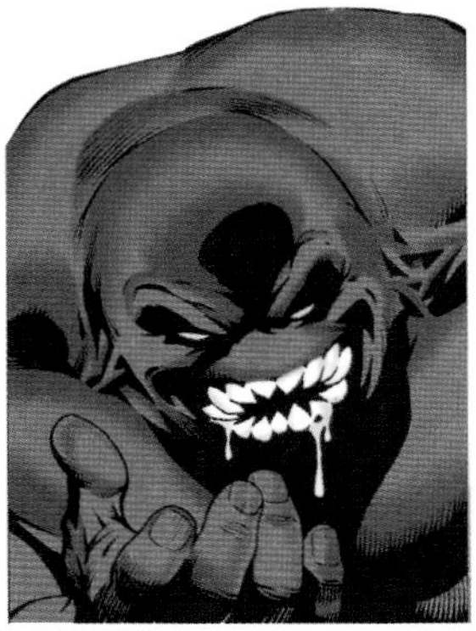

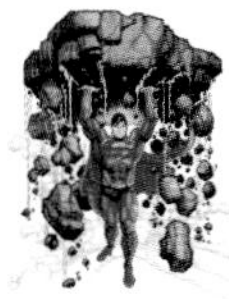

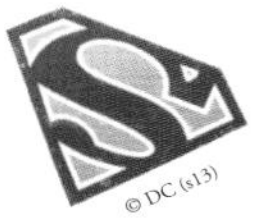

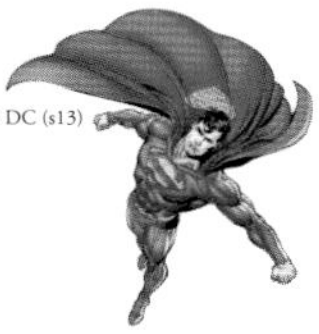

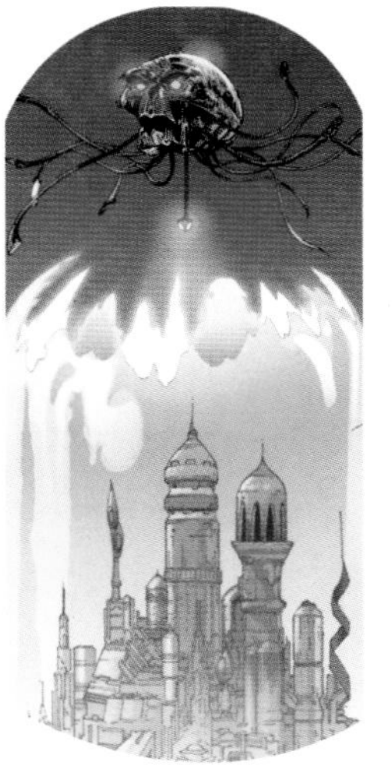

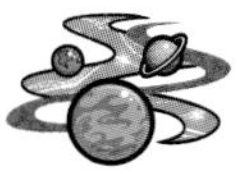

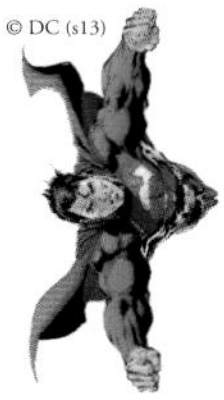

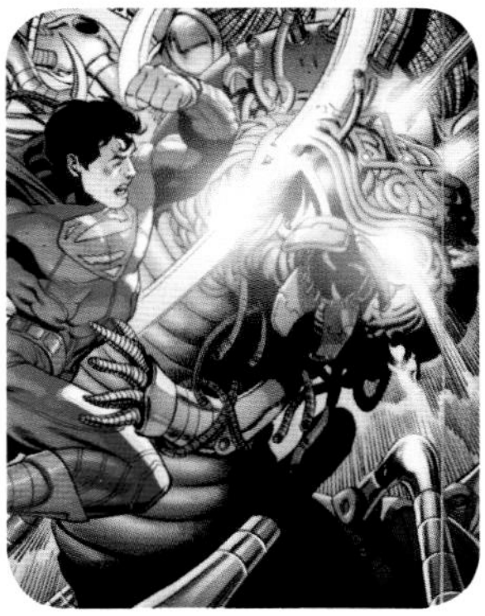

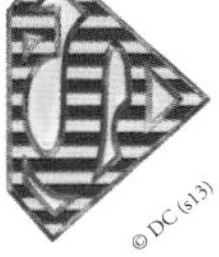

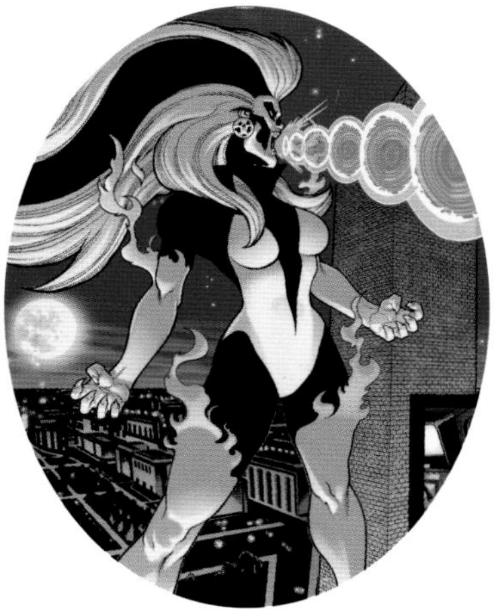

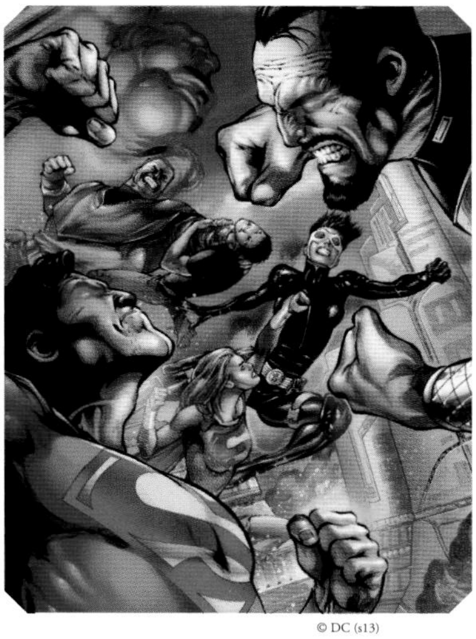

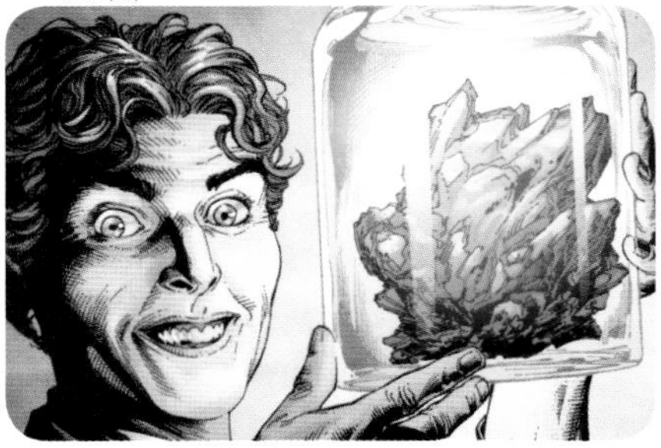

Extra Stickers

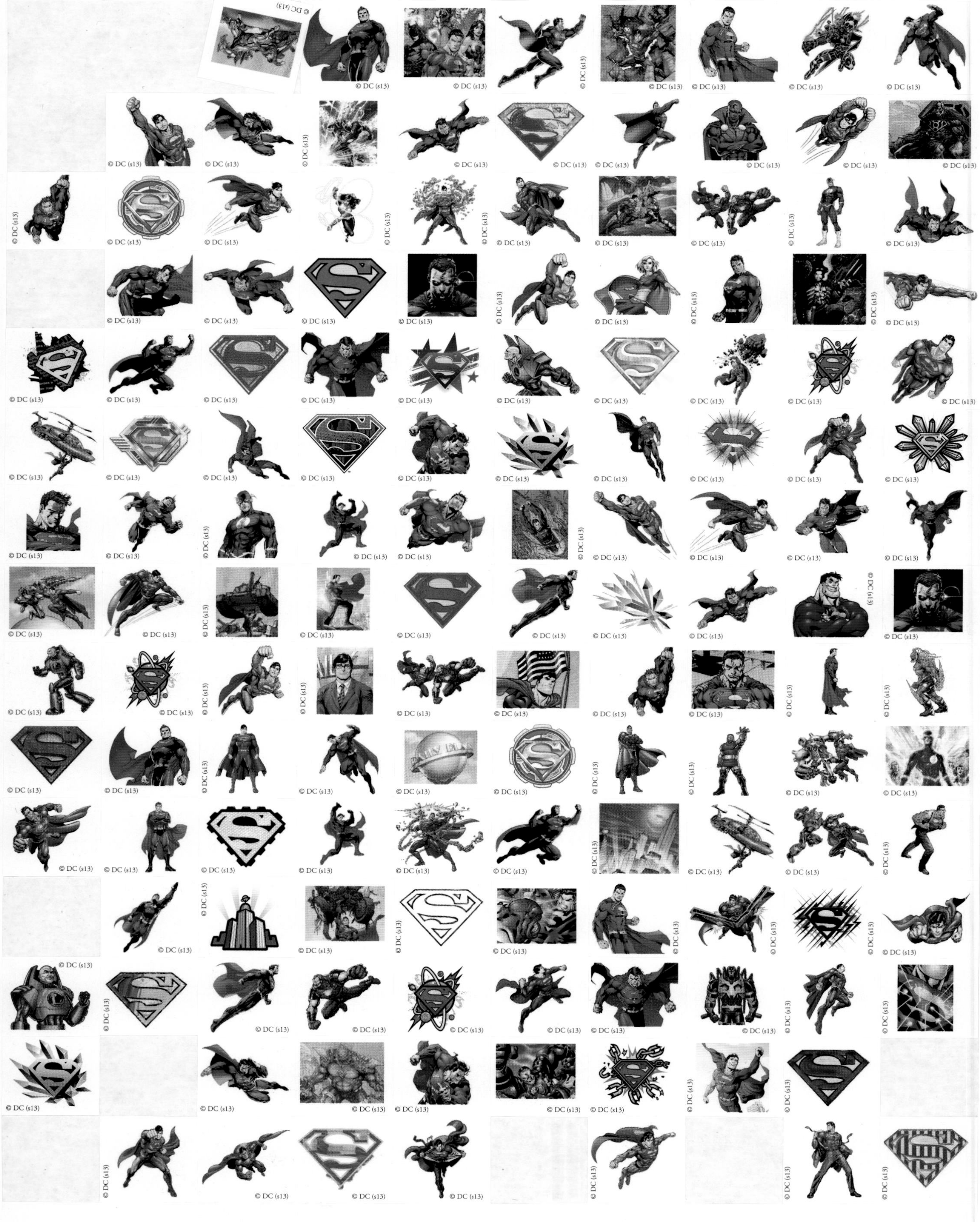
© DC (s13)